My Perfect World
is
A Path to Real Heaven

OTHER WORKS BY ADAM WISEMAN:

Warning
Published 1995
ISBN 91-630-3462-X

My Motivation For Writing This Book:

EXISTENCE OF MANY CRISES ON EARTH AND THE POSSIBILITY OF TURNING THEM INTO WORLD WAR III:

Given the possibility of a third world war, and given the abundance of nuclear arsenals around the world. It is estimated that humans could blow up the EARTH more than hundred times over.

At any moment, these threats may turn into tragic and irreparable catastrophic events.

I hope that before is too late, vanguard Intellectual scouts and libertarians around the world will take steps to save the EARTH from any risk of possible destruction.

The existence of armies in different countries and enmities of different religions, nations and races with each other brings us closer to the destruction of the EARTH each day.

Feeling of this great danger was my main motivation for writing this book.

In the world, most of the energies are spent to build military equipment, like tanks, Missiles, bombers and many other distractive devices for the possible war with other humans of different cultures, different races, religions and anyone who thinks different then them. I believe instead of all these hostilities, campaigning and building various means to kill each other and destroy cities, houses, infrastructures and all other facilities. We should spend energies to build more modern cities, life appliances and facilities for people to have more opportunities and fun to live better on EARTH and enjoy their life enough to stay healthy. Instead of making people to work so hard and still being poor, with no fun and not enough vacations, we need to find ways to make human life easier, with less working hours and more time to be with family, do sport, hobbies, read books and rest. Imagine a time when all the industries, services and all other facilities work only for the benefits of people for health, prosperity freedom, social justice and comfortable life for everyone equal on EARTH?

For example, instead of building a fighter jet, make ultra lights manpower aircrafts for sport purpose or making small modern flying machines for short and long distance trips for the use of people. Instead of building tanks for war, they can build and mass produce comfortable cars can move on heavy snow even in the Arctic with a cold weather of minus 60 degrees or hot weather in the desert above 60 degrees Celsius, without endangering the drivers or passengers. Right now, all these facilities are available for construction and distribution of all these opportunities among all human. Only the will of the majority of the people of the world is needed to provide all these possibilities to them.

THAT IS WHEN I CAN SAY THE REAL HEAVEN ON EARTH HAS BEEN ESTABLISHED.

The unwise and irrational actions of the current world leaders were another reason for me to write this book for reminders and souvenirs, which I dedicated to humans.

If one-day human beings realizes that they did not come to this world to fight and kill each other and destroy the nature, but they came to build the world and have peaceful coexistence. Then the EARTH will be a better place for them and future generations to live their life.

ONE OF THE DIFFERENCES BETWEEN ANIMALS AND HUMANS IS THAT:

Humans make and write the history of the world, but animals are not able to do so. This was another motivations for me to write this book.

I believe that, the wise people of the world are aware of these dangers, each of which I discuss in detail in this book.

As the wise know, currently 3 evil-minded groups rule the world that I call them three Amigos.

*Amigo#1 Insatiable greedy capitalism.
*Amigo #2 Mercenary political dwarfs.
*Amigo #3 Superstitious and deceiver religious leaders.

I believe that if the humans of Earth do not take steps to save our only home (EARTH) from these dangers, nor if they make no effort for developments, peace, security, prosperity, freedom, social justice and comfort for all living things equally, it will be very sad because no one else will come to Earth from another planet to do these things for us.

MY CONSCIENCE KEPT TELLING ME THAT SOMETHING HAD TO BE DONE TO SAVE THE EARTH FROM THE DANGER OF THESE 3 AMIGOS AND THAT WAS WHY I START WRITING THIS BOOK IN 2017.

An idea that sprouted in my mind in 1979 and has grown to present day. 37 years later, finely the idea of My Perfect World has become an efficient and complete philosophy for solving social problems and confusions, which is already in your hands.

Despite daily work and every other type of surprises and responsibilities in life, and due to the linguistic differences between my mother language (Persian) and English, after 43 months, with the help of technology and my publisher (Page Master), I was able to publish this book on May 20th 2021 in the virtual and real world. Now that 9 months have passed since the publication of this book, I am proud to announce that, it has been well received by the people. I'm sure it will be better received in the world over time, especially after My Death.

If you have any unanswered Socio, Political, Religious questions that have been troubling you since childhood, be sure to read this book to find the answers.

IF YOU AGREE WITH MY LOGIC AND WANT TO SHARE THIS SACRED GOAL, FIRST OF ALL READ THIS BOOK CAREFULLY, THEN YOU WILL KNOW WHAT TO DO NEXT.

I am sure that if one-day the good and wise people of the world decide to prepare a universal constitution for a new world order, they will definitely benefit the rules of this book.

The contents of this book are a treasure trove of historical, religious and philosophical studies with personal experiences that are intertwined with the undeniable reality of human societies. I dedicate this treasure as my only valuable wealth to the people of the world. I hope this book will be welcomed by most of the people in the world and will accompany me in this holy way. I believe this book is the key to opening the doors of real heaven to humanity.

I WOULD LIKE TO KNOW YOUR OPINIONS ABOUT THIS BOOK.

Please don't forget to leave your review in the virtual world when you finish reading the book.

Best wishes to the wise and virtuous people of the world.

Adam Wiseman
www.adamwiseman.ca
February/23/2022

My Perfect World

Adam Wiseman

MY PERFECT WORLD

Published by Ahmad Yousefi, Edmonton, Canada

Version 4

ISBN
paperback: 978-1-77354-204-1
paperback including WARNING: 978-1-77354-298-0
ebook: 978-1-77354-205-8

The views expressed in this book are those of the author .

Publication assistance by
PAGEMASTER
PUBLISHING
PageMaster.ca

About this Book

After many greetings to you dear reader who has chosen this book to read. Let me briefly present its most important topics to you:

This book contains materials such as;

From this chapter onward, most topics are about My Perfect World.
An alternative system to replace all the current systems across the world.
A global system without currency, banks, intermediation, weapon factories, borders or military.
In My Perfect World there will be equal opportunities for everybody on this planet. It would be one country on planet EARTH. Two flags (one universal and one provincial flag). Two languages, one international and the other mother languages. A global e- government runs by philosophers, various scientists and technicians. The task of these e-government groups is to restore peace, freedom, security, welfare, prosperity and social justice for all living things on EARTH.

Here I focus the extravagance in the consumption of human's energy and other energies in the useless ways, which I have explained with all the details and answers.

(PAGE 141)
TALIBAN IN AFGANESTAN:

(PAGE 142)
HONESTY IS THE BEST POLICY:

In my perfect world we use the philosophy of honesty, logic, scientifically and efficiently to solve society's problem instead of politics.

(PAGE 148)
CHAPTER 4
WHAT DO WE NEED TO DO TO MAKE A PERFECT WORLD?

WHAT STEPS DO WE NEED TO TAKE, AND WHEN CAN WE START?

(PAGE 150)
HERE IS MY PROPOSAL ON HOW WE CAN BUILD THIS PERFECT WORLD

In this chapter I have explained about My Perfect World from A to Z, with all the details.

To portray my Perfect World, I have included all the puzzles together in one frame to display a complete image of a flawless Perfect World.

NOTE:

Of course this Perfect World is the product of my personal thoughts, studies, researches and experiences. But to build and establish this Perfect World requires the collective effort of all people around the world. To do a great and global work, requires all the people of the world to be united, and to unite the people of the world requires a common denominator to bring them together around specific goal.

I believe that in order to build a perfect world, we need to unite everyone around the world, and in order to achieve that unity; we need a common belief or religion that can bring us together. I believe that there are only two phenomena in the universe that all living beings on EARTH have in common. The SUN and the EARTH, which we cannot survive, not ever for one second without them.

All humans and other living beings have absolute need to these two planets to survive. In the order of being united for building a Perfect World, every human being should know that we have only one energy source which is the SUN, our great father and only one home which is the EARTH our great mother.

FINAL SECTIONS

IT IS NOTEWORTHY THAT THE EXCITEMENT PART OF THIS BOOK STARTS FROM CHAPTER 3.

Starting date and place:
November /21/2017, in St Albert, Alberta.
Adam Wiseman

Contents

Preface:

MY PERFECT WORLD IS TOTALLY A PHILOSOPHY OF A NEW WORLD ORDER.

A worldwide hundred percent Democratic Social Council Meritocracy system with no money, no bankers, no military, no weapon factories, no war, no intermediaries, no poverty, no homelessness, no prisons, no prisoners, no corruption, no terrorists, no stress and no anxiety.

It's a system with equal possibility of social peace, security, justice, freedom, education, medication, housing, nutrition, and everything else for everyone on earth – from the very first minute of birth, until the last moment of life, equally without trading, buying or selling anything with money.

My perfect world not only does not conflict with a good and prosperous life, but also considers a stylish and aristocratic life necessary for all human societies.

The spark of this philosophy was hit my mind in 1979 when I was 24 years old, during the so-called Iran revolution.

That was the time when Ayatollah Khomeini came to power in Iran, in my opinion, with the help of American C I A and British intelligence services M I 6— and of course that happened with a predetermination to overthrow the king of Iran.

In my opinion, the plan to overthrow the King of Iran was determined by American politicians, British, French, Germans and other industrialized countries, as well as oil companies and weapons factories. They were all members of capitalism, and thirsty for more wealth and power.

Two Weeks in January: America's secret engagement with Khomeini
BBC News (excerpt)

From his home in exile outside Paris, the defiant leader of the Iranian revolution effectively offered the Carter administration a deal: Iranian military leaders listen to you, he said, but the Iranian people follow my orders.

If President Jimmy Carter could use his influence on the military to clear the way for his takeover, Khomeini suggested, he would calm the nation. Stability could be restored; America's interests and citizens in Iran would be protected.

At the time, the Iranian scene was chaotic. Protesters clashed with troops, shops were closed, public services suspended. Meanwhile, labour strikes had all but halted the flow of oil, jeopardizing a vital Western interest.

Persuaded by Carter, Iran's autocratic ruler, Mohammad Reza Shah Pahlavi, known as the Shah, had finally departed on a "vacation" abroad, leaving behind an unpopular prime minister and a military in disarray - a force of 400,000 men with heavy dependence on American arms and advice.

Khomeini feared the nervous military: its royalist top brass hated him. Even more worrying, they were having daily meetings with a US Air Force General by the name of Robert E Hisser, whom President Carter had sent on a mysterious mission to Tehran.

The ayatollah was determined to return to Iran after 15 years in exile and make the Shah's "vacation" permanent. So he made a personal appeal.

– BBC.COM

....

The last time, when the King Mohamad Reza Pahlavi was leaving Iran on 1979

When Khomeini arrived in Iran from France, although the King had previously left Iran, the ruling system of the country was monarchy and Mohammad Reza Pahlavi was the legal king of the country.

The king left Iran because he felt the street riots were due to his presence in Iran and his involvement in the country's policy making.

Ayatollah Khomeini had no power other than some people's support when he arrived in Iran, but before his arrival the king had already left Iran because of rising tension, chaos and blind street riots.

The first day Khomeini arrived in Iran, he gave a speech in Behesht Zahra (the greatest graveyard in south of Tehran).

(The Khomayni's first speech in the largest cemetery of Tehran [Behesht Zahra])

He began his speech by threatening king Mohammad Reza Pahlavi, saying in the near future he would form his own new government with national support. Then, he directed his speech to encourage the military to join the chaos he and his masters had made for Iran. Then, he changed his subject again to give people absurd promises like: if I come to power I will make water for free, electricity for free, transportation for free, housing for free and so on and so forth. He also promised the people to bring humanity to their society (Khomeini was so illiterate that he used the status of humanity instead of human dignity).

He never implemented any of his promises when he got into power a month later. Not only he did not honour any of his promises, but also all living necessities became more expensive for the people, in a very short time. Now after 39 years, with the regime of Ayatollah Khomeini and his successor Khamenei being in power, the currency's value of Iran is almost 3,600 times smaller than the first day of regime change and inflation has risen relative to the country's currency.

I was a young man in those days, but I wasn't naive, I didn't believe any of Khomeini's promises. When he came to power and established his arbitrary government in Iran, he never fulfilled his promises.

It was clear to me it would be impossible for an illiterate person like Khomeini to make such a great reform, because he wasn't an educated man and he didn't have any scientific and efficient plan to provide the services that he had promised to the people. But, at the same time I liked the idea of free housing, free electricity, free transportation and everything else being for free! Why not?

These words of Ayatollah Khomeini motivated me to start to think about a new world order, a new *philosophy* which I call it *My Perfect World*.

What is wrong with working for free and getting all the necessities of life for free? Obviously we weren't born with money, right? So free housing, free food, free education, free medication, free car and every other thing being for free is not unnatural.

It is a great idea and it should be normal, but how that big change and reform could be implemented, was a big question?

Human societies have lived with our current system for hundreds of years and do not know anything better. Having money and wealth is the first and foremost desire of human beings.

Everything in this system works with money and exclusive capitalism and people don't know any better system for alternative. But in fact we weren't born with money, so why not live without it? Why do we have to look at each other as customers and dollar signs all the time?

Why do some people have so much money that they don't know what to do with it except keeping them in the banks; and at the same time many other people have no money at all, not even enough money to buy food and have shelter over their heads?

Why happiness and misery, poverty and wealth are inherited? Why? And why? There are many other related questions in my mind that I will discuss them in the following pages.

From the moment Khomeini was promising people, the essentials of people's lives will be for free, this idea was born in my mind and grew over time for the last 39 years. In the beginning I had no idea how that ideal reform could be implemented and how to convince people to agree with this new idea?

After more than 35 years of thinking and reading different books and search different ideas, I found answers to all my questions of creating such a practical logical and free-living societies.

Now as I am writing this book, the idea is already 39-years-old; and it has grown big and powerful in my mind as a beautiful practical and logical dream for global society.

This philosophy was living with me all these years, days and nights, in happy and sad times; my mind was always busy thinking about this supper reform ideal society and the questions around it. For me to find the answers for each question it was necessary to take time thinking, reading more historical and philosophical books and also I was talking about the idea to other people almost every day in my life, just to know how other people are thinking about my new idea, and mostly young and educated people were agree with me.

What shall we do to have such a society? What do we need to start that system? What will humans lose or gain in this new system? What kind of change will happen to rich people and what change will happen to poor people?

Over time, I found many answers one by one to put the entire puzzle together to make a complete picture of this ideal system for global society.

My knowledge may not be complete about all aspects of life, but it is enough to give me an idea of the alternative system of all current systems on earth.

Now, by publishing this book, I want to present my hidden treasure of 39 years, to all the people of the world, this book – My Perfect World.

To learn how to build and complete this ideal society, I went over above and beyond all the questions to find the right and perfect answers to every question. I talked to individual people about this idea to challenge myself and to find out what other people think about this idea.

Many people, I can say 99 percent, agreed and loved the idea, and they supported me by nice words and good comments. And, maybe one percent of people disagreed and were against it, but they didn't know how to express their opposition logically to justify why they disagreed with my idea.

I think those who disagreed with my philosophy were not at that level of knowledge to be able to judge my philosophy. There are people in the world are just negative and we see some of them every day.

Now, after 39 years I strongly believe this non-monetary idea can be a practical, philosophical logical and social solution for healthier, peaceful, happier, longer life; with social justice, freedom, security and prosperity for everyone equally on planet earth.

This book was originally written in the Persian language in 2015 and it was published at one time on Facebook, but now I have rewritten the book in English because this idea belongs to all the people and different nationalities living on earth.

CHAPTER #1

Self-Introduction My Story

I am a Persian man from Iran. I was born in July 1954 in Iran and grew up in Tehran, among a low-income family with four brothers and two older sisters. I was the middle child of the family.

I went to school at the age of six and every summer when school was closed I worked in various stores. I finished my elementary school, and then, because of family financial problems, I didn't continue into high school.

I started working full time at the age of 12. I went back to high school a few years later when I realized I needed to educate myself more, but before that I had to save enough money for high school.

When I was 18-years-old, I was working in a small machine shop and going to high school to get my diploma in the evening. Five years later, in 1978, I owned a small machine shop with two lathe machines and three workers. I was successful at work and successful at the school, I was an A+ student and making good money at work.

In 1979 Iran fell into a deep political disaster with the regime change — what Europeans and Americans called it a revolution; and many people, like me, called it a coup. I believe that some colonial countries for their own benefits planned that revolution.

In that year, political problems started in my country with the intervention of these colonial countries. Extremist Muslims were supported through these countries, especially by the United States and Britain. The good fairly rich, free and peaceful country I used to know suddenly changed to a totalitarian regime; poor, messy and insecure in the Middle East.

Everything in society had changed to black and white; bullying and dictatorship. I was not only opposed to the new regime but I was fighting it in my own style. I fought against the new regime with all my power and abilities. I wrote many anti- regime slogans on the walls and talked against the new Islamic regime to other people, loud and clear with lots of courage and anger. I tried to bring people together to fight back against the new regime and prevent more damage to our country and to our people, but at that time, people like me fighting the new regime were in the minority.

Soon, I had to close my machine shop and sell all my machinery and tools, because the business was no longer any good with the regime change.

BEING ARRESTED

One day around sunset in the summer of 1981 when I was chatting with a friend close to his home's door, the revolutionary guards surrounded me and pointed their guns at me. They ordered me to put my hands up and freeze, and then they came closer and handcuffed me with no explanation.

They just told me, "We want to ask you a few questions and then we will let you go home." They said they had been following me everywhere since the morning of that day.

First, they took me to my mother's home where I was living with my family. They started to search the whole house and took all the books and magazines belong to me and my other brothers and sisters. Then, they took me and one of my brothers who happened to be at home – the rest of my family were out of the city for a few days vacation at the time, except me and him and my father.

The guards took me and my brother, with many books and other things, into custody.

IN CUSTODY

They kept us in a dark and wet basement for a few days. I told them my family had nothing to do with the books and other items; everything belonged to me. I signed to accept the responsibility for all items that they took from our home. With that signature, they let my brother go free.

From that day on, they began torturing and interrogating me, while I was blindfolded. They were looking for the names of friends who worked with me against the regime and what operations we had planned for the future. An interrogator would beat me with a lead baton. He hit me on my head, my finger bones and on my knees, while he asked questions; but he couldn't get any useful information from me because I had nothing to say.

A week later they transferred me to a real prison called EVIN. They put me into a 4x3 metre room only 2.5 metres high, where 28 prisoners were already held.

CHARGES AND TRIAL

I was accused of leading a large group intending to stage a demonstration and overthrow the regime. After several interrogations in a period of a few weeks, and without getting any useful information from me, I was eventually taken to court. I was blindfolded and did not have any lawyer to defend me.

During all interrogations, I played dumb, illiterate and ignorant with the interrogator, so the interrogator was unable to obtain any useful information or evidence against me. In that "so-called" courtroom I had to defend myself without being able to see my judge or accusers.

After the prosecutor read my charges I tried to defend myself, with calm nerves and simple words. Within 10 minutes the court was finished and they condemned me to one-year in prison for having banned books and magazines in our house. From the Islamic regime's point of view, every book except the Quran is no good, illegal and forbidden.

A POLITICAL PRISONER

After two months in EVIN prison, they transferred me to a prison named GAZEL HESAR in the city of Karaj.

The first night in the new prison, they kept many of us in one dark room in which we couldn't even sit on the floor. We stood up stuck to each other for the whole night. The next day, the guards divided us into different cells and they put me into one crowded cell (with an area of 120cm by 240cm by 350cm height) with 22 other prisoners already in there. It was hard for me to even imagine that I could fit in that cell, but I lived there for more than 3 months and I learned that everything is possible when is necessary.

The prison chief named Davood Rahmani kept telling us that we keep you in these dark and tight cells because the Islamic regime wants your bones to soften and become flexible. He meant they wanted us to accept and obey the new regime without any questions or any objections.

The above image is the same cell in Ghezel Hesar prison with a bunk bed, where i lived with 23 other prisoners for more then 3 months with no sunlight.

In this prison there were six sections called (Band) and each Band, had one-hallway with12 cells — 6 cells each side of the hallway. Each cell had one bunk bed with about 22 up to 27 prisoners in each cell. Each Band had about 280 up to 320 and some times more prisoners. It is worth mentioning that, during the monarchy's regime, the same cells held only 2 prisoners and all together in the whole Band there were 24 prisoners for 12 cells.

The new regime followed Islamic law – they treated their prisoners with Islamic sharia. From the Islamic regime's point of view, the greater the pressure on political prisoners, the sooner they will calm down and repent from their past. Freedom and democracy were what the superpowers demanded from the king of Iran before they supported Khomeini get into power, but when Khomeini came to power these demands were dropped and journalists no longer came to Iran to interview the new leaders about democracy. The situation for political prisoners was getting worse everyday until now, 39 years later.

For 12 rooms and up to 300 prisoners, there were only 3 showers and 3 toilets. Each of us was allowed to use the toilet two times a day for 2 minutes for each. We were allowed a cold shower once a week, 5 minutes for every prisoner. Lice were living under the prisoners' skin and I was one of those infected.

No change was made for three months. We lived in those tight and dark cells with no sunlight and no fresh air, with a small plate of disgusting food. There was mental and physical torturing in different ways by the prison guards almost every day, with different excuses.

Finally one morning by the order of the prison chief they moved us to a larger band with bigger cells and we were allowed to use the prison backyard one hour a day for refreshing. But the night before we were transferred to that larger prison, the guards entered our section with guns and lashes and they beat us with a hundred lashes to each prisoner, under the pretext of planning a riot. The scenes of that night will never fade in my mind.

After spending one year of my conviction, they still didn't release me. I had to stay two extra months.

Finally, after two months extra imprisonment, I was released, but I owe my freedom to my mother's efforts. She was after my case all the time I was in jail. The total time I was in jail was 14 months, but to me it was like 14 years.

PLANNING TO ESCAPE THE COUNTRY

After I was free, I knew they are watching me. Every day a different person was following me everywhere; they just wanted to know where I am going and whom I am in touch with. I knew if they caught me again, they would kill me for sure with no questions.

I started a plan to escape from Iran. In the new regime I was not even allowed to leave the country legally, so I had no choice but to escape the country illegally.

My passport was issued under the previous regime and it was already expired. I started looking for a smuggler. After a few months I found a Pakistani man who was working in my friend's machine shop. I talked to him about my plan and he introduced me to another Pakistani man who was a human trafficker (smuggler). This man had some people on the border city of Iran and Pakistan called Zahedan. Those men were working for him, were familiar with the desert route. I paid a few thousand U.S. dollars to him to take me to Pakistan and from there, send me to the United States.

Early one morning in July 1983 I flew to Zahedan, the border city of Pakistan and Iran. Around noon, I met the guides in the designated place. I also found out there was another young man escaping the country with me at the same time.

With the three guides, who were caring a few watermelons to quench our thirst in the desert, we started the journey. We left Zahedan in a truck for a few kilometers and when we got out into the desert we changed our clothes to indigenous local clothes and continued our journey on foot through the desert toward Pakistan.

Part of the desert between Iran and Pakistan

We walked mostly at nights and rested during the days, because we didn't want the border guards to see us, until we reached to the first village, called Quetta, in Pakistan. We stayed there one night and the next day we flew from Quetta to Karachi.

All together, it took us three days to arrive in Karachi. It was a very hard journey for me because my brand new shoes, which were a gift from my sister's husband. They tore and the board under the shoe was completely detached right in the middle of desert. I had no choice but to take the shoelace off and wrap it around the shoes to continue the journey until the first town. Anyway, I was very happy to be able to escape Iran.

Although I had to face a new world from then on, the horror of the past was far more frightening than the fear of the future.

My planned destination was the United States, but after three weeks being in Karachi, I found another human trafficker who could send me to Canada right away for $2000 US, instead of going to United States. I paid off the old smuggler for the services he provided to me until Karachi and I got the rest of my money back from him. I got some more money from Iran by selling my car, and hired the new smuggler to arrange my trip to Canada.

On August 15, 1983 I flew from Karachi to Montreal, Canada with two stops, the first stop was Riyadh in Saudi Arabia and the second stop was Rome in Italy. I was travelling with a Turkish passport, which didn't need a visa from Canada at the time.

When I arrived in Montreal I applied for political asylum and the only document I had to prove my identity was my liberation letter from prison.

A NEW START

I started my new life in Montreal in a refugee camp with zero money, zero knowledge of the French or English language, except a little bit of knowledge of Canadian culture from studying world history and geography in the past.

A few weeks later I found work in the kitchen at the same camp where I was living. Three months later I was able to rent an apartment shared with a buddy from the camp.

As I began a new life in Canada, I was also thinking about my idea of a Perfect World. A free-living life for every one on earth; isn't it wonderful?

At first, the name I chose for this philosophy was " A Path to Real Heaven" because I always wondered how humans could live in real paradise on earth. But recently, with the suggestion of a friend, I changed the name of my book to My Perfect World.

As I grew older, the idea of free living continued to grow in my mind; greater and brighter everyday — until 37 years later, in 2015, I started to write this book in Persian and then released it on Facebook.

Two years later I decided to rewrite the book in English so it could reach more people. I believe this idea is a perfect, valuable and unique philosophy to live better life on earth.

I think this philosophy is really worth being considered and read carefully by everyone, at least once, because I feel like I'm the last person to bring the message of peace to humanity.

I'm worried about the day when a great explosion on earth will end everything. My attempt is to make the human conscience overcome the devil of their existence and triumph, before is too late.

The conclusion I want to make is, if we want peace, freedom, prosperity, security and social justice, we need to listen to the ideas of others and choose the best options from them for society. This philosophy is my belief, dream, and imagination and I am not expecting that everyone will perfectly understand and be in agreement with it right away, because I believe, not everyone can have the same dream or imagination at the same time. But I expect and I hope, everyone will carefully read this book at least one time, because today's dream can be tomorrow's realty. I believe that all human beings who claim to have the intelligence and understanding of the foresight and the construction of human societies should be responsible and active in the improvement of the earth and life on it. In fact all human beings have a duty and responsibility to express their views and opinions in order to develop and improve their living conditions on earth, so that the best of those ideas can be selected and implemented.

One thing that I am sure about is, every game has an end, and capitalism will eventually end one day. My philosophy of a perfect world is an alternative system that can replace capitalism, fake communism and other useless isms. This philosophy belongs to the future and it will be more understandable for new generations as time goes by and perceptions change.

WHY AM I PUBLISHING THIS BOOK?

My intention to publish this book is,

1 - To save the mother earth and its belongings from the danger of human destruction.

2 - As a responsible human being, I have a duty to share my views and opinions about the preservation and security of the earth and the creatures on it with others.

3 - This planet is our only home, therefore I must try and make sure that it will be a better place to live for us and for future

generations, and much better than when I was born; not only for myself but also for every other living things that lives on this planet.

4 - I think after we die, we all come back to this life again, but with a different form and shapes; so if I don't try to fix and solve our social problems in this life, I will definitely face the same problems in the next life when I come back. So I must try my best to solve our social problems once and for all before this life of mine ends.

For example: If a person writes a book about the harms of animal hunting and succeeds in convincing hunters not to hunt and harm animals, this book can be his own saviour if he or she is reborn as a bird or other animal after death. Why? Because people learned from that book not to harm or hunt any animals.

The above story may seem a bit dreamy and unscientific, but on the other hand no one can prove the opposite side of this unscientific dream – that there is no life after death.

5 - I believe that there are many important motivations in our life and one of these motivations is to be more developed and more complete then when we were born. We can only be a perfect human if first we take steps to make progress on ourselves and then on our environment and finally participate in development and prosperity for the whole earth.

Also, in my opinion, there are many more important and valuable motivations in life that can stimulate the flourishing of new ideas for the building and development of human societies and making a better life for all people on earth, rather than money. Capitalism's motivation can only raise tensions leading to crimes, corruption and war; just to amass more wealth, money and power, for one percent of the world population.

6 - The last reason for me to publish this book is, because I am old enough and I don't know when my heart and my brain will stop working. I write and publish my philosophy so I don't take them to my grave with me, therefore I have no debt to the

development and evolution of the world. This book is one of my valuable treasures and I want to pass it on as inheritance to the people of the world and future generations. I leave this treasure to mankind as an inheritance.

WHY I AM PUBLISHING THIS BOOK IN ENGLISH?

This book is carrying very important messages to the global society; to all nations, all ages, all classes, to men and women. Right now, English is the only international language that many people on earth speak and understand.

Translation

It was very hard for me to translate my original Persian book to English, so I rewrote the whole book all over again. I know it is not going to be exactly the same book, but I promise it carries the same message and it might be a lot better.

One more important thing about this book is, I try to use the simple dialect that I am using in my daily life – I want to make sure that all classes of people at any age with any level of education will understand the content of this book.

CHAPTER 2

Capitalism is a Path to Real Hell

In my opinion, the current path of the capitalist system is a path to real hell.

Why?

In this book I try to show the disadvantages and losses of capitalism and show how this system will eventually take us all to a real hell. Also, I will introduce my perfect world, a system which I strongly believe will take us all to a real heaven in our lifetime and on this planet (starting in Chapter 3).

My perfect world is hundred percent based on the power and ability of the people (socialism). In my proposed system, the foundations of the ruling power are based on the people's will and power. It means anyone who is at the top of the triangle of society to advance social works, (government) receives his ability from the base of the triangle, (people).

It is a Democratic Social Council Meritocracy System that has never existed in any country on earth up to now. With my perfect world, it is possible to build a real paradise on earth in our lifetime. This paradise will be built by cooperation, universal unity, and correlation with our best knowledge, wisdom, dedication, perseverance, sympathy and contemplation.

To build and complete such a paradise on earth requires an efficient, Social Council, Democratic, Meritocracy system, capable of meeting all the essential needs of society.

A system in which good thought, good speech and good deeds are at the forefront of everything, and its officials and government servants have the necessary knowledge of science, philosophy and competence.

The following is from www.worldsocialism.org and based on from Marx and Engels work in the 18th century?

> The word capitalism is now quite commonly used to describe the social system in which we now live. It is also often assumed that it has existed, if not forever, then for most of human history.
>
> In fact, capitalism is a relatively new social system. For a brief historical account of how capitalism came into existence a couple of hundred years ago, see the Communist Manifesto by Marx and Engels.

But what exactly does 'capitalism' mean?

CLASS DIVISION

Capitalism is the social system, which now exists in all countries of the world. Under this system, the means for producing and distributing goods (the land, factories, technology, transport system etc.) are owned by a small minority of people. We refer to this group of people as the capitalist class.

The majority of people must sell their ability to work in return for a wage or salary, which we refer to as the working class. The working class is paid to produce goods and services, which are then sold for a profit. The capitalist class gains the profit because they can make more money selling what workers have produced, than they pay the working class for labour. In this sense, the capitalist class exploits the working class.

The capitalists live off the profits they obtain from exploiting the working class whilst reinvesting some of their profits for the further accumulation of wealth. This is what we mean when we say there are two classes in society.

This claim is based upon simple facts about the society we live in today. This class division is the essential feature of capitalism. It may be popular to talk (usually vaguely) about various other 'classes' such as the 'middle class', but it is the two classes defined here that are key to understanding capitalism.

It may not be exactly clear which class some relatively wealthy people are in. But, there is no ambiguity about the status of the vast majority of the world's population.

Members of the capitalist class certainly know who they are, and most members of the working class know that they need to work for a wage or salary in order to earn a living (or are dependent upon somebody who does, or depend on state benefits).

THE PROFIT MOTIVE

In capitalism, the motive for producing goods and services is to sell them for a profit, not to satisfy people's needs. The products of capitalist production have to find a buyer, of course, but this is only incidental to the main aim of making a profit, of ending up with more money than was originally invested. This is not a theory that we have thought up, but a fact you can easily confirm for yourself by reading the financial press.

Production is started not by what consumers are prepared to pay for to satisfy their needs, but by what the capitalists calculate can be sold at a profit, those goods may satisfy human needs but those needs will not be met if people do not have sufficient money.

The profit motive is not just the result of greed on behalf of individual capitalists, they do not have a choice about it and the need to make a profit is imposed on capitalists as a condition for not losing their investments and their position as capitalists. Competition with other capitalists forces them to reinvest as much of their profits as they can afford to keep their means and methods of production up to date.

— WWW.WORLDSOCIALISM.ORG

••••••••••••••••••••

HERE ARE 5 QUESTIONS ABOUT CAPITALISM, WHICH I WILL EXPLAIN ONE BY ONE:

1-What is the meaning of capitalism?
2-When was the exact time the capitalism has been born?
3- what is wrong with the capitalism?
4-Is there any possibility to reform the capitalism?
5- what could it be the best alternative system to replace it with capitalism?

ANSWER 1-WHAT IS THE MEANING OF CAPITALISM?

DEFINITION OF CAPITALISM

#1-WHAT IS THE MEANING OF CAPITALISM?

The capitalism is a social system that is formed on the basis of private capital, salaried workers, production, supply, demand and finely profits from the sale of products for the capitalist.

A simple diagram can illustrate capitalism by a triangle of products, customers and profit. Balance of these three categories is the foundation of the capitalist system. It means that if there were no product in the market there would be no customers and if there were no customers, there would be no profit.

#2-WHEN EXACTLY CAPITALISM WAS BORN?

Marx labelled a period as "pre-history of capitalism". In effect, feudalism solidified the necessary roots and foundation for development of the capitalist system.

Feudalism: Feudalism was mostly confined to Europe and some other countries, and lasted from the medieval period through the sixteen-century.

In the order of better understanding where capitalist system came from, we should go back through the human history to before and during the beginning of feudalism.

The capitalist system may have been born when a paleolithic man, while making an axe for hunting and cutting down trees, thought that it would be better to make two axes and exchange one of them with a neighbour and make a profit from it.

I would like to talk a little bit about the human evolution history to make it easier to understand how feudalism began.

Feudalism became the base of capitalism and these two systems became so powerful one after another to spread throughout all over the world, but only for the benefit of one percent of population. Feudalism and capitalism have had many pleasant affects on one percent and many unpleasant affects on 99% of people. The root and foundation of capitalism is based in feudalism and feudalism started when agriculture was discovered.

BEFORE AND BEGINNING OF FEUDALISM:

Caveman era

When the early human were living in the caves and doing animal husbandry, daily work was split between men and women. Men were hunting and women were harvesting grass for animals kept in caves. In the spring and summer times, when ladies were going out to pick up some grass for their animals, slowly and over time, they realized that the seeds were falling from the grass they were caring to the caves, it grew up few weeks later on their ways going back and forth, on their passageways trails and that was how ladies discovered how to farm, about 9,500 BC.

After the development of agriculture, those early human started to move out of caves and they built huts near the lakes, rivers and wherever there was water for drinking and farming. Each tribe fenced around their own farm, huts; and they kept their family, animals and other belongings inside the fence, and that area became their territory.

This time was the beginning of feudalism – from this time on, land lording and ownership began.

LANDOWNERS STARTED THE FIRST OWNERSHIP AND SLAVERY.

Feudalism is a system that drives its power from being a big landlord and having more slaves and more animals for work on land or to sell, and that's how the power concentration by oppressor, greedy and ambitious people began.

Anyone who owned a land was able to hire some guards to protect their family and belongings. Also, landowners were able to gather farmers to work for them for a bite of food and place to sleep. Over time, these landowners with their guards and slaves became much stronger, until they started to have a little army for themselves and ruled over larger territory.

Sometimes for different reasons and problems, they fought with other tribes and defeated others killing the men and taking possession of the land, women, children, animals and other belongings. They took the women for working at home, farming and for sexual abuse, and they kept children for slavery to work on the farms and other misuse.

So any tribe leaders who had more lands, more slaves and more soldiers, began governing other tribes and they were collecting taxes from ordinary people. Those big landowners in different continents with different languages were called with various adjectives, like: King, Queen, Lord, Khan, Khalifeh, Sahib, Sir, Master, Duke, etc.

In order to continue their lives, people had to pay taxes and other gifts to these leaders who had land, gold, slaves, a protective army, and power. Strong tribal leaders became stronger – with every battle they won, they controlled more tribes, more territory and more people.

SLAVERY SYSTEM

As the agriculture was developing, landlords became more powerful, because they had much more capital, more land than average people and they were able to take over any other lands they wanted. Many times, they could force others to work for them for food and a place to sleep. The biggest slavery system was in Egypt and the memorial of that period is the Pyramids.

Slavery system is a system that allows rich people to buy and sell poor people as property.

– .WIKIPEDIA.ORG/WIKI/SLAVERY

Slavery is any system in which principles of property law are applied to people, allowing individuals to own, buy and sell other individuals, as a de jure form of property. A slave is unable to withdraw unilaterally from such an arrangement and works without remuneration.

In many cultures, slavery began before written history. A person could become enslaved from the time of their birth, capture, or purchase. Historically, slavery has been legalized institutionally in most societies at some point, but now is outlawed in all

Recognized slavery countries: The last country to officially abolish slavery was Mauritania in 2007. Nevertheless, there are an estimated 40.3 million people worldwide subject to some form of modern slavery.

The most common form of modern slave trade is referred to as human trafficking. In other areas, slavery (or unfree labour) continues through practices such as: debt bondage. The most widespread form of slavery today; serfdom, domestic servants kept in captivity; certain adoptions in which children are forced to work as slaves; child soldiers; and forced marriage.

Iran is a country that sits on large oil reservoirs, but there are millions of children working instead of going to school. Many of them are working in brick kilns and many of them are working on waste recycling.

For example; nowadays many countries are forcing unaccompanied children to work for little money only to survive.

I saw a documentary video clip, a long time ago about wealthy Saudi men who buy young kids from poor countries in order to take part in camel races, because kids are light in weight and camels can run much faster, but these kids were kept in the camels' stables, and when they get older or obese, they are buried alive in mass graves, which is hard to believe, but I think it's true.

Even England, France, Portugal, United States of America and many other countries had the slavery system until about 150 years ago. Other countries, like Saudi Arabia still have slaves because in Islam any infidel can be Muslim's slave as it said in the Quran. In any battles between Muslim and other religions, when a captive is captured by a Muslim that Muslim can use that captive as a slave and they can do anything they want to the slave.

WHAT DOES ISLAM TEACH ABOUT SLAVERY?

Does Islam condemn slavery? Does Islamic teaching allow Muslim men to keep women as sex slaves?

Islam neither ignores nor condemns slavery. In fact, a large part of the Sharia is dedicated to the slavery. Muslims are encouraged to live in the way of Muhammad who was a slave owner and trader. He captured many slaves in different battles; he had sex with his slaves; and he instructed his men to do the same.

The Quran actually devotes more verses to making sure that Muslim men know they can keep women as sex slaves.

This is one of several personal-sounding verses "from Allah" narrated by Muhammad – in this case allowing a virtually unlimited supply of sex partners. Other Muslims are restricted to four wives, but they may also have sex with any number of slaves, following the example of their prophet.

Quran (23:5-6) " Who abstain from sex, except with those joined to them in the marriage bond, or (the captives) whom their right hands possess.

This verse permits the slave-owner to have sex with his slaves. See also Quran (70:29-30).

The Quran is a small book, so if Allah used valuable space to repeat the same point four times, sex slavery must be very important to him. He was relatively reticent on matters of human compassion and love.

Quran (4:24) "And all married women (are forbidden unto you) save those (captives) whom your right hands possess."

Even sex with married slaves is permissible.

Breeding slaves based on fitness.

Quran (2:178) "O ye who believe! Retaliation is prescribed for you in the matter of the murdered; the freeman for the freeman, and the slave for the slave, and the female for the female."

The message of this verse, which prescribes the rules of retaliation for murder, is that all humans are not created equal. The human value of a slave is less than that of a free person (and a woman's worth is also distinguished from that of a man).

Yet another confirmation that the slave is not equal to the master. Slave owes his status to Allah's will. (According to 16:71, the owner should be careful about insulting Allah by bestowing Allah's gifts on slaves – those whom the god of Islam has not favoured).

– THERELIGIONOFPEACE.COM

••••••••••••••••••••

SLAVERY IN THE WEST

Slavery in Great Britain existed and was recognized from before Roman occupation until 1833. Britain sent musketeers to Africa to sell goods and for the return kidnapped black people and transported them to the bottom of the ship to row the ship to return to England and upon their in England they were forced into debt on their farm land. The black people are living in England and united States today are from the same African generation.

Slavery in United States was ended When Abraham Lincoln won the 1860 election on a platform of halting the expansion of slavery. Seven states broke away to form the Confederacy. The first six states to secede held the greatest number of slaves in the South. Shortly after the Civil War began Confederate forces attacked the US army's Fort Sumter, and four additional slave states then seceded.

Due to Union measures such as the Confiscation Acts and Emancipation Proclamation in 1863, the war effectively ended slavery, even before ratification of the Thirteenth Amendment on December 1865 formally ended the legal institution throughout the United States.

Slavery Prohibition and its Aftermath

Abraham Lincoln banned slavery, but since capitalism cannot live without slaves, as a result, regardless of skin color, anyone who lived below the poverty line became a slave – they were first slaves of feudalism, then of capitalism until now.

One of these two different forms of slavery is the old fashioned Feudalist system; which was forcing the slaves to work for them, and the other one is the modern slavery system, which works on free-will for capitalism. That means people must choose to work for the low wages for capitalists to survive; or not to work for them and become homeless and die of hunger.

THE DESTRUCTIVE RESULT OF THE SLAVERY SYSTEM AFTER CENTURIES:

Today, as I'm writing this book, although the slavery law in the United States and Europe has been abolished all together and no trace of black slavery is seen, racism still remains, and from time to time we hear in the news that a white policeman killed a black man during the arrest. If white Europeans in past centuries did not kidnap black Africans from their homelands and bring them to Europe, there might not be an issue called racism today, and all races may have more respect for each other. Combining different races and cultures can cause many problems when one is forced to leave their homeland.

But, we must also consider the fact that the slavery system in the past was the cause of constructions and progress of human societies due to forced and collective teamwork. So, we must admit, today's modern society is indebted to the slavery system of the past, but also we must realize the continuation of modern slavery can lead human to the destruction of life and can be a path to real hell on earth. Slavery in any form must end because time and needs have changed and the slavery system will have no use and no place of any form on this planet anymore.

First of all there is enough of everything for every one living on this planet, so there is no need for anyone to be greedy or to keep others captive and hoard the essentials of the people in warehouses. Secondly the level of consciousness, understanding and education of people is much higher than 200 years ago and everyone knows their needs and their rights. Therefore, the rights of all human beings on earth must be respected equally without any conditions and with full executive guarantee.

The tense political situation and people's resentment in the whole world is due to Greed, Jealousy and Hate.

The presence of armies, nuclear warheads and intercontinental ballistic missiles that have been created all over the world in many countries just to defend their lands, religions or nations make the possibility of the third world war much greater than global peace among human society.

All different religions, various beliefs between nations and large gap in class differences in each society are a clear proof that we are close to a great war. This time, if any world war happens, life on earth will probably end; or in best-case scenario, maybe life will be continued but we have to start everything all over from scratch (Paleolithic Era).

I only imagine that if any war happens and accidentally a missile with nuclear warhead falls into one of the oil reservoirs under the ground, what will happen in that reservoir? I can imagine a big explosion and large piece of earth will separate. And, the earth drop off its axis and will go back to where it came from billions of years ago; of course it goes straight to the sun and our current life will end.

DEVELOPMENT

Inventions, improvements and progress in the agricultural system (feudalism) and its transformation into capitalism.

The development of civilization has relied heavily on the discovery of metals. Agriculture itself needed tools, which could be made of metals. Prehistoric man used metals to build tools and weapons as their knowledge of metallurgy developed. Metals played an essential and important role in the development of human society to advance the agriculture, various industries, construction, transportation and arts. By discovering metals, blacksmiths were born and from then progress in agriculture and various industries continued to grow.

Blacksmith shops made sickles, farming instruments, war instruments like swords, shields, armour and helmets. For transportation they made shafts, wheelbarrows, horseshoes and other basic tools. Since blacksmiths were able to form metals, other craftsman started to invent various machines such as metal cutting and the lathe.

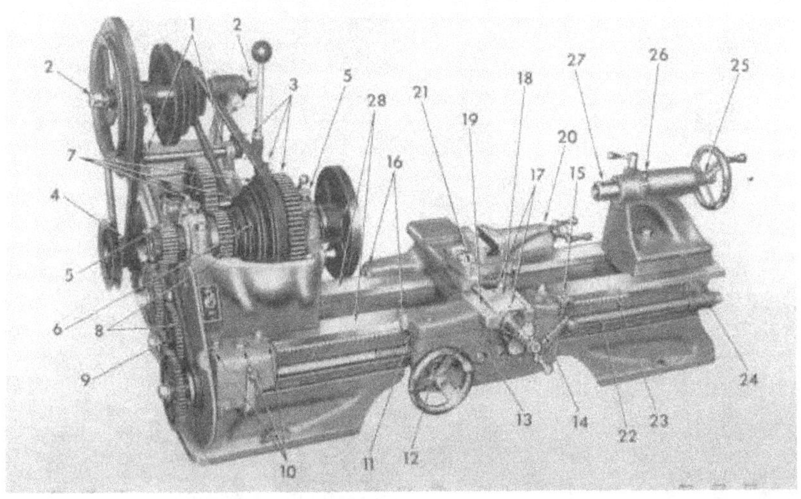

(An old lathe machine)

(An old sewing Machine)

With the lathe machine, machinists were able to make parts for printing machine, stitching machine, ball bearings for engines and shafts for engines and so many other parts for different machines. As a result, other industries made different engines to make automobiles, trains, airplanes, large cargo and warships, etc.

Benjamin Franklin (January 17, 1706 – April 17, 1790) was one of the most innovative Americans of all time. Indeed, his work and experiments resulted in several important discoveries and inventions including electricity, bifocal glasses, a usable battery and many more.

Transportation: The history of Railroads: From Tramways to Hyper loop Trains. www.thoughtco.com/history-of-railroad-4059935

While George Stephenson (born June/9/1781, died August/12/1848) is credited as the inventor of the first steam locomotive engine for railways, Trevithick's invention is cited as the first tramway locomotive. In 1821, Englishman Julius Griffiths became the first person to patent a passenger road locomotive.

– THOUGHTS.COM

(1792-1871)

When was the first computer invented?

English mathematician and inventor Charles Babbage is credited with having conceived the first automatic digital computer. During the mid 1830s, Babbage developed plans for the analytical engine.

- WWW.BRITANNICA.COM

••••••••••••••••••••

Then came telecommunication invention by Alexander Graham Bell:

Bell's Telephone

A pioneer in the field of telecommunications, Alexander Graham Bell was born in 1847 in Edinburgh, Scotland. He moved to Ontario, and then to the United States, settling in Boston, before beginning his career as an inventor. Throughout his life, Bell had been interested in the education of deaf people. This interest leads him to invent the microphone and, in 1876, his "electrical speech machine," which we now calls a telephone. News of his invention quickly spread throughout the country, even throughout Europe. By 1878, Bell had set up the first telephone exchange in New Haven, Connecticut. By 1884, long distance connections were made between Boston, Massachusetts and New York City.

Bell imagined great uses for his telephone, like this model from the 1920s, but would he ever have imagined telephone lines being used to transmit video images? Since his death in 1922, the telecommunication industry has undergone an amazing revolution. Today, non-hearing people are able to use a special display telephone to communicate. Fiber optics is improving the quality and speed of data transmission. Actually, your ability to access this information relies upon telecommunications technology. Bell's "electrical speech machine" paved the way for the Information Superhighway.

Thomas Alva Edison (February 11, 1847 – October 18, 1931) was an American inventor and businessman, who has been described as one of America's greatest inventors. He developed many devices that greatly influenced life around the world, including the phonograph, the motion picture camera, and the long-lasting, practical electric light bulb.

Dubbed "The Wizard of Menlo Park", he was one of the first inventors to apply the principles of mass production and large-scale teamwork to the process of invention, and is often credited with the creation of the first industrial research laboratory.

Our world has been brighter ever since this grate invention made the second revolution in the cities and industrial world.

Industrial electrical machines invented one after another and by these inventions; life in the cities began to grow faster.

The factory owners became stronger then landlords with more profits, because they owned bout land and factory and this was the beginning of the city development and capitalism.

The fact that factories were producing more products, they needed more workers and more customers and more markets therefore, transportations to deliver their goods and to sell their products in to other countries and other cities was needed.

••••••••••••••••••••

Transportation
The invention of automobile.

The very first self-powered road vehicles were powered by steam engines, and by that definition Nicolas Joseph Cygnet of France built the first automobile in 1769 — recognized by the British Royal Automobile Club and the Automobile Club de France as being the first.

So why do so many history books say that the automobile was invented by either Gottlieb Daimler or Karl Benz? It is because both Daimler and Benz invented highly successful and practical gasoline-powered vehicles that ushered in the age of modern automobiles.

Daimler and Benz invented cars that looked and worked like the cars we use today. However, it is unfair to say that either man invented "the" automobile.

At last:

Henry Ford

American car manufacturer, Henry Ford (1863-1947) invented an improved assembly line and installed the first conveyor belt-based assembly line in his car factory in Ford's Highland Park, Michigan plant, around 1913-14. The assembly line reduced production costs for cars by reducing assembly time. Ford's famous Model T was assembled in ninety-three minutes. Ford made his first car, called the "Quadra icicle," in June 1896. However, success came after he formed the Ford Motor Company in 1903.

This was the third car manufacturing company formed to produce the cars he designed.

He introduced the Model T in 1908 and it was a success. After installing the moving assembly lines in his factory in 1913, Ford became the world's biggest car manufacturer. By 1927, 15 million Models had been manufactured.

Another victory won by Henry Ford was patent battle with George B. Selden. Selden, who had never built an automobile, held all American car manufacturers paid royalties a patent on a "road engine", on that basis Selden. Ford overturned Selden›s patent and opened the American car market for the building of inexpensive cars.

****

Then came Airplane invented by wright Brothers.

Airplane invention:

The Wright brothers, Orville (August 19, 1871 – January 30, 1948) and Wilbur (April 16, 1867 – May 30, 1912), were two American aviators, engineers, inventors, and aviation pioneers who are generally credited with inventing, building, and flying the world's first successful airplane.

They made the first controlled, sustained flight of a powered, heavier-than-air aircraft on December 17, 1903, four miles south of Kitty Hawk, North Carolina. In 1904–05 the brothers developed their flying machine into the first practical fixed-wing aircraft. Although not the first to build experimental aircraft, the Wright brothers were the first to invent aircraft controls that made fixed-wing powered flight possible.

The brothers' fundamental breakthrough was their invention of three-axis control, which enabled the pilot to steer the aircraft effectively and to maintain its equilibrium. This method became and remains standard on fixed-wing aircraft of all kinds From the beginning of their aeronautical work, the Wright brothers focused on developing a reliable method of pilot control as the key to solving "the flying problem".

This approach differed significantly from other experimenters of the time who put more emphasis on developing powerful engines. Using a small homebuilt wind tunnel, the Wrights also collected more accurate data than any before, enabling them to design and build wings and propellers that were more efficient than any before. Their first U.S. patent, 821,393, did not claim invention of a flying machine, but rather, the invention of a system of aerodynamic control that manipulated a flying machine's surfaces.

They gained the mechanical skills essential for their success by working for years in their shop with printing presses, bicycles, motors, and other machinery.

Their work with bicycles in particular influenced their belief that an unstable vehicle like a flying machine could be controlled and balanced with practice. From 1900 until their first powered flights in late 1903, they conducted extensive glider tests that also developed their skills as pilots.

Their bicycle shop employee Charlie Taylor became an important part of the team, building their first airplane engine in close collaboration with the brothers.

++++++++++++++++++++

In the United States, after the Bethlehem steel factory in Pennsylvania, started to make large beams (girders) in 1908, some investors start to build railroads, others start to build bridges and others built skyscrapers for offices and residential use. So the result of the Bethlehem steel plant became the main reason for more development, more jobs and more facilities.

⁂⁂⁂

The first desktop and mass-market computer was invented by Pier Giorgio Pronto and manufactured by Olivetti. About 44,000 Programmer 101 computers were sold, each with a price tag of $3,200. In 1968, Hewlett Packard began marketing the HP 9100A, considered to be the first mass-marketed desktop computer.

⁂⁂⁂

From the beginning of human civilization until now, there have been thousands and thousands of researchers, inventors, scientists and artists who have always been a minority and deprived of society and lived in spite of all the material deficiencies and wealth of the world. With the least facilities have been engaged in construction, innovation, inventions and discoveries to advance human life towards development and progress. The majority of these elites community in any society has lived in absolute poverty and has died in poverty. But after their death, others have benefited financially from their creative effects. Unfortunately, I have not been able to mention all of them here because it is not related to the subject of this book, but in any case, the memory and name of these super humans is unforgettable in human history and as long as the earth is alive, their names will remain immoral. Truly, the name of goodness and immortality is the most valuable inheritance left by wise and virtuous people. Anyway, let me remind you of the latest major invention in the world of communication and new technology, which is credited to IBM, which was launched in 1994.

The first smartphone was named Simon. It featured a touchscreen, email capability and handful of built-in apps, including a calculator.

Mobile phone/Inventor
Martin Cooper- Eric Tigerstedt – W . Rae Young

These inventors and explorers whom I have mentioned so far not only did not disturb human beings with their existance, but also made life much easier for everyone, and after their deaths, others exploited their inventions.

••••••••••••••••••••

LAST 100 YEARS

After all, over the last 100 years the capitalist system has become more modern then ever before.

MODERN CAPITALISM

Capitalism was getting more modern, stronger, with more profit, more work for workers and as a result, more class division between the poor majority and rich minority. Modern industry factories and modern agriculture, made capitalism more advanced, enhanced and stronger. With modern and advanced industry the speed of production is constantly increasing. By advanced systems products were transported to different cities, and different countries; but at the same time, prices were rising sharply every day. The rich became richer and the poor became poorer and the class divide continues to rise.

Also the middle class is increasingly falling into the lower class or below the poverty line. As the Capitalists built more buildings and houses, the apartments rent and house prices are constantly rising. Now days almost every one knows that only one percent of the earth population has 99 percent of the earth's wealth and 99 percent of the population owns only one percent of the earth's wealth; yet neither of these two classes are really happy, enjoys life enough, or lives longer then the another.

Power and authority have always been in the hands of those who owned oil, gold, guns, money and land. Sometimes the position of the power-holders is replaced by a revolution or a coup or a blind rebellion and the weak and poor classes of the society overthrow the rich. But, because they do not know of any better system that can replace the old system, they repeat the old system again, which results in a monopoly, and power concentration and ultimately leads to dictatorship. Again the wheel spins on the old axis of where the richer and stronger class oppress the poor and weak majority. A rich minority with an armed army and authority rules over the poor and weak majority of people.

In most countries the majority of the people are the working class and they build and produce every essential need for their society, yet they do not own any of the products they make.

The carpet weaver makes the most beautiful carpets; most of them live on an old rotten carpet. The construction worker who builds multi-storey houses, lives in small, dilapidated rooms. Car builders travel by bicycle, an old car or public transportation. Hardworking farmers working in hot summer and cold winter on lands to produce the community's food are living in the worst condition houses and they survive with the lowest food quality.

As long as the financial system is alive, this weak majority and strong minority cycle will keep going and rotating around its axis until one part of this circle become heavier than the other side, than the centrifugal phenomenon occurs and everything will mess up. Small minority with money, land, guns and power will rule the poor and weak majority to the point of explosion.

Summary: the people who are directly involved in the construction of building or producing essentials needs of living, mostly own none of their products, and many of them live below the poverty line.

Let's go back to the subject of birth and emergence of capitalism. By expanding the supply of goods to the markets and bazaars, capitalism entered to a new stage and became much stronger then ever before. With the invention of various industrial and agricultural machines, many farmers became unemployed and therefore went to industrial cities to earn a living, perhaps in factories.

Most farmers moved to the cities to find better jobs in a factory to make more money to survive and continue their life. Many land-owners and big farm owners also started to invest their capital in the cities as well.

#3-WHAT IS WRONG WITH THE CAPITALIST SYSTEM?

The capitalist system creates many problems for human societies, but since I want to summarize this book so that its final message is concise and useful to readers, in the following I bring a few more examples of disadvantages of capitalism.

Capitalism is like a contest and in that contest whoever has more money is the winner of the contest. It doesn't really matter how they find that money, they may have acquired it through theft or the sale of drugs, or they may have killed some people for it. A limited number of them may have inherited wealth from their parents, but it is not clear where their parents got all that wealth. No one needs to know about these details in the contest.

In this contest no one has mercy on others. Having more money and capital is the first rule and condition for winning the competition. But, in this shameful and disgraceful competition the only things are regarded as not important are actually human dignity and the public interest. These capitalists competitions remind me of the struggles of Roman gladiators who did not have any mercy on their rival for survival.

PROBLEMS, LOSSES AND DISADVANTAGES OF CAPITALISM:

In modern times, the capitalist system tried to adopt itself with the time and the conditions of its societies. So the capitalist system changed the method of old fashion slavery to modern slavery.

Consequently since then, they stopped going to Africa to kidnap people for slavery, because so-called democratic capitalists were ashamed to have an obvious slavery system in the constitution of their country. As a result of this reform in name and appearance, colonial societies from the beginning of 19th century began to talk about human rights and democracy and so on. It's not because the capitalists have accepted such change for the benefit of society, but because the new world of communication and speed of news transmission has prevented them from continuing their old ways of slavery.

Those called democratic governments had to appear that they are democratic and support freedom; so as a result they changed their policy plan from forced slavery, to modern, democratic and free will slavery.

HOW DOES THIS NEW SLAVERY SYSTEM WORK?

Instead of going to other countries and kidnapping people and forcing them to work for free as slaves, they changed their policy behind closed doors, plotting to colonize the third world countries. By tearing into those countries' government with media propaganda and spending money to buy traitors in those weak and poor countries; or taking over with military force to remove the good elected leaders from power and replace them with corrupt and criminal people to run those countries that capitalists gained control.

Corrupt so-called politicians have taken the place of good elected leaders and the result is unemployment, destruction, corruption, crime and devastating the economy of that country. In addition, these corrupt politicians killed or imprisoned the country's youth for various poor reasons. The result of these pressures was many young educated people fled from their homeland and applied for asylum to the colonial countries which used to have the old fashioned slavery system before calling themselves democratic government; specifically England, France, Portugal, Spain, Italy, and the United States of America, and even Russia and China.

There is no need for colonial countries to start a war to destroy a country, but by giving bribes to the traitors of those poor countries, virtuous patriots and progressive developers can be replaced with evil-minded, criminal and corrupt people who will destroy the country very easily and fast because they have no knowledge of how to run a country.

It is an evil idea, but it works very well, and many people couldn't figure out the secret. Compared to the traditional slavery it is much easier and more economical – with a more democratic appearance for capitalists to manage and control with this new approach. Plus, no one ever asked them how and when they suddenly become a democratic system and how and why do you let refugees enter your country so easily?

Isn't it funny that white Europeans with the massacre of Natives conquered the American continent, and now the countries formed on this continent consider themselves supporters of democracy and human rights? Although many governments have been in power since American independence, no Native Americans have ever been a country president. However, they still consider themselves supporters of democracy, freedom, and human rights.

Do those colonial countries really care about the people and youth of other countries? Millions of migrates leave their countries and leave their loved one behind and come to the developed colonial countries for peace, work and good life. Could they not have had peace, work, prosperity and a good life in their own home country? The answer is clear, the countries of these people are brought into chaos by the global capitalists for their own benefits and these people have no choice but to flee their own countries and leave their loved one behind and go to a far destination to colonial countries which provide them with so-called security, work, peace and better life.

The young generation run away from their countries and when they arrive in these developed colonial countries, they beg asylum to become a refuge, then they have to wait a long time in the camps for a work permit and then residency. After spending a long time waiting in refugee camps they start to work for minimum wage, with the lowest life standard and what ever money they make, they spend on rent for a room in a house (shared with 4 or 5 other people), food, clothes, phone, electricity, and if they have a car they pay for insurance and gas, and other expenses, and by the end of the year, what ever is left for them, they must pay as income tax, GST, PST, HST to the federal and provincial governments and this will be the routine for the rest of their life. Yet these refugees think they are free and safe and are thankful for their destiny. But these poor refugees have no idea that this fate had already been decided for them by the colonial powers.

No savings, no vacations and no fun in life, if some of them become rich in those societies, they must have done something really special like the invention of one of the essentials of the people's life or they do something wrong, like stealing, selling drugs, smuggling or some other illegal thing. Of course doing illegal things will end them to prison and they have to pay whatever they have saved, to the lawyers to defend them and keep them out of jail.

In capitalism nothing is in the right place. Most people are in jobs that are not related to their field of study or profession. In many parts of the world, educated people are either imprisoned or killed or in exile, or working in jobs other than their profession. Instead, illiterate and ignorant religious people rely on power and are given important work because the ruling colonial system wants it that way. Why? Because the religious and ignorant people do not have questions, answers, logic and reasoning and they can be easily deceived and looted. Backed by colonial countries, the most illiterate, ignorant, corrupt criminal person can become a leader of a country; and this selected leader of the colonial regimes, can kill or imprison all educated, intellectuals, journalists, scientists, environmentalists, writers, artists and many other wise people, or he can make them run away to different countries. So all these peaceful educated people that are able to make this world a better place for all of us are killed, jailed or exiled by one corrupt and criminal leader – someone who wants to return a developing country back to thousands of years ago with his superstitious religion, only because the big brother and big sister wants more money and more power and they can only achieve their ambitious aspirations by creating more corruption, crime and terror among the people.

One more example to show how modern slavery works in developed (colonial) countries like United States of America, United Kingdom, France, Germany, Russia, and even China; they sacrifice other countries for their own benefits; in other words, they make a big mess in third world countries for their own big profits. Their technique is like a fisherman who muddies the water to catch more fish.

For example, in the summer of 1953 England and American politicians planned to remove Mohammad Mossadegh, the elected prime minister of Iran, with a coup. Why? Because Mosadegh was kicking all the British Petroleum workers out of Iran. The Prime Minister was saying, the oil is in Iran and it belongs to the Iranian people, no one else should make more profit then Iranians.

The 1953 Iranian coup d'état, known in Iran as the 28 Mordad

Winston Churchill, who was the British Minister of the Navy armed forces during the days of war, urged the Iranian & British Petroleum Company, arguing that the replacement of liquid fuels instead of coal for the supply of fuels was critical. He ordered the Iranian & British oil company to carry out a secret pipeline to the Persian Gulf to provide fuel for British ships, and that was without paying any money to the Iranian side. Also, the British weren't using Iranian experts to work in the oil company, but they were using exploited Pakistani, Palestinian, Indian and others rather than Iranian people. That is why Prime Minister, Mohammad Mosadegh was angry and considered the contract no longer valid.

* SEE FOOTNOTE #1

As a result, the coup was orchestrated by the United Kingdom and USA, organized by one CIA agent seated in the American embassy in Tehran. He spent only a few million US dollars to finish the coup. In 2013 the United States finely admitted to their involvement in overthrowing a democratically elected government as reported by CNN.

Mohammed Mossadeq was Time Magazine's "Man of the Year" in 1951.

> The 1953 Iranian coup, known in Iran as the 28 Mordad coup d'état, which was the overthrow of Prime Minister Mohammad Mosaddegh in favour of strengthening the monarchical rule of Mohammad Reza Pahlavi on 19 August 1953, orchestrated by the United Kingdom (under the name Operation Boot) and the United States (under the name TPAJAX Project or Operation Ajax). I believe this was an internal political problem between the king and Prime Minister, and the Iranian people could solve their problem without external interference.

There are rumours that the British wanted to replace Mossadegh with Mullahs at that time but the American President Dwight D Eisenhower did not agree. Maybe the Iranians should thank president Eisenhower for the past.

Then, when King Mohammad Reza Pahlavi became older, and wiser, he wanted to make his country's economy strong for his people. He decided to raise the price of oil, to spend the money to develop the country and helping the Iranian people have better living conditions.

The logical reason for the king to raise the oil price was, everything he needed to buy from Europeans or Americans or any other country was increasing in price, so he also wanted to sell the country's oil at a higher price to make it fair. But for Capitalism is not normal that a leader of a third world country being logical and nice to his people, because in this case it will not benefit the colonial countries and that's why the super power colonial countries, stabbed him in the back.

Mohammad Reza Pahlavi also was the mediator of peace between India and Pakistan, Egypt and Israel. The mediation of the King of Iran for the peace of other countries was not acceptable to those weapons factories. It is clear that weapons factories can sell their weapons and make profit from them only in a state of war.

Then, 26 years after the coup against Mohammad Mosaddegh in favour of Mohammad Reza Pahlavi, in the beginning of 1978, Britain and Americans came back to Iran for another coup, but in a different evil plan. They sent many journalists to Iran to interview the King about democracy and the freedom situation in Iran.

The Shah didn't realize the Americans and British and other European politicians were preparing a secret coup against him. They were doing all this things because they wanted to remove him from power, because he was blocking their interests.

He accepted all the journalists and he interviewed them all, one by one. In those interviews he was very calm and confident and the King gave logical answers to their questions.

But democracy and freedom were only an excuse for the UK and USA. They wanted regime change. In 1978 under the western countries pressure, the King started to give more freedom to other parties like the radical communists and radical Muslims parties and he let the opposition say whatever they had to say against the regime and the king. He called it political open space. His new Prime Minister Shapor Bakhtiar also let much radical opposition, Muslim and communist prisoners free from jail. He was a freedom-loving and patriotic man who released all prisoners to show his goodwill to the protests of the people at the beginning of his rule.

But, that was a big mistake, because it created an opportunity for American and British politicians to back-stab King Mohammad Reza Pahlavi and knock him down faster and easier. In 1979, Radical Communist and Radical Muslims were free from prison and they were the ones who helped the big oil companies and weapon factories get Khomeini into power. They created real chaos in Iran, but those colonialist countries shamelessly called that disgraceful rebellion a revolution.

....

William Engdahl in A *Century of War: Anglo-American Oil Politics and the New World Order*, states:

> In November 1978, President Carter named the Bilderberg group's George Ball, another member of the Trilateral Commission, to head a special White House Iran task force under the National Security Council's Brzezinski. Ball recommended that Washington drop support for the Shah of Iran and support the fundamentalist Islamic opposition of Ayatollah Khomeini. Robert Bowie from the CIA was one of the lead 'case officers' in the new CIA-led coup against the man their covert actions had placed into power 25 years earlier.

....

American and British politicians specifically supported the most radical, fanatic, superstitious and illiterate Muslim to take power in Iran. They chose and supported an evil man to lead a country with an ancient civilization and culture and at that time, these powerful decision makers didn't imagine what consequences their wrong choice would create in the future for them.

We see that the CIA and MI6 created another disgraceful political movement in their history.

WHO WAS AYATOLLAH KHOMEINI?

The king of Iran exiled ayatollah Khomeini to Iraq. He was living in Iraq for almost 15 years but suddenly western intelligent services (CIA and MI6) miraculously arranged a passport for Ayatollah Khomeini and they took him from Najaf, a city in Iraq, to Kuwait and when Kuwait didn't accept him because of their political affiliation with the King of Iran, or for another mysterious political reason. then they took him directly to Novel Le chateaux, a city around Paris, France. Every day thousands of educated young people want to enter France but they wait in line for years, but an illiterate person like Ayatollah Khomeini receives a visa to enter France overnight – a miracles in politics.

During Khomeini was living in France, BBC news and other media from London and all over Europe and America backed by US dollars flew him around like an angel, advertised and tried to show him as a hero for the Iranian people. They prepared everything to bring this great Satan into power.

When Khomeini was in Iraq, he never made a speech against the King's regime nor was he threat to the King – if that was the case, the Iranian regime could easily get rid of him either through its intelligence agents or even through Saddam Hussein's regime, because Saddam had a good relationship with Iranian's regime at the time.

Opponents of the King took Khomeini as a winning card away from the reach of the Shah's agents. They took him first to Kuwait and when Kuwait didn't accept him, they took him directly to France where it wasn't easy for the Shah's agents to destroy him.

The Western media made Khomeini look like a religious hero and supported him as a replacement for the King of Iran, as a great leader. I remember when Khomeini was in Paris it was rumoured that Khomeini's image had been seen in the moon and Khomeini himself never denied the rumour. All the rumours about Khomeini were heard from foreign media.

....

> "There were illusions at the beginning, with Khomeini in France," according to the former French ambassador Nicoullaud . "Khomeini's speech was on 'peace and love'. He appeared to international media and governments like a kind of guru, a kind of Gandhi, who would re-establish democracy and so on.

"In fact this language was precisely by those intellectuals around him to seduce international opinion. Khomeini didn't care about that at all."

– AMBASSADOR FRANÇOIS NICOULLAUD

A few months later they sent Khomeini with a bunch of his idiot followers and journalists by Air France to Iran, to take over a 2,500 year old Monarchy. Of course, he had to thank the USA president Jimmy Carter and British government support. US dollars and BBC news made a most illiterate, ignorant, evil-minded person to be a leader of one of the most powerful and peaceful countries in the region. A country that had very friendly relationship with all other countries especially with Americans and Europeans until the last day. Unfortunately, the King Pahlavi only realized in the last days of his life that Westerns stabbed him in the back.

In this picture Jimmy Carter apparently drinking a cheers in the Iranian king's {Mohammad Reza Pahlavi} health but in secret, he holds a dagger on his back, to knock him down.

If that power replacement didn't happen because of some greediness and personal profit of big brother and big sister, then why did it happen? It doesn't make sense to me; to turn peoples life around and disrupt the lives in one country for the sake of a few Capitalist's interest. Why should this terrible event take place in the Middle East? Or any other places on this planet? How long must the people of the world be captive by the greed of some limited minority?

Ayatollah Khomeini was a Mullah (religion student) from Hozeh Elmieh (religion school) in which they only study one so-called holy book, the Quran. In that school many Mullahs supported Khomeini. Since Shah gave more freedom to the opposition, they used that opportunity for more demonstrations against the king and his regime.

*SEE FOOTNOTE # 2

UNITY OF EXTREME MUSLIM AND EXTREME COMMUNISTS:

The King Mohammad Reza Pahlavi called the radical Muslims and the radical communists a red and black alliance. These two radical groups came together and worked together with solidarity and unity. With the help of the colonial countries media and money, they dragged the King down. Mohammad Reza Pahlavi himself was the first man who called his opposition a Red and Black Alliance; he meant the supporters of the Soviet red flag and supporters of the Islamic black flag.

But, even though Western politicians were the conductors of this chaos in Iran, they were completely unaware of the formation of this alliance. Anyway, the opposition started marches, protests and demonstrations in different cities of Iran and then suddenly started to call Ayatollah Khomeini EMAM in Arabic – which means leader in Persian. Khomeini's supporters tried to make a holy Islamic figure of him.

An important point about Ayatollah Khomeini: Before I say what I want to say about Khomeini, first I must explain what Ayatollah means: Ayatollah means God's sign. What you'll read below about Ayatollah Khomeini is not a joke but facts that can be found on line.

Now about Ayatollah Khomeini's philosophy, the man who used to call America a great Satan: He wrote a book before he came to power titled *Tahrir Allvasileh* in which he explains about if a man have sex with animals, what they should do? He recommended that, if someone has sex with a domestic animal such as cow, sheep, camel, pig or a donkey, it is better to take that animal out of town and kill it and set it on fire and then pay the damages to the owner of the animal.

On page 17 in that book, he writes that lust is also permissible with an infant as long as the penis does not enter the baby's uterus, a man can rub his legs to a child's legs and put his penis between the baby's legs for lust. That book is full of nonsense, mostly about sex and lust.

Two other important things about Khomeini that I would like to mention here are that in one of his speeches Khomeini was commenting about economy as belonging to donkeys. In another speech, he said the danger of a university is much greater than that of a cluster bomb. I really must congratulate the British and European political leaders and especially congratulate Mr. Jimmy Carter, the president of United State of America in 1979, for electing Khomeini for 80 million innocent people with a history of 2,500 years of civilization. I doubt you have a good name in human history.

The political leaders of so-called democratic countries chose such a person and placed him in the power of an old and cultural country like Iran and this way of thinking has ruled in that ancient country for the last 41 years. Anyone who protests against the current situation is either sentenced to prison or shot in the brain as if human life in Iran is worthless. The funny part is that such a regime scares people away from ISIS and yet ISIS learned everything from Khomeini's regime. Throughout its 2500 year history Iran has gone through many wars and tragic events, but the current Islamic Regime in Iran has overtaken all the Cannibalistic and criminal regimes in human history.

Eventually the Iranian people will overthrow this corrupt, criminal and ignorant regime as well, soon or later, but Iranians will never forget the damage that colonial countries have caused in Iran over the past 100 years by their behaviour.

As a result of the activities of American and European politicians, Iran has become an insecure, unstable and a weak economy with a population that has been plagued by years of war. Corruption, crime, unemployment, looting, terrorist and intercontinental ballistic missiles and nuclear warheads are the 41 year-old products of this regime. If we evaluate the results of the actions and decisions of many world-famous leaders and politicians from a meritocracy point of view, they don't even deserve to lead a small village with several families.

The Western choice of regime for Iran, after 41 years can shoot at cargo ships and oil tankers, they can shoot at Aramco oil refinery in Saudi Arabia, they also can shoot more than 4,800 people in the streets of Iran in three days, because of the peaceful demonstrations that people had against the regime decision of tripling the gasoline prices in one night. They can shoot at US bases in Iraq, they can shoot a passenger airplane with 176 passengers and keep it as a secret for three days and not give back the black box to the country it belongs to for a long time. And they have done many other evil things in the past 41 years all over the world, and they have many other surprises in the future if they remain in power.

In my opinion, colonialism countries create a scarecrow for colonized countries and set them in power to scare the people and liberation movement, but after a while, these scarecrow makers suffer a deadly fear of what they have made themselves. They don't even dare to approach the scarecrow to destroy it.

All these pre-planned problems for one country were only for the benefits of some specific peoples. They created chaos in a country and destroyed the lives of its people just for the exploitation of a certain group. Enmity with Iran for how long? How much money and power is enough?

IN (GUADELOUPE CONFERENCE, 1979):

These leaders reached the conclusion that Shah could no longer stay in power and his stay would only raise tensions. In Guadeloupe, European and American leaders gathered together and planned to remove Mohammad Reza Pahlavi the king of Iran from power and replaced him with ayatollah Khomeini, the most ignorant, illiterate, liar, and corrupt-minded person, who was the worst enemy of Iran and enemy of Iranians.

Today I can boldly say that the Islamic regime that Khomeini founded in Iran was not only to destroy Iran and Iranians, but also to destroy the whole world. What I am saying today will be proven to everyone, once this Islamic regime stays in power for a few more years and gains access to nuclear weapons and inter-continental missiles. They are far worse than the North Korean regime.

WHAT WAS THE MAIN REASON FOR WESTERN COUNTRIES FOR THE SHIFT OF POWER IN IRAN?

I believe they had two different plans; their first plan was to draw Islamic Green belt countries around the Communist Soviet Union, so that idea of communism did not go beyond the soviet borders. The second plan, was to start the Iran-Iraq war, so they can buy cheap oil from those two countries, and they can sell all the old and rusty ammunition and guns held for years in weapons depots to them.

They may have succeeded in buying cheap oil and selling their rusty weapons, but no success in keeping Russia quarantined. Nowadays Russia and Communist China benefits the most from the Middle East, especially from Iran.

Guadeloupe Conference on Iran

> The Guadeloupe Conference attended by heads of four Western powers; U.S.A., UK, France and West Germany, was held in the first week of January 1979 on the island of Guadeloupe. Their agenda concerned world issues and the political crisis in Iran, where a popular revolutionary

upsurge was about to topple Mohammad Reza Shah. The dimensions of the agreements achieved before and after the conference have been kept secret.

French President Giscard d'Estaing hosted the Guadeloupe Conference. US President Jimmy Carter, British Prime Minister James Callaghan, and German chancellor Helmut Schmidt attended the four days meeting.

These leaders had reached the conclusion that Shah could no more stay in power and his stay would only raise tensions. In a press conference, the US secretary of state Cyrus Vance announced that Shah was getting ready for holidays outside Iran adding that Shah's political role on shaping Iran's future had come to an end.

– MIR M. HUSSEINI.

••••••••••••••••••••

From the very beginning of the turmoil, the real Iranian people have had much loss and problems with racial and religious discrimination, imprisonment and exile, losing the youth in war or getting shot in the streets during peaceful demonstrations by the regime since taking over 41 years ago, and all these continue until today in 2020

SEE FOOTNOTE # 3

Before that turmoil, Iran was one of the most peaceful, stable and strong country in the whole world, in many different ways; plus the king was friendly to Western countries, especially to Americans. At that time the whole Middle East was in peace, because Iran was in peace.

Khomeini came to power in Iran and he stole everything from people. He took away relative prosperity, freedom, security, peace and justice. His followers destroyed many things we had for thousands of years; they burned many Persian books and destroyed many historic buildings. Proponents of the regime, in the name of construction, have destroyed all of Iran's natural resources. They are trying hard to destroy our historical monuments, and cultural heritage but they are not able to destroy everything; because the Iranian or Persian culture is so old and rich with strong roots that no enemy ever could destroy it.

Iran is the cradle of human civilization and will never die. Iran as a country used to be called Persia. The people of that country have been defending themselves from savage, hungry attackers, which have come from all over the world during the last 2,000 years. Alexander the Macedonian was the first attacker. He died there, but his commanders Salukis and his descendants stayed in Iran for 182 years. Eventually, they were expelled by a group of Iranians

* SEE FOOTNOTE #4

When Khomeini's plane was flying to Tehran, inside the airplane a reporter asked Khomeini, "How do you feel going to Iran after all those years?" The man sitting beside Khomeini (Shadegg Ghotbzadeh) had to translate the question to Khomeini. Khomeini said calmly, "NOTHING." From that moment on, some Iranian's realized there would be no freedom nor any progress or development from Khomeini for Iran. Many others didn't get what nothing means from someone who wants to be a leader of a great and ancient country, which he has no feeling about.

From a person who has never went to school or worked in his life, and has never seen a movie in a theatre, and only boarded a plane twice, (once to go to Paris and once to return to Iran,) you cannot expect to hear more than NOTHING from him.

Hostage taking:

On November 04, 1979, about eight months after Khomeini got into power, he ordered his followers to attack the American Embassy. They attacked the embassy in Tehran and they held fifty-two hostages for 444 days. I think that was Khomeini's way of saying thanks to Jimmy Carter and his entire Democrat party members who helped him to get into power.

The funny part of the hostage crisis happened many years later. Throughout all these years at every ceremony and even in the Islamic parliament, they burn the American flag and shout "Down with America". But now all those who climbed the embassy wall to take the hostages are high-ranking government officials and sending their children to the United States to study in universities. Masomeh Ebtekar is one of them and her son is living in US. The grandchildren of Ayatollah Khomeini are in Canada and many others are in Europe.

The question is, how is it possible that Americans have no embassy in Iran but US emigration gives visas to Khomeini's supporter's children to enter their soil – like there is no problem and no hostage crises ever happened?

From the first day the Islamic regime got into power in Iran up to now with the command of Ayatollah Khomeini and his successor Ayatollah Khamenei supreme leaders, 5,000,000 people were killed in public or in secret and more than 7,000,000 escaped the country and 5,000,000 are still in public or secret prisons. Also, 80,000,000 Iranians are in the captivity of the Islamic regime, in a prison the size of Iran.

REPEATED – THE SAME TRAGEDY IN AFGHANISTAN AND OTHER COUNTRIES:

Those colonial countries pursued the same destructive policies in Afghanistan and many other countries. They removed the King Zahir Shah with a peaceful regime in Afghanistan and they replaced it with most radical Muslims like the Taliban. They made Afghanistan go back 1,400 years; a huge regression. Even in the 21-century they still have the law of stoning women. Many Afghans have died and many others escaped the country, and who knows how many are in prisons. Even since the American military kicked the Taliban out of power after 9-11 and replaced them with Hamid Karzai and others; nothing is changed. Everyday Taliban suicide bombers blow themselves up and kill many defenceless and innocent people inside Afghanistan.

AMERICAN FRIENDSHIP WITH SAUDI ARABIA AND THEIR ENMITY WITH THE FRIENDLY SAUDI TALIBAN!

Americans are best friends with Saudi Arabia and leaders of Saudi Arabia are the best friends with Taliban. Saudi Arabia helps the Taliban financially to teach Quran to children to make them ready to be suicide bombers to kill American soldiers or others. I cannot figure out the American policy, because it doesn't make sense to me at all, how can any one fight with his friend's friends? Can you? They fight with Taliban whom are friends of Saudi Arabia and Saudis are friends with Americans!

These so-called democratic countries did the same thing to Egypt, some radical Muslim assassinated Amber Sadat, the peaceful president of Egypt, and they replaced him with Hosni Mubarak.

NOTE: The islamic regime of Iran named the killer of Anwar Sadat on a street near the Egyptian embassy

In Chile they had coup against Salvador Agenda, democratic elected president and replaced him with dictator Pinochet.

They did the same in Pakistan, in Iraq and many other countries. I am sure they are planning to make more mess in many other countries in the future, but unfortunately whatever these developed countries do today, they have no idea about the end of their career, they don't know what will come back to them in the future. They just think of instant profits and interest, they don't think of the consequences.

* SEE FOOTNOTE #5

After those political changes, millions of people, young and old with their children try to flee their country. Many are smuggled into overcrowded small boats to seek asylum in other countries if they survive the sea safely.

NOTE: Just a few months ago, an iranian couple with three children drowned in the English Channel while travelling to England in a small boat with too many people.

Some others head to Australia to have a better life but they end up in horrific refugee camps on Manus Island. Many others bought their own tickets and were smuggled out of their country to colonial countries like England, America and other European countries, and when they arrive, they beg for refugee asylum.

Then they work as a cheap labour all their life, and if they don't work for one month, they will be homeless with no roof above their head and no food in their bellies. Yet, they are very happy that they are living in a free and safe country; all because they don't know that big brother and big sister had designed such a life for them beforehand (a man-made destiny).

MODERN CITIES:

With all the inventions and new ideas mentioned earlier, little by little the cities started to grow and they became big and modern with more facilities; like faster transportation, easier communication, digital television with bigger screen, computers, robots and advanced medical remedies.

Capitalists are saving more money by replacing human workers with high technology robots and computers. That replacement automatically decreases the cost of running the company, so it would bring more profit and fewer headaches for capitalists. More production making every day with modern machines and robots, transporting them to different cities and different countries by plane, truck and train, at the same time the prices of the productions are going up and higher everyday for more profits.

It is strange that the lower the cost of different companies' products, the higher the price of the same products are sold at, and there is no will to lower the price or control it by authorities.

That is why the rich become richer and the poor become poorer and the class difference has become extremely high.

Now days, almost every one knows that one percent of the earth population has 99 percent of the earth's wealth and 99 percent of the population owns only one percent of the wealth. Yet neither of these two classes is really happy nor do they live longer than another.

In capitalism everything revolves around self-interest, greed and selfishness. These selfish rules are the foundation of the system. Nothing is about "we" or "us" or other people's interest. No one cares for the interests of others; the rich want to be richer and the poor want to survive.

Company owners think about themselves and their own family interests and profits. In the capitalist system, the public interests and social rights of the people have no special meaning; in fact, there is no such thing as public interest. The majority of the society is made up of workers and they are also customers of the same one percent capitalist elite.

An example:

> A gun factory makes guns and other dangerous harmful weapons to sell, only for the purpose of making itself a profit. Now, if someone buys a gun and goes out to a public place like a market or school and starts to shoot others and kill many people, that is not the gun factory owner's problem. It doesn't matter to the owner who kills who, to them the profit is more important then anything else. As a matter of fact, they have expert people working for them in a secret, to plan wars between other countries so they can sell more of their products as well. Although war brings destruction, displacement, famine, death and calamity to ordinary people, it also brings great economy prosperity to the weapon factories, oil companies, and corrupt politicians and religious leaders.

A real example of what happened in the past:

The gulf war between Iran and Iraq 1980-1988. About a year after Ayatollah Khomeini came to power in Iran, war started between Iran and Iraq. I believe that colonial countries for the benefit of oil companies and weapons factories orchestrated that war. They secretly planned a war between Iran and Iraq, and these two countries fought each other for more than eight years. Who won that war and who lost it? The weapons factories and the big oil companies won the war and Iran and Iraq lost the war. That's my answer.

How? War needs a big budget to buy weapons to give them to the solders to fight. Also solders need food, clothes and other things, other professional soldiers need a salary as well. All these things need money. Iran and Iraq needed money to pay for the war expenses and the only way they could provide the war's budget it was to sell oil for very low price to the big oil companies.

Iran and Iraq had to sell good quality oil with a low price to the oil companies from the same countries that planed the war. After selling their oil, they had money to buy the old rusted weapons from gun factories of the same countries that planned the war in the first place.

That is not a bad deal for those colonial countries. They made a very good profit for eight years of war; selling old rusted weapons with a high price, and bought good quality oil for a very low price. But, all that money goes only to the one percent rich people's pockets and the rest of people get nothing out of that; but instead they have to pay more money for petrol they use in their cars and pay more money for the natural gas they use for heating their homes and pay more for other essentials. The gun factories and the oil companies are the best partners and they help and support each other to make more profit. Maybe the both companies belong to the politicians? Who knows?

The war makers don't bother to plan war for the countries have no oil or other valuable mineral resources, unless they do it for the attraction of cheep labourers. Munition factories are making and producing a variety of weapons every day. They don't make them to keep in the museum but only for war to make profit.

Another example of disadvantages of the capitalist system for the human communities is: Cigarette factories.

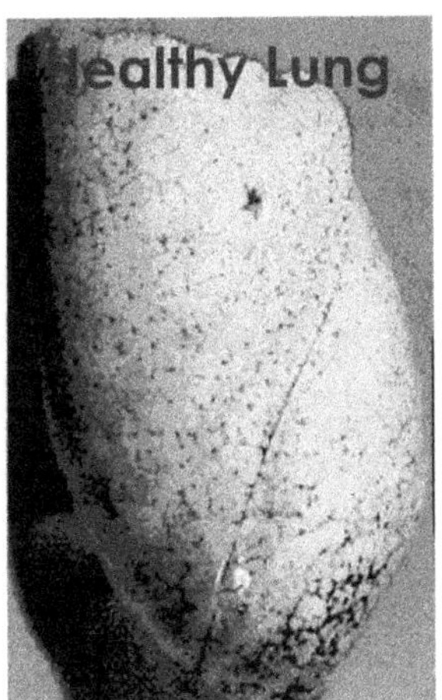

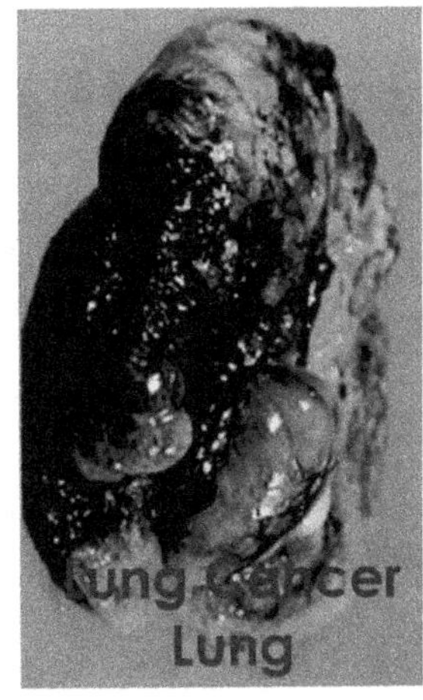

The cigarette factory owners don't care if people loose their teeth or get lung cancer or heart attack, or even if they die, just because of smoking cigarettes. The cigarette factories add so many different chemicals to natural tobacco; to make sure that anyone who tried smoking once, can never quit until they die. The only important thing for the cigarette company owners is to make more money and more profit. For the capitalist, morality and humanity have no meaning at all.

I have heard from some people that they were addicted to heroin and they were able to quit that dangerous chemical mixed with opium in a laboratory, but they weren't able to quit smoking cigarettes. It is hard to imagine, but it's true. When many different chemicals come together, they produce the worst and most dangerous poison, but the amazing part is when you can buy that poison in any gas station legally and we call it CIGARETTE.

Have you ever wondered what is in a cigarette?

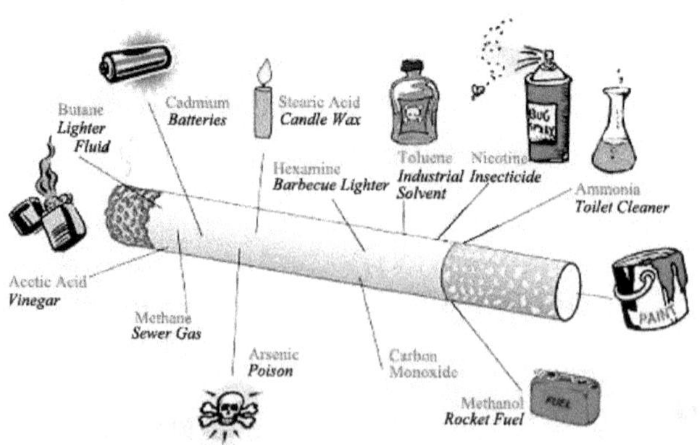

Cigarette ingredients:

Over 4,000 chemicals, including 43 known cancer-causing (carcinogenic) compounds and 400 other toxins. Cigarette ingredients include nicotine, tar, and carbon monoxide, as well as formaldehyde, ammonia, hydrogen cyanide, arsenic, and DDT. Nicotine is highly addictive. Smoke containing nicotine is inhaled into the lungs, and the nicotine reaches your brain in just six seconds.

> They say cigarette are not as serious as heroin addiction, but addiction to nicotine also poses very serious health risks in the long run and it is very difficult to quit. Nicotine in small doses acts as a stimulant to the brain. In large doses, it's a depressant, inhibiting the flow of signals between nerve cells. In even larger doses, it's a lethal poison, affecting the heart, blood vessels, and hormones.
>
> Nicotine in the bloodstream acts to make the smoker feel calm. As a cigarette is smoked, the amount of tar inhaled into the lungs increases, and the last puff contains more than twice as much tar as the first puff. Carbon monoxide makes it harder for red blood cells to carry oxygen throughout the body. Tar is a mixture of substances that together form a sticky mass in the lungs. Most of the chemicals inhaled in cigarette smoke stay in the lungs. The more you inhale, the better it feels—and the greater the damage to your lungs. You can ask anyone working on a bachelor degree in any medical field and they will be able to tell you what damage smoking does to the lungs.

An exhaust is a pipe that is installed in each engine to direct smoke out of engine, because the designers and inventors of various engines have realized by experience that if the smoke stays inside the engine, it will fail the engine in a very short time. But some of those inventors while they were installing the exhausts on their own invented engine, had a cigarette on their lips and they were smoking heavily and directed the smoke into their own body. Isn't that really weird?

So as long as those companies they pay tax (if they pay any) to the governments, they are allowed to sell their products in any markets legally, without any hindrance even if it is proven in laboratories that these products are real poison. To prevent any complaints or legal barriers from public, owners of cigarette factories also put up a images of human body parts destroyed by cigarettes and even warn people that smoking can cause cancer. But they don't explain, if they care so much and they are worried for people's heath, why they add so many chemicals into tobacco? We know that pure tobacco is much less harmful to the body.

When people smoke for so many years, as they get older they become sick and they cannot even breathe easily. They must quit when they reach the point that they must carry an oxygen tank with them wherever they go. They must also use other medicines to cover heart diseases or lung cancer.

ANOTHER DISADVANTAGE OF THE CAPITALIST SYSTEM IS ALCOHOLIC BEVERAGE COMPANIES:

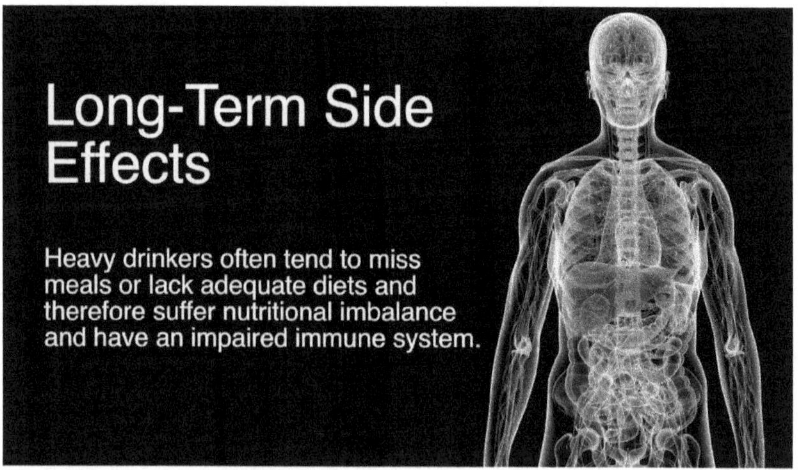

Long-Term Side Effects
Heavy drinkers often tend to miss meals or lack adequate diets and therefore suffer nutritional imbalance and have an impaired immune system.

What happen when some one is alcoholic?

Disadvantages of alcohol consumption:

1. Loss of self-control: Alcohol drinking loses self-control on the body and thereby leads to accidents.
2. Damage to liver: Heavy consumption can damage parts of their body, especially liver, stomach, brain are affected the most. It can also lead to cardiovascular troubles and high blood pressure, etc.

Cigarette and alcohol factories are also best partners because one matches the other one.

Who first discovered alcohol and for what use?

Muhammad Zachariah Raze also known by his Latinized name Razes

Born 854 CE [1], Ray, Persia [2]

Died 932 or 925 CE [2], Ray, Persia (Iran)

Era Islamic golden age

Main interests: Medicine, philosophy, and alchemy. He also wrote on logic, astronomy and grammar.

A comprehensive thinker, Raze made fundamental and enduring contributions to various fields, which he recorded in over 200 manuscripts, and is particularly remembered for numerous advances in medicine through his observation and discoveries.

An early proponent of experimental medicine, he became a successful doctor, and served as chief physician of Baghdad and Ray hospitals. As a teacher of medicine, he attracted students of all backgrounds and interests and was said to be compassionate and devoted to the service of his patients, whether rich or poor.

According to the Encyclopedia Britannica (1911), he was among the first to use humeral theory to distinguish one contagious disease from another, and wrote a pioneering book about smallpox and measles providing clinical characterization of the diseases. He also discovered numerous compounds and chemicals including alcohol and sulphuric acid, among others.

Through translation, his medical works and ideas became known among medieval European practitioners and profoundly influenced medical education in the Latin West. Some volumes of his work Al-Mansur, namely "On Surgery" and "A General Book on Therapy", became part of the medical curriculum in Western universities. Edward Granville Browne considers him as "probably the greatest and most original of all the Persian physicians, and one of the most prolific as an author." Additionally, he has been described as a doctor's doctor, the father of paediatrics and a pioneer of ophthalmology. For example, he was the first to recognize the reaction of the eye's pupil to light.

– WIKIPEDIA

••••••••••••••••••••

The discovery of Vodka to drink.

Zachariah Raze had discovered white alcohol for pharmaceutical purpose, like disinfection in 9th century, but in the 18 century, in Poland and Russia some people started to make alcohol out of potatoes, rice, sugar, corn and other nutrients for drinking purpose; just to make people drunk, and make money off of that..

Wine has a long history from thousands of years ago especially red wine from Shiraz, but vodka was first made in Poland and Russia in the 18th century for consumers.

Why alcohol makes the drinker thirsty?

UT South-western researchers, in their study, have identified over use in alcohol can cause a number of adverse effects in the morning, including headaches, nausea, body aches and fatigue, as well as dehydration, which can leave you feeling thirsty. This is due to the effects of alcohol on your body.

A hormone that acts on the brain increases the desire to drink water in response to specific nutrient stresses of consuming **more** alcohol that can cause dehydration. That's why, when we drink one beer we become thirsty, we need the second one and after drinking the second beer we need more and more.

When mostly people drink alcohol, they like to smoke a cigarette as well and vice versa; some people smoke a cigarette and then they like to drink some alcohol.

WHAT IS THE REASON FOR ATTRACTING PEOPLE, ESPECIALLY YOUNG PEOPLE TO SMOKING CIGARETTES AND DRINKING ALCOHOL?

I believe the owners of these companies make up stories and spread them among people in the form of rumours to convince the community that smoking and drinking alcohol is a sign of growth and maturity and intellectual intelligence of individuals. But these imaginary stories can only affect the brains of teenagers, which is the best age to deceive and target them to be new costumers for any addictive substances. (Don't be a sissy la la, have a cigarette and let's drink some booze together to grow up, a teenager boys or girls says to each other) These taunts have been whispered in our ears since we were teenagers to encourage the constant consumption of goods that have accustomed us to them, and now it has become part of our language and culture.

NOTE: In the country where I live now, there are four, sometimes five alcohol shops in every neighbourhood with at least two grocery stores.

The cigarette and alcohol producers are supporting each other and these two industries also support pharmaceutical companies, because the cigarette and alcohol eventually cause all kinds of cancers and diseases. At old age medication must be used to treat these diseases. Consumers of these two products ultimately will need different medications to recover the side effects of alcohol and cigarettes. Therefore, we know alcohol drinkers and cigarette smokers eventually will be the medicine factories customers in the future.

In the capitalist system, all these companies are attached or related to each other like a chain. Who knows, maybe all those companies are belongs to one family or one company and if they are not owned by one person with his family now, maybe they will be owned by one company or (one family) in the very near future. As we see, big companies are buying the smaller ones everyday.

DISADVANTAGE OF CAPITALISM IN THE FOOD MARKETS:

Wasting food in every small or big supermarket.

I was working in Wal-Mart for a few months and I saw many tons of food going to the trash bin every day, some of the fruits like bananas had only some scratches and they were absolutely fine to eat, but the system chooses to trash them rather than give as a charity to poor people.

It is true that some organizations gather and distribute food for low-income families from food banks, but most of these foods are close to expiration date and it must be quickly consumed or thrown in the trash. Also there are many low-income people that never like to go to the food banks because of their pride. What can society do for these kinds of people?

Why do we waste the farmer's energy for nothing? I believe this is because the capitalists think the price must stay high and they don't care for food wasting. Many people in the world have a shortage of food, nutrients and the right vitamins. This nutrient shortage has caused a variety of diseases for them.

NOTE: There are many disadvantages of fast food restaurants that everyone knows about, and I do not need to comment on them.

Why does it have to be that way?

Is it because in the capitalist system everyone thinks of, and cares only, about their own interests? Why? Why is everything in human society about "me", "I", "myself" and "my family"? Why nothing is about "us", "we", or "everyone"? What is wrong with our brain?

DISADVANTAGE OF CAPITALIST IN COLLECTING MONEY FROM PEOPLE, EVEN WHEN THEY HAVE LITTLE INCOME:

People get paid limited money every two weeks or every month for their daily hard work, but they receive monthly payment bills from many different companies such as internet, phone, electricity, TV, water and dozens of other bills; in addition to paying rent or mortgage payments, food and many other expenses must be provided with one salary.

There are many different companies that send bills to people and people have no choice but to pay those bills, otherwise suddenly they don't have electricity or if they don't pay for gas they have no hot water or heat; or if they don't pay for their phone line, the next month they will have no more phone line and no internet; if they don't pay for TV line there would be no more TV and so on, yet all the above is needful in our society.

One day a long time ago someone invented an alternator to generate electricity. Nowadays many companies in all over the world sell electricity at a very high monthly price compared to people's low monthly income. Someone else invented the phone, and now many companies charge people lots of money every month for having a phone line and Internet. Other people have discovered many other things but they lived poor all their life and they died poor, but after their death other people started companies with their own names to exploit these inventions and charge people monthly for these services.

One of the main motivations for me to write this book is the danger of the destruction of the earth by the greedy, aggressive and ridiculous capitalist system. I call the capitalist system ridiculous, because in this system humans are all looking at each other as a customer or dollar sign.

MEDICATION IN CAPITALISM

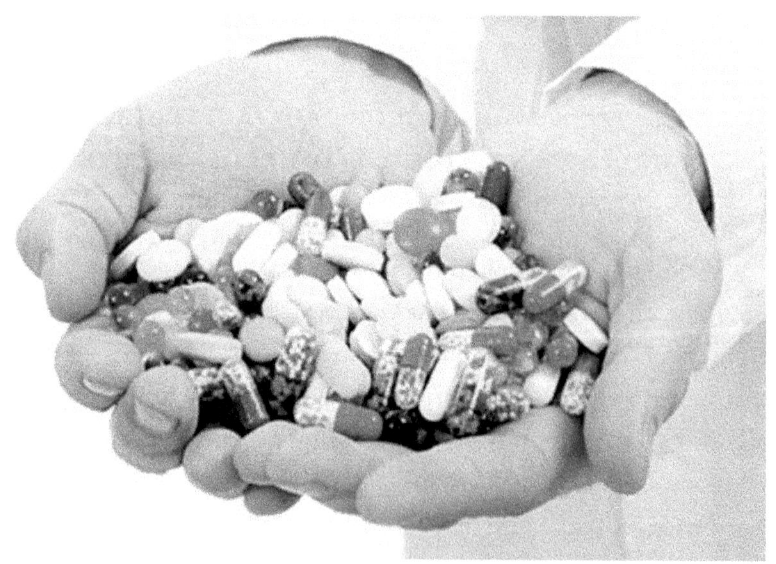

MEDICATIONS SYSTEM IN EVERY COUNTRIES ARE DIFFERENT

In some countries, visiting a doctor is more expensive than the medicines and in other countries medicines are more expensive than visiting a doctor. In some other countries medicine and visiting a doctors are both expensive, for example in Canada if someone is working and have no insurance, when they get sick they can visit a doctors for free but to buy the medicine they must pay for it themselves, like my self, I was owner operator working for a taxi company but I wasn't covered by insurance for any medical treatment. I had to pay almost $2,000 a year for my medicines. The government pays for the medicine of those who do not work and live under government aid, but their medicine must be one of the cheapest.

In United States it is worse, because a patient must have insurance or they must pay out of their own pocket for visiting a doctor and for the medicine. Also, there are various medications at different prices for one type of illness. Some of the medicines are cheaper then others but they have side effects and will make the patient more sick than before; and there are other medicines for a higher price for the same illness, but apparently they have less side effects.

Why? Are diseases controlled by human? Or is it within our power to prevent diseases? Is it possible to decide not to be sick? Why we must pay so much more money for the right medication?

For example: For diabetes there is Metformin, a round white pill which is the cheaper medicine but it has side effects, and there is Janumet a brown cylindrical tablet, which is much more expensive, almost one dollar each tablet, but it has fewer side effects. Can anyone tell me, why should there be discrimination between the poor and the rich in various diseases? Do the rich people deserve better treatment than poor people, because they have more money?

If researchers and pharmacists around the world discover the Corona (Covid-19) vaccine, but the price will be so high that poor people can't afford to buy it, what shall they do? Should they just wait for death? Perhaps this discrimination treatment in human health between poor and rich is part of the world population control policy, by the big brother and big sister?

Disadvantage of capitalism in treatment of diseases:

Physicians and pharmacists discovers the treatment of various diseases and cancers:

I believe researchers have found cures for many diseases but the medicine company owners don't release those secret cures, because it would be bad for their business; so usually the medicine company owners buy the cure from the researchers and they throw them in the garbage because they don't want to loose their business. And if that researcher doesn't want to exchange the result of his medical research for money and his goal is to improve and cure all the patients with that specific disease and serve his community, than suddenly an accident will happen and the medical researcher will be pressed between two trucks on the road and dies, and no one talk about his medical research anymore.

To the capitalist, money is more important than human health, because if all humans are healthy and fine, then they wouldn't buy medicines. The result would be no profit for the company's investors and after while the company must shut down.

Pharmaceutical companies are more interested in the production of soothing pills than in the production of curative and healing medication, because sedatives are a constant source of income and always beneficial to the owners.

It is not far-fetched to say that the spread of certain viruses by some pharmaceutical companies is deliberately distributed in the community so they can sell the particular drug matched to that disease. Also, it makes it easier and cheaper to control the earth's population, because in many poor countries, many people are not able to buy these drugs. Many people will die as either they don't have access to the medication or through physically weakness they are not able to resist these sicknesses.

Coronavirus:

The subject of the coronavirus is not something that can be easily overcome because this virus has come to take the lives of many of the world's vulnerable, old, poor and weak people and weak companies.

The story goes that the virus has been transmitted from bat to Pangolin anteater and from pangolin to humans.

I do not agree with this theory. Why? Because humans have been eating different kinds of animal meat since the ice age and this carnivore continues to this day, all over the world. Some people, out of hunger, consider every animal they see to be their food and they don't care if the animal is a sheep, a pig, a dog, a cat or a bat or anteater. But throughout the long history of humans eating meat, nobody has been infected with such a virus that spreads quickly and kills so many people so easy. It doesn't make sense to me that nature created such a virus.

Throughout history, there have been thousands of hungry people hunting bats and pouring them into pots and cooking and eating them and no virus has been ever infected them.

Now what happened all of a sudden coronavirus it came from eating Pangolin meat and it spread all over the world?

In my opinion this virus has not been transmitted from animals to human, rather the virus is being tested in high-cost virology laboratories, to control the population of the earth in favour of the rich and so-called superior genes. They also want small businesses out of the global economy. The vaccine will soon be available to public, but the price will be so high that the poor will never be able to afford it in many countries.

The reader of this book may ask me what is your solution to destroy the Corona-virus and save the people of the world from this dangerous virus?

My answer to this question is as follows:

First- Compulsory public quarantine of one month except for sensitive and all other essential jobs such as hospitals, fire departments, electricity, water, telephone, taxi, police, gas stations , delivery drivers and all essential jobs which they can not be closed .

Second- For the quarantine of the public, we must have an efficient and logical program can include the provision of people's necessities and be delivered to people's homes for free of charge, at least for one month.

Note: The doors of the people's food and other essentials where houses should be open 24/7 days a week to meet the people's need and everything should be deliver to people's homes for free. I think this would be a good opportunity for the capitalist system to prove its kindness and generosity in this important month.

Third- Anyone who is forced to work during this month is required observe of 3 to minimum 2 meters of social distance and observance of hygiene principals.

NOTE: Governments should give them extra benefits or a month off paid after the quarantine.

Fourth- Forced masking of the mouth and nose in public and free to walk for exercising with keeping distance between one group living together in one house with others 3 to minimum of 2 meters and observance of hygienic principals.

Note: It should be mandatory of only 2 people of one family (or roomate) be allowed to walk together at a time.

Fifth- All travel, sightseeing and air travel must be stopped for one month.

Sixth- No family should visit each other unless they live in one place.

Seventh- No landlord should have any right to request rent from their tenant during this one month.

Eighth- No companies such as electricity, telephone, water, gas, internet and other services should have right to charge anyone for that month.

Note: People should be given a week to prepare the necessary food and other materials for the month of quarantine. This could also be an opportunity for those who are travelling for any reason to return home before the start of one month quarantine.

I think that observing and following the above eight principals can destroy the CORONAVIRUS for good.

....

Dentist Services in Current System of the World

There are so many dentists in every country and every city but they are there only for the people who can afford to pay the price. When I was in Rosemont, California, I met many toothless people, something that really surprised me a lot, and I asked a few of them,

"Why don't you repair your teeth?" Their answers were all the same; they didn't have enough income and they couldn't afford to repair their teeth. They were not even able to pay for artificial teeth, so they can chew and digest their food properly. In the long run most of those people become sick, because of indigestion disease.

One good example that happened few years ago when I started to write this book and I was a witness of it:

My roommate had toothache for a few weeks and she didn't have enough money to go to the dentist. She was a newcomer to Canada and did not speak English very well. So I took her to a dentist in our town to find out what was wrong with her wisdom teeth and how much it would cost to fix them. They took x-rays and dentist told us that he had to pull out three of her teeth and the cost would be $1,250 and I already paid $125 for her x-ray. Although she was working at the time, but she was working part-time and she has low income, so she couldn't afford to pay that money.

I took her to the social welfare office and I asked them for financial assistant to help her get rid off the rotten teeth and pain, which was making her suffer every night and she wasn't able to sleep. So the reception made an appointment time for two hours later and she asked us to bring some documents for review. We came back on time and met the social worker. She took all the documents and went through all of them and in the end she told her, "You have enough money in your bank account to cover your dentist fee."

I told her she has only $1200 and in one week from now she must pay $640 for her rent and then she must pay for her diabetes medications, pay for food, pay for her phone and she has other expenses as well and after paying for all this expenditure, there would be nothing left for her to pay the dentist. The social worker referred us to go to the university dentist, the students don't charge, she said.

I called the university right in front of her face, and someone answered me I told her about my roommate situation. They said that we must pay $280 for registering and we must pay for other fees that she didn't know upfront how much that would be and also she wasn't sure when they have time for my roommate to go there to fix her teeth problem. That was the end of telephone conversation.

Then the social worker was suggested that we should go to a church or mosque. I told her we are not religious and I don't think it is right to go around and beg money for her pain; it is the government's responsibility to assist her, not a church or a mosque. So in the end, we left the social welfare office with no positive response. That was the end of the social assistance for an emergency situation in a capitalist system. I don't blame the social worker, because she does exactly what the law asks her to do.

ANOTHER EXAMPLE OF THE DISADVANTAGE OF CAPITALIST SYSTEM IS THE BANKERS:

The bank owners don't make any useful products that are used by people, but they are the wealthiest people in whole world and they own the best of everything. How?

Easy, they keep peoples money with close to zero percentage of interest in their banks, but if they have to give loan or they lend mortgages to the same people to buy a house, first of all and foremost they look at every bank account and all available information of the borrower, then they ask for all kind of guarantees from the person who wants to borrow money; and after all, most of the money that is taken out of the home buyer's account as a monthly instalment, payment is calculated from the interest of the loan, to the extent that monthly instalment interest is much higher than the principal of the debt. For the borrower there is no choice but to accept all terms and conditions of the loan, or buy a smaller/cheaper house if one is available.

Why? Because the bank has the money and they like to make big interest on it by lending it to borrower – it is what it is, take it or leave it. They do what ever they want to do and no one can do anything about it. That's how capitalism works. Bankers are the best friends of factories, builders, investors, oil companies, and business owners – who ever is making lots of money – banks are working with them. Banks are built in the best locations and they have many employees working for them; they make money out of money and nothing else, they have no useful production. Bankers have skyscrapers in every city centre in all countries on this planet. Where does all the money came from to build those skyscrapers? The bankers provide no essential products for people's needs! Have you ever wondered how many people these global bankers employ?

DISADVANTAGE OF CAPITALIST SYSTEM IN GROWING DIFFERENT TERRORIST GROUPS, WHICH ARE GROWING LIKE MUSHROOMS EVERYDAY AND EVERYWHERE

When I was a teenager, 50 years ago, I heard in the news that some Palestinians terrorist groups like Hamas or AL Fatah were hijacking airplanes and kidnapping some Jewish people here and there; but now days we have many Islamic groups from Iran, Saudi Arabia, Algeria, Somalia, Pakistan, Afghanistan, Syria, Iraq and even in Philippine islands; Islamic Jihadi, Al Qaida from Saudi Arabia, Al Shaba, Boca Haram in Africa, Hezbollah in Lebanon, Hashed AL shabby in Iraq and many others from Iran and Saudi Arabia. Most of these groups are being supported either by some arabic countries which are Sunni, or the Iranian Islamic regime, which is Shia.

Many countries are claiming that they are at war with terrorists, (even Iran and Saudi Arabia,) pretend they want to destroy terrorists; but in reality, those countries are taking immediate political and economical advantage and benefits from the existence of terrorism. Apparently European, American, Russian, Chinese and some Arabic regimes have been fighting with terrorists groups for more then 20 years on different fronts, but it seems those terrorist organizations will never be destroyed and they become bigger and stronger everyday.

No one knows who gives them guns, missiles, tanks and ammunition? In the distance past, terrorist groups appeared in masks to hijack an airplane or kidnap hostages. These days, terrorists have removed masks from their faces and continue terrorist activities with more courage, more boldness and less fear; to the extent that the world's superpower countries sit at the negotiating table with them. Instead, the repressive government officials of the Islamic republic of Iran wearing masks to suppress the protesting people.

NOTE: A terrorist group in an African country attacked a girls school a few years ago, and kidnapped several hundred girls and took them away. Now, many of those girls are the mothers of the children of that terrorist group, and no government has taken any action against them so far. These new babies will be the soldiers of that terrorist group in the future.

Isn't it weird?

Terrorist phenomenon and its problems and consequences
How to eliminate this phenomenon:

Terrorism is a phenomenon born of the capitalists, religions, politicians and mafia. People who form terrorists groups are mostly illiterate, ignorant, unemployed, without any income and any family. Their leaders are experienced agents of industrialized and dictatorial countries, and these agents are often irrational cowards, materialistic and power-hungry; without having any logic and knowledge of argument about wrong or right of paths in lifestyle.

Therefore, these people do not know any other ways of achieving their goal other than physically eliminating others through cowardice and from behind. The work and mission of the terrorist is to promote fear and panic among the common people through their brutal behaviour so that their masters (older siblings) can achieve their sinister goals and achieve their desired result of taking their share of power and wealth.

How to destroy the terrorist phenomenon?

In my opinion, in order to eradicate these evil and filthy social problems, we must first and foremost restore prosperity, freedom, peace, security, and social justice to the international community. Secondly, there must be no banks and no money where anyone can take any action against people. They shouldn't be able to live secretly in caves and buy whatever they need from the city with money, and provide everything for their group members, and escape the consequences, thirdly collect and destroy all the weapons and destructive tools and guns from society.

> NOTE: Just as human have developed a vaccine to eradicate a deadly virus, logic dictates that we think and find a way to eliminate terrorists before they can destroy us.

Fourth, Individuals from terrorist groups who have committed crimes against humanity should be brought to justice and those who have not committed crimes should be educated and released on condition that they must be monitored by legal authorities.

Corruption and crime in the capitalism:

In the capitalist system, many criminals commit crime in one country and they escape the law and punishment and runaway to a different country where they continue living freely and no one even can find them. Why? Because they have lots of money and by investing their capital in those countries, they can get a residency permit in any country they want. Each country has set aside a certain amount of money for investment for residence permit applicants.

In some countries a criminal who is a head of mafia with hundreds of people working for him selling drugs or they do other crimes with no hindrances. That leader can do anything he wants and no one can even touch a button on his shirt. Police usually don't want to get involved because these mafia leaders are able hurt anyone and their family.

Even if they do catch mafia leaders by the army and imprison them, they have the best lawyers to defend them and if they go to jail they will have the best cell and all the living conditions in that cell and everything will be provided for them all the time. Also, from inside the prison they can harm or kill anyone inside or outside of the prison. How? They pay people working for them to do the job. They can also buy the prison director and get out of prison and come back anytime they want. Why and how can one person have so much power in the capitalist system? Because he has lots of money so he can do anything he wants to do and from the laws point of view, it doesn't matter how and from where he got all that money.

The Iranian regime and the corrupt and criminal authorities are a clear example of the above subject. There have been countless instances of robbery, embezzlement and corruption by top Islamic officials over the past 41 years, all of whom stole billions of US dollars and fled with all that money which belonged to National Treasury of the country. So they escape and they enter to any country they want; in Europe, in Canada, in USA. This includes Mr. Mahmud Reza Khavari, the chairman of Iranian National bank who embezzled 3000 billion Tomean, equivalent to 3 billion US dollars. He fled to Vancouver, Canada and now he lives in his luxurious home in northwest Vancouver and no one is asking him where did you get all this money from?

This is just one example of embezzlement. There are thousands of other embezzlers in the Islamic government of Iran whose names are not disclosed, because the leader of the Islamic regime does not like the names of embezzlers to be revealed, because he is the leader of them all. In that system, whistle-blowers are usually imprisoned and government thieves are all free and no one goes after them.

But if a person in another country has political activities against the Islamic Republic, the security agents in disguise will go after him or her to kill them or kidnap and return them to Iran and force them to confess against themselves in front of a national TV camera and then execute them.

For example, on December 12, 2020, the regime hanged a journalist named Roholla Zam, someone who lived in Paris but was tricked, brought to Iraq, kidnapped, taken from there to Iran, and was forced to confess before he was executed just to show their power, and instill fear in the hearts of the people.

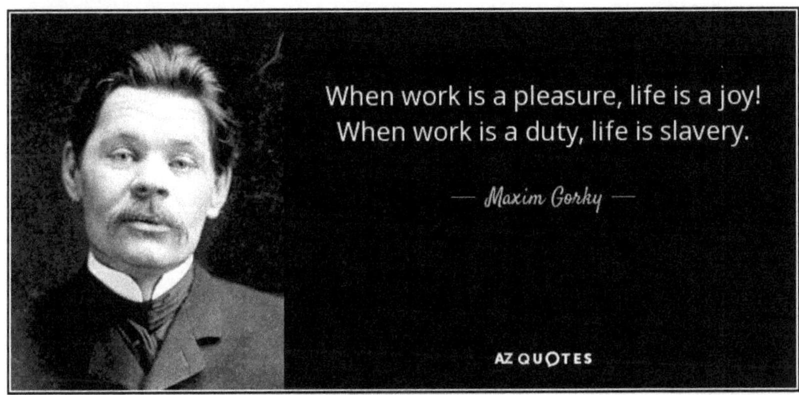

When work is a pleasure, life is a joy!
When work is a duty, life is slavery.
— Maxim Gorky —
AZ QUOTES

Maxim Gorky

Here I remind you of a very clear and understandable definition about various thieves by Russian author Maxim Gorky.

Born: March 28/1868, Died: Jun/18/1936

He said there are three types of thieves in the world: ordinary thieves, political thieves and religious thieves.

Ordinary thieves are those who steal your wallet, gold, watch and household items to feed their bellies.

Political thieves are the ones who steal your future, your dreams, your aspirations, your work, your livelihood, your salary, your education, your ability, your credit, your prestige, your national capital and even your taxes and they keep you in misery.

Religious thieves are those who steal your beautiful world, your dare of thinking, your science, your knowledge, your wisdom, your happiness, your health, your soul and they sell you some expensive things like god, religion, and heaven. Instead, they give you superstitions, sorrow, grief and depression. Religious thieves lie, they deceive, they keep you in poverty, misery and they are proud of what they do.

The interesting difference is that ordinary thieves choose you, but you choose your political thieves. You are also the one who chooses your religion and respects and magnifies religious thieves.

Another difference is that ordinary thieves are chased by the police, arrested, tortured, flogged, imprisoned, have their left hand and right foot cut off and are humiliated and so on.

But both political and religious thieves are protected by law and by the police. They hold higher positions, they force and oppress you and yet they are indebted to you.

What would be the international action against corruption?

I have the necessary detailed explanation against corruption later in the book but my short explanation for action against corruption and economical crimes in my perfect world is: By eliminating banks, money, any currency or credit cards and in total dismantling the capitalist system from our society, the way to concentration of wealth and power will be blocked and no one can do any corruption or economic crime anymore.

In the capitalist system, money and capital are the tools and these tools can do anything for the person who have them; legally or illegally.

> NOTE: When the wealth, weapons and media are concentrated in the hands of one person in a society, the result would be widespread corruption and crime.

The relationship between crime and law

In the capitalist system there is a direct relationship between the judiciary and the criminals.

In a society where there is no crime, the presence of lawyers and judges and courts become unnecessary and useless. Therefore the existence of the court, judges, lawyers and other crews need funding, and violators of the law can only provide this funding.

In a nutshell, if there is no thief, criminal or transgressor in the society, there will be no need for the judiciary. The judges, lawyers and crew will be useless.

There are so many other examples of disadvantage, loss and wasted energy in the capitalist system, which I will try to mention later in the book.

Now we should look at human rights in the capitalist system. Are human rights of all people on earth equally respected? Is justice provided equally for all human beings living on this planet, or not?

HUMAN RIGHTS IN CAPITALISM

I believe politicians who never worked and have never been under any pressure for anything in their life, wrote this declaration through the United Nations in Paris. They wrote these human rights poetically, but they were never able to implement them.

THE UNIVERSAL DECLARATION OF HUMAN RIGHTS

The Universal Declaration of Human Rights (UDHR) is a milestone document in the history of human rights, drafted by representatives with different legal and cultural backgrounds from all regions of the world. The Declaration was proclaimed by the United Nations General Assembly in Paris on December 10, 1948 (General Assembly resolution 217 A) as a common standard of achievements for all peoples and all nations. It sets out, for the first time, fundamental human rights to be universally protected and it has been translated into over 500 languages.

Article 1.

All human beings are born free and equal in dignity and rights. They are endowed with reason and conscience and should act towards one another in a spirit of brotherhood.

Article 2.

Everyone is entitled to all the rights and freedoms set forth in this Declaration, without distinction of any kind, such as race, colour, sex, language, religion, political or other opinion, national or social origin, property, birth or other status. Furthermore, no distinction shall be made on the basis of the political, jurisdictional or international status of the country or territory to which a person belongs, whether it is independent, trust, non-self-governing or under any other limitation of sovereignty.

Article 3.

Everyone has the right to life, liberty and security of person.

Article 4.

No one shall be held in slavery or servitude; slavery and the slave trade shall be prohibited in all their forms.

Article 5.

No one shall be subjected to torture or to cruel, inhuman or degrading treatment or punishment.

Article 6.

Everyone has the right to recognition everywhere as a person before the law.

Article 7.

All are equal before the law and are entitled without any discrimination to equal protection of the law. All are entitled to equal protection against any discrimination in violation of this Declaration and against any incitement to such discrimination.

Article 8.

Everyone has the right to an effective remedy by the competent national tribunals for acts violating the fundamental rights granted him by the constitution or by law.

Article 9.

No one shall be subjected to arbitrary arrest, detention or exile.

Article 10.

Everyone is entitled in full equality to a fair and public hearing by an independent and impartial tribunal, in the determination of his rights and obligations and of any criminal charge against him.

Article 11.

(1) Everyone charged with a penal offence has the right to be presumed innocent until proved guilty according to law in a public trial at which he has had all the guarantees necessary for his defence.
(2) No one shall be held guilty of any penal offence on account of any act or omission, which did not constitute a penal offence, under national or international law, at the time when it was committed. Nor shall a heavier penalty be imposed than the one that was applicable at the time the penal offence was committed.

Article 12.

No one shall be subjected to arbitrary interference with his privacy, family, home or correspondence, or to attacks upon his honour and reputation. Everyone has the right to the protection of the law against such interference or attacks.

Article 13.

(1) Everyone has the right to freedom of movement and residence within the borders of each state.
(2) Everyone has the right to leave any country, including his own, and to return to his country.

Article 14.

(1) Everyone has the right to seek and to enjoy in other countries asylum from persecution.
(2) This right may not be invoked in the case of prosecutions genuinely arising from non-political crimes or from acts contrary to the purposes and principles of the United Nations.

Article 15.

(1) Everyone has the right to a nationality.
(2) No one shall be arbitrarily deprived of his nationality nor denied the right to change his nationality.

Article 16.

(1) Men and women of full age, without any limitation due to race, nationality or religion, have the right to marry and to found a family. They are entitled to equal rights as to marriage, during marriage and at its dissolution.
(2) Marriage shall be entered into only with the free and full consent of the intending spouses.
(3) The family is the natural and fundamental group unit of society and is entitled to protection by society and the State.

Article 17.

(1) Everyone has the right to own property alone as well as in association with others.
(2) No one shall be arbitrarily deprived of his property.

Article 18.

Everyone has the right to freedom of thought, conscience and religion; this right includes freedom to change his religion or belief, and freedom, either alone or in community with others and in public or private, to manifest his religion or belief in teaching, practice, worship and observance.

Article 19.

Everyone has the right to freedom of opinion and expression; this right includes freedom to hold opinions without interference and to seek, receive and impart information and ideas through any media and regardless of frontiers.

Article 20.

(1) Everyone has the right to freedom of peaceful assembly and association.
(2) No one may be compelled to belong to an association.

Article 21.

(1) Everyone has the right to take part in the government of his country, directly or through freely chosen representatives.

(2) Everyone has the right of equal access to public service in his country.
(3) The will of the people shall be the basis of the authority of government; this will shall be expressed in periodic and genuine elections, which shall be by universal and equal suffrage and shall be held by secret vote or by equivalent free voting procedures.

Article 22.

Everyone, as a member of society, has the right to social security and is entitled to realization, through national effort and international co-operation and in accordance with the organization and resources of each State, of the economic, social and cultural rights indispensable for his dignity and the free development of his personality.

Article 23.

(1) Everyone has the right to work, to free choice of employment, to just and favourable conditions of work and to protection against unemployment.
(2) Everyone, without any discrimination, has the right to equal pay for equal work.
(3) Everyone who works has the right to just and favourable remuneration ensuring for himself and his family an existence worthy of human dignity, and supplemented, if necessary, by other means of social protection.
(4) Everyone has the right to form and to join trade unions for the protection of his interests.

Article 24.

Everyone has the right to rest and leisure, including reasonable limitation of working hours and periodic holidays with pay.

Article 25.

(1) Everyone has the right to a standard of living adequate for the health and well-being of himself and of his family, including food, clothing, housing and medical care and necessary social services, and the right to security in the event of unemployment, sickness,

disability, widowhood, old age or other lack of livelihood in circumstances beyond his control.
(2) Motherhood and childhood are entitled to special care and assistance. All children, whether born in or out of wedlock, shall enjoy the same social protection.

Article 26.

(1) Everyone has the right to education. Education shall be free, at least in the elementary and fundamental stages. Elementary education shall be compulsory. Technical and professional education shall be made generally available and higher education shall be equally accessible to all on the basis of merit.
(2) Education shall be directed to the full development of the human personality and to the strengthening of respect for human rights and fundamental freedoms. It shall promote understanding, tolerance and friendship among all nations, racial or religious groups, and shall further the activities of the United Nations for the maintenance of peace.
(3) Parents have a prior right to choose the kind of education that shall be given to their children.

Article 27.

(1) Everyone has the right freely to participate in the cultural life of the community, to enjoy the arts and to share in scientific advancement and its benefits.
(2) Everyone has the right to the protection of the moral and material interests resulting from any scientific, literary or artistic production of which he is the author.

Article 28.

Everyone is entitled to a social and international order in which the rights and freedoms set forth in this Declaration can be fully realized.

Article 29.

(1) Everyone has duties to the community in which alone the free and full development of his personality is possible.
(2) In the exercise of his rights and freedoms, everyone shall be subject only to such limitations as are determined by law solely for the purpose of securing due recognition and respect for the rights and freedoms of others and of meeting the just requirements of morality, public order and the general welfare in a democratic society.
(3) These rights and freedoms may in no case be exercised contrary to the purposes and principles of the United Nations.

Article 30.

Nothing in this Declaration may be interpreted as implying for any State, group or person any right to engage in any activity or to perform any act aimed at the destruction of any of the rights and freedoms set forth herein.

....

FAILURE TO ENFORCE HUMAN RIGHTS LAW THROUGHOUT THE WORLD.

All these 30 human rights articles prepared and funded by capitalists, are excellent and complete, but only on paper, because these human rights have no executive guarantor.

Which of these articles have been implemented in which country?

In China? In Russia? In North Korea? In Syria? In Iraq? In Afghanistan? In Iran? In Chile? In El Salvador? In Venezuela? In Vietnam? In India? In South Africa? In Egypt? In Europe or in the United States? In which country?

In which country are human rights fully respected and all people are satisfied with their human rights?

Of course, if I want to make a fair judgment on this subject, I have to say that human rights are relatively more respected in some European and North American countries than in most Asian, South American and African countries.

I do not believe that human rights are being enforced and fully respected in the capitalist system because in this system human rights are a hereditary issue. If a person is born in a royal family his or her human rights will be fully preserved. If a person is born in a wealthy family their human rights will be almost preserved. But, if someone is born in a poor family, human rights will not be held for them because they have no money to hire a lawyer to defend their human rights.

Human rights are violated everywhere in the world. The only people who can have human rights are the people who can hire a lawyer to defend their rights.

Who are the guarantors of implementation of human rights?

In the capitalist system none of the human rights cases for poor people has a guarantor. There are millions of cases of breaking the human rights code, happening everyday in this world and nobody cares about them. Millions of children who should be in schools are working hard for little income and many of them are hungry and homeless. Cruel and greedy people hire these children and make them work hard for little money. These working children are not even seen in some countries, let alone human rights. Some of them don't even have proper clothing or a pair of shoes on their feet. Hundreds of ordinary and defenceless people are dying everyday under chemical bomb attacks or terrorist attacks in many countries and no organization has any power to do anything about it. All the human rights organizations have meetings and talk and talk about many things and they condemned any act against human rights, but they have no enforcement guarantee to ensure human rights.

Example: From November 15 to November 18, 2019 there was a non-violent demonstration in many cities in Iran to protest the three-fold increase in gasoline prices by the government. The Islamic regime's response to these peaceful demonstration was internet disconnection nationwide, and the killing of more than four thousand eight hundred people with their sniper rifles and no action has been taken by human rights organizations against the Islamic regime so far. Thousands of people were also arrested in that demonstration and imprisoned. A young wrestler man named Navid Afkari has been executed just a month ago because he took part in those peaceful demonstrations. Hundreds of other young protesters are hanged every month, under various titles in secret places. In many countries even the news did not mention the massacre. Human rights organizations are all about condemnation of human rights violators and nothing more.

> NOTE: Reuters put the death toll for the three days of protests at 1500, but when a few weeks later the coronavirus killed some in Iran there was no place for them in the forensic morgue, which housed 5000 bodies. That is why I say that the number of people killed in that demonstration was more than 4800.

Another example: For more then seven years, people have been dying in Syria in different ways everyday by ISIS or Russian or Iranian regime or Bashar Al Assad military, (the permanent president of Syria), but no human rights organization and no superpower governments have yet done anything about it. The massacre that is taking place in Syria is more like a prewritten program written by big brother and big sister in a closed-door room.

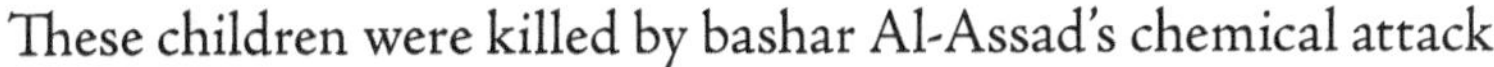

These children were killed by bashar Al-Assad's chemical attack

Take a look at Syria since 2011, no matter how many children are killed, how many millions are displaced and how many cities are destroyed, big brother and big sister have decided to keep Bashar Al Assad in power at any cost. These decision makers do not answer to anyone and if someone insist on asking the big brother and big sister of the society for an audit and accountability, there will be an accident and the annoying questioner will be killed mysteriously, so no one can find out what happened and how he or she suddenly died without any disease or previous symptoms. These incidents happen everyday in Iran and other dictatorship countries.

Human rights and capitalism are two separate categories, such as day and night that do not tolerate the existence of one another. In fact, for a variety of reasons, discrimination between rich and poor is impossible to be eliminated due to class differences in the capitalist system. Thus, human rights are not implemented equally.

Human rights are achieved when there is no capitalist system and class differences are gone and no one has more power than the other. Capitalism and human rights is not a match. Why? Because if everyone has equal human rights, then there would be no class difference and that means there is no capitalist system ruling the societies any longer.

I believe these human rights are only a symbolic statement written by capitalists in whom they are religious, superstitions without any experience of unemployment, poverty, hunger, homelessness or misery, plus they don't have power to enforce their written human rights.

I hope my honest words in this book do not offend anyone; I am also using my freedom of expression in accordance with articles 19 of the same United Nations human rights code, commenting about this system and about my vision for a perfect world. Although if I assume human rights law are protecting my rights and they empower me to write this book in a free atmosphere without being worried about any insecure situation from any dictator regime.

I can say whatever I want to say, but still there is a possibility that some pro-capitalism or pro-religious or pro-politician and finely big brother and big sister don't like my ideas and decide to get rid of me. I have to say something in advance to those people who don't want me alive. We're all born once, and we all die once, sooner or later and no one knows where, how and when we die. But we will be free of need and we can relax for a while when we die, I love that moment when I am gone and it doesn't matter when, where and how. But it's important to me that I die for my idea, the time and place is not the issue for me, I am only ready after publishing my book. My body can be destroyed but my mind and my philosophy will never be destroyed. Whoever reads this book and believes in it, they will become a leader and will not need any more leadership from me or anyone else. The conclusion I want to draw from the above is that my body is mortal, but my mind will live as long as the Earth is alive.

Not only I am not afraid of dying, but also I believe, the characteristics of death are much greater than the characteristics of birth, and for people who know about that secret the joy of welcoming death is much greater than the joy of birth because our birth is not in our control, (and we are not able to think about our birth before we are born,) nor our death is in our control but we already know about the characteristics of death and it's something that we see it in our future, and we have lots of time to think about our death. The death is always waiting for us and we know about it. For me the pleasure of death is the same pleasure as birth; therefore I love to die, when the right time comes.

I believe that there are countless transformations, changes and flourishing happens after death, that unfortunately science has not yet uncovered these facts yet.

Many people are afraid of death, because they are not aware of the benefits of it. I believe when we die all our pains, diseases, addictions, anger, greed, jealousy, hate, depressions, dependency and our needs will go away from us and we will reborn fresh and healthy all over again in a different form and different shape. Plus, when someone dies for his or her goal and useful beliefs – something that benefits human beings – their name will be eternal. I believe the sooner we leave this world, the sooner we will return to this world again.

Finally, I must say to those who want to kill me in the future, if they do so, in fact, they have done me a great favour, because I do not want to live with all the old-age pains. Besides, when I get killed, my philosophy will come into action much faster

••••••••••••••••••••

CYRUS THE GREAT AND HIS HUMAN RIGHTS CHARTER:

Now lets find out about the human rights written by Cyrus the Great, King of Persia, about 2,500 years ago, and compare it to this new human rights charter that has been written in the 19th century.

Cyrus the Great, also called Cyrus II, (born 590–580 BCE, in Persia [Iran plateau]—died c. 529), conqueror who founded the Achaemenids Empire, centred on Persia (Iran Plateau) and comprising the Near East from the Aegean Sea eastward to the Indus River up to the Macedonian border almost 3,000 miles (4828 km) to the west.

He is also remembered in the Cyrus legend—first recorded by Xenophon, the Greek soldier and author, in his Cyropedia—as a tolerant and ideal monarch who was called the father of his people by the ancient Persians. In the Bible he is the liberator of the Jews who were captive in Babylonia.

The release of thousands of Jewish prisoners in Babylon by Cyrus the Great was the greatest liberation in history. He saved 40,000 Jews who were imprisoned by Nebuchnezzar or (Nabonidus), the king of Babylon. Cyrus the great released them from those prisons and presented them with his human rights charter. He set them free to go to their homeland to live freely, safely, in peace of mind to build their own religious synagogue.

(This is the Cyrus the Great's human rights charter Cylinder.)

Cyrus the Great, was the king of justice, king of liberation, and the great father of his nation, he was always carefully monitoring the proper implementation of his own written human rights in the societies under his rule. King Cyrus was seriously the executive sponsor of his own human rights charter.

The artwork carved on the wall of the Persepolis shows the Plantiff people are standing in line for judgement in front of the Achaemenid king

Cyrus was a Zoroastrian himself and he had learned from Zoroastrianism that the good Thoughts, good Words and good Deeds are the best way to guide mankind to the path of excellence. But he never forced the defeated countries to follow his religion; instead he respected the defeated people's god. In Babylon he attended one of the religious ceremonies to honour their god.

Cyrus the Great was a saviour of mankind at his time, but unfortunately after his death, the whole world has never seen such a great king up to this day.

With the knowledge that I have about Cyrus the Great and his regime from the history I know the form of his regime was a Council Democratic, Meritocracy system, which means he chose competent people in specific fields for specific positions where they had enough knowledge and awareness of that position. I must add that since the Persian Empire was established by Cyrus the Great 2,500 years ago, until 41 years ago, Iran's Plateau has never had a slavery system until Khomeini's Islamic regime came to power. This also proves that Cyrus, the architect and founder of the Achaemenids, Persian Empire was a wise, knowledgeable and compassionate King and Leader of many nations.

....

KNOWLEDGE, AWARENESS, COMPETENCE AND MERIT OF DIFFERENT PEOPLE IN DIFFERENT DISCIPLINES:

Human talents are very different from each other and not everyone can have talent of making money or collecting wealth to be rich. Some people were born artists but they don't know how to sell their own art, never mind selling someone else's products, so he or she wouldn't be a good salesperson. Other people are scientists and they know a lot about many different scientific articles but they don't know, or do not want to know how they can get rich through their knowledge, to make money. Other people are creative and inventors but they don't invent things to make money, they are just genius and invent things without thinking of profit. Other people are born to be spiritual and they don't have any interest in making money or to be rich, they have different philosophy about life. Others are born to do sports and they can become champions, but they don't know how to make money.

There is also a small minority of the community who only has knowledge of raising money and gather wealth and nothing more. So all these people are living together on this planet with different talents in life, none of them are the same. Most of these people have a naturally variety of talents other than wealth accumulation and they are moving in the same direction that they were interested in from their childhood. They don't make things for profit; they do it only because they like to do it.

With all these explanations the question is, do all these people deserve to eat and have place to sleep? Do they deserve to have car, home, computer and free education, free medication or having other living appliances for free? Or all those people who do not have the talent of collecting wealth and money should die? I believe everyone who lives on earth deserves to have all essential needs of life, even if they don't have any money. Unfortunately in this system it's impossible to be equal and have all the needs without having money. But the needs are there and we all have the same needs in life and those needs must be met anyway.

In the capitalist system, in order to become rich, people must either be a genius and invent something very useful for the public, or they must be a gangster and know how to steal, lie, scam, or fool others to become wealthy. If someone wants to make big and fast money they must know how to walk all over everyone else. For example, if a car dealer doesn't lie about an old car which was in a heavy accident and worth only $1,000, how can he sell that car for $5,000 and make $4,000 profit? Or if a broker doesn't buy a farmer's products at a cheap and unfair price, he can never sell them to the markets with higher price and make more profit for himself.

No one is able to sell anything with a big profit if they don't buy it at a low price, or if they don't lie about it.

I don't believe anyone can ever be richer than others in any system if they respect human dignity and be honest. In this system we are all customers to each other and to the big companies. We must pay money for everything we need, regularly; everyday or every month. We must pay rent to the landlord as much as they ask, pay for electricity, pay for phone, pay for TV channels and internet, pay for food, pay for transportation, pay for gas, pay for clothes, pay for medicine, pay taxes, and pay for many other things that are essential to our life. Some people also pay more for their addictions like cigarettes and alcohol or other drugs as well.

For many people there is no chance of saving any money for yearly vacation; the majority of people must work regularly until they are retired; for many others until they die. I think I am one of those people, working non-stop for the last 55 years and for the last seven years I wasn't able to go on any vacation. Not only do I not have money for the vacation but also if I don't work for one week I will be behind of paying my bills, and that is because I have had no interest in accumulating wealth since my youth. I love working until the last moment of my life, but we also need vacations and fun.

....

EXISTENCE OF ALL FACILITIES EQUALLY FOR ALL:

I believe there is more than enough wealth for everyone living on this planet, and no one needs to be greedy anymore; nor anyone should be homeless, hungry or poor. But, unfortunately the capitalist prefers to keep the products in the warehouse, or throw them out in the garbage when the products are out of date, rather then give them to people for free or to charity, because the capitalist wants to keep the price high. It doesn't really matter to the capitalist if they have fewer customers, but they want the rich customers who can pay the high price for their products and I believe that is not fair.

Money-makers are becoming richer and the poor become poorer everyday and yet neither of them is superior to the other in terms of health and longevity. In this system rich and poor, they both have lots of stress, worries, anxiety, and they both eat and drink chemicals every day. The stress, anxiety, worries, and chemicals we consume daily are factors that help shorten our lives.

ANXIETY, CHEMICALS AND WORRIES ARE THE MOTHER OF ALL DISEASES.

Rich people are always thinking of how to make more money and they are always worried about how and where to keep their money and wealth in a safe place so that no one can steal them. They have so much money that they do not know where to keep it or how to spend it, so they pass their time mostly in nightclubs, drinking alcohol, using drugs or spend their money on other foolish things like loosing it at the casinos or gambling at home. At the same time, poor people are struggling to survive with canned foods from charity and they need a roof above their heads and they deal with all kind of diseases due to lack of vitamins in their body and not taking a shower. That is why we can easily say poor and rich people both live with different stress and anxiety, and both classes are consuming chemicals every day and non of them cares for another, poor doesn't like the rich and rich don't like the poor, it seems like they hate each other very deeply. These two main factors (STRESS and CHEMICALS) cause human deaths prematurely and the cause of all these misfortunes are the GREED, which grows in the Capitalist system to accumulate money and wealth; and JEALOUSY which is born and grows out of lack of self-confidence in people. Hatred is the result of jealousy and greed.

So we can easily say, MONEY is the first real enemy among all human beings, there is an old saying that they say, "money is the root of all evil". All other problems come from money. Jealousy, which comes from lack of confidence and the idea that everyone is better than us, is mostly due to lack of money and shortage.

Hate, grudges and resentment, are born and grow in response to monetary and material problems between two or more people and the lack of justice on that problem makes it stay for long time, and its main basis and root is money, wealth and the capitalist system.

My perfect world is not against wealth, richness, happiness and a high standard of living; but it is against poverty, lack of resources and a miserable life for the majority of the world population.

My perfect world is a philosophy to eliminate greed, hate and jealousy at the lowest cost and the best outcome.

In the capitalist system, human beings spend their maximum energy to make the minimum of products and services for everyday community needs, although not all members of society participate in production or giving services to others. However, not only are the products of the international community produced by a small number of workers, but many of their products are thrown in the trash after all. Not all people are able to use social production and use services, because everything belongs to the capitalist monopoly and the capitalists prefer to make more profits out of their products rather than meet the needs of society.

For example: After the products are ready to be used by artisans and farmers, the mediators buy the products from them and keep them in the warehouses for a period of time, then they distribute the products to the shops and supermarkets. The products stay in the markets for a while, waiting to be sold, then whatever is left over and are out-of-date is thrown in the trash.

So, first the industry workers and farmers spend energy to make the products. Second other energies are spent to keep the products in the warehouses. Third other energies are spent to take the products to the shops and markets to sell them, and after all, for the fourth time, some of those products are dumped into the trash because they are out-of-date and they are no good anymore, so they are discarded. Yet there are so many people are in need of those products to use them, but because they don't have enough money to buy them they cannot have them. Just consider how much space, how much electricity, how much water, and how many people, must be involved from production to consumption, or from production to destruction? What will be the final end of the capitalist system by wasting so much human energy?

Countless examples illustrate the various obstacles that the capitalist system poses to the progress of human society are just wasting energy and stopping the communities development. This system is all about exclusive capitalism for one percent of the world population, and it doesn't care about the society's essential needs and progress to the benefits of 100% of people. The character and direction of the capitalist system is the path to concentration of capital into very small minority. Ultimately perhaps the global capitalism may be summarized into only one family. At that point Capitalism will transfer to Imperialism or Socialism, depending on the level of philosophical social knowledge of the people.

We can easily conclude that, slowly and over time capitalism will eventually be concentrated in one family and by that time the game of capitalism will be all over. Then humans need a new alternative system to run the global society. That system will be either Social Council Democratic and Meritocracy system or Imperialism. Imperialism is (a policy of extending a country's power and influence through diplomacy or military force).

••••••••••••••••••••

WHAT WILL BE THE FUTURE SYSTEM OF THE WORLD?

Either will be an imperialist system controlling all members of society through surveillance cameras or digital necklaces and reporters; and ordinary people have to do exactly what they are asked to do, like Robots.

Or, if the level of philosophical consciousness of the people reaches such high level that they can choose their own destiny, they will choose a system that dominates their destiny, like a real free-will Socialism.

So-cial-ism {Socialism} is a philosophical and economical theory of social organization, which advocates that the means of production, distribution, and exchange should be owned or regulated by the community as a whole.

In my perfect world, all able-bodied and healthy people must participate in production and everything must distributed free of charge, equally among people according to their needs. Peace, securely, freedom, prosperity, comfort, and social justice also must be provided by the government to everyone equally.

………………….

QUESTION #4 -IS THERE ANY WAY TO REFORM CAPITALISM?

Answer #4-Absolutely not.

Because the capitalist system is all about monopoly. The essence and nature of this system is irreversible because the capitalists are by no means willing to divide their wealth among society and will not give up their greed as long as capitalism is valid, and if they do give up their wealth, than the system will be called my perfect world.

In the essence of the capitalism, the interest and benefits of the capitalist are the most important issue of the system. There are few benefits for the majority of people, because the main return from the investment is to the capitalist.

As time goes by, the monopoly capital circle becomes smaller and tighter, to the point where global capitalism focuses on one point and one family.

At that point there will be a change to one of two states. The great capitalist (Imperialism) that owns everything and will establish an electronic super modern slavery system and all humans will be at their services with a digital collar; or by then people will have reached a high level of social, philosophical education, understanding and will establish a Social Council Democratic and Meritocracy system), which we can call it a perfect world.

COMPARING THE ANT COLONY WITH HUMAN SOCIETY:

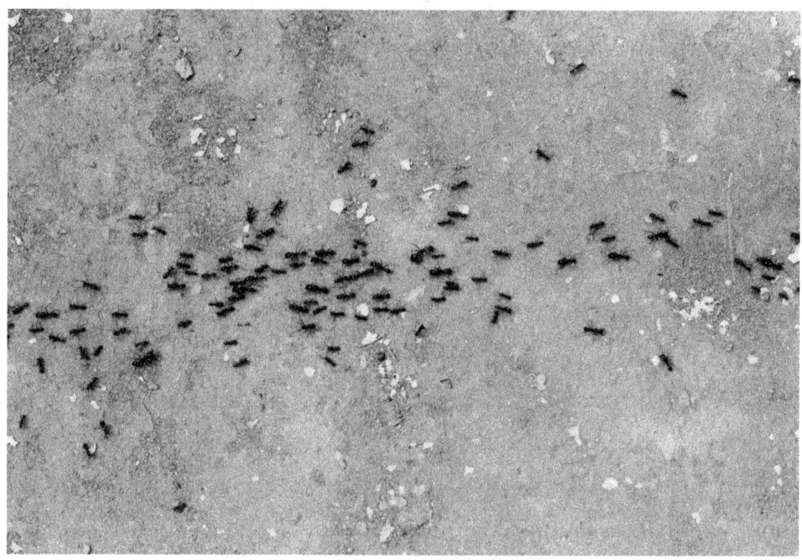

In one scene from the *Culture high* documentary video I saw a scientist comparing an ant colony to human society. It showed how simply ants live and work together, and what can distract their work and daily life.

The scene showed how the ants were gathering food together. When the ant workers are gathering food, all of them are travelling and moving in a very narrow road to get the food and then bring it back to the granary. Then it showed what could distract their daily work life.

If some of those ants start to surround and hoard the food storage and not let others have access to it, the hoarding action creates an obstacle for worker ants traveling back and fort and that barrier starts a big problem in the colony. Chaos and panic are the two main components of this problem.

Human life is the same as an ants life, because ants and humans, both have social lives. So, the same principles that can interfere and disturb the ants' daily life, can interfere with humans lives as well.

The monopoly of essential supplies and daily needs of the people by one percent of a community can disturb and interfere with 99% of people's life.

The ant's society example is similar to human society, that some people keep food and supplies, in their warehouses until the day they are sold, or they are out of date and thrown into the trash. But people outside those warehouses need those appliances for themselves and their family but they have no access to them unless they bring money to buy them, then they can own food and other supplies. That is the real problem because many people don't have enough money to get what ever they need. We can easily say, capitalists are obstacles to the societies' prosperity, health, development, progress and happiness. The result is that when all these problems build up, one day society will explode and uncontrollable uprising will take place.

When people are supplied in every way in the community, they will step up to invention, progress and development of their society and this will benefit every body. The history and evidence of the capitalist system doesn't show a good picture of the future. As far as I remember to this day, prices have risen and purchasing power has diminished compared to the past, while accelerating various products with superior technology. That is not a good history record for the capitalist system.

Capitalism is not an ideal endless system to run the global societies and it's hard to imagine a bright future and a happy ending for it. In the end of this system, I can imagine a real disaster and bad ending for all of us, even for capitalism itself, because all of us in this system are captives of Greed, Jealousy and Hate and the results are; hording, monopolization and selfishness. We all fear the future and because of that, we have no mercy for each other. Everyone wants to save more money, more food, more capital and more land for themselves and for their family. But it looks like the leaders; elites, big sister and big brother forgot that we are all living in one planet and if there will be a big deadly explosion on earth, the life will end for everybody, rich and poor, black and white, young and old, literate and illiterate, religious and infidel, king or queen. That explosion will end life for all of us humans and other creatures on earth. So let's share life with all its possibilities and have peace, security, freedom, justice and endless happiness for everyone equal, before is too late.

In my perfect world – the new system that I am offering – I planned that everything will be equally shared with everyone living on planet earth without existence of money or any credit cards, and no class differences in our society. I guarantee one hundred percent that the kids living in my proposed system will live much healthier, happier, with a much longer life.

I believe after a few generations, mankind can live at least 150 years. How? Because there would be no more chemicals, no stress, no anxiety and nothing else to be worried about for the past or future. We no longer need to run from morning to night to earn money to pay the bills and make a living. No more chemicals in our food or in our drinks, free housing, free food, free medication, free education, free life facilities and so many other opportunities will make it possible for human beings to live much longer than now days.

The global 100% Social Council, Democratic and Meritocracy system guarantees to eliminate greed, monopoly of capital and power concentration, by removing money, credit cards and banks from our society. Money is one of the main tools that allow greedy and monopolistic people to accumulate wealth and concentrate power to them. In my perfect world life must be shared equally to everyone living on earth. Everyone must be able to use all opportunities available, to enjoy living of prosperity, freedom, peace, security and justice.

Dictatorship and abuse of power comes true when the capital of a society is concentrated in the hands of one person, but in my perfect world no one will be able to attract the capital of a society to themselves because there will be no more money that anyone can keep to himself or herself.

We all must pay more attention to global benefits, interests and happiness, because we all live on one planet and the happiness of each of us depends on the happiness of others. Our happiness is provided when the happiness of others is fulfilled. We are all brothers and sisters and we are all children of the earth. To complete our happiness, we must respect nature and other living things as well. We must be nice to ourselves, nice to mother earth and nice to other creatures living on this planet with us. All living things on earth have rights that must be respected and protected by humans.

ABOUT HUMANS AND HOW THEIR RELATIONSHIP SHOULD BE TO EACH OTHER ON EARTH:

I refer you to one of the Persian poet Saadi Shirazi's poems, titled Benny Adam (human kind) from the 13th century. A carpet containing this poem was installed in the United Nations building in 2005.

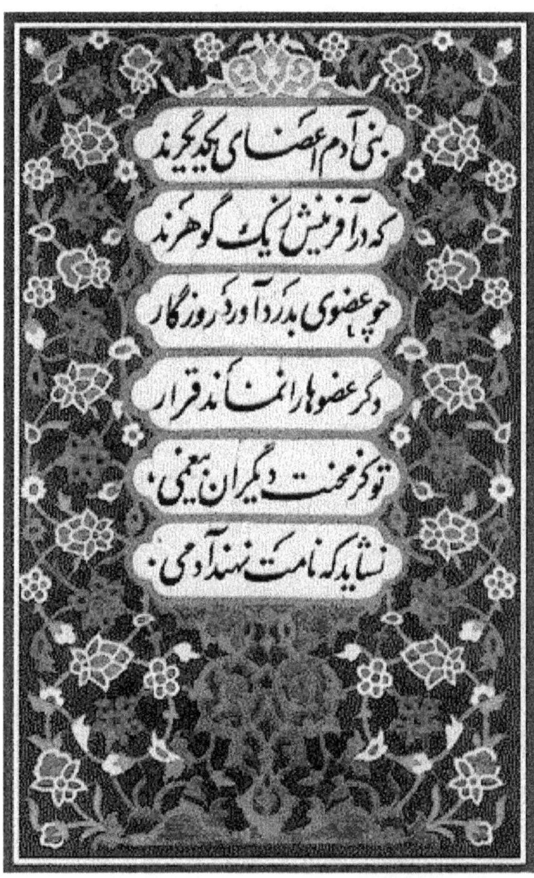

Translation (A rhyming translation by M. Aryanpoor)

Human beings are members of a whole,
In creation of one essence and soul.
If one member is afflicted with pain,
Other members uneasy will remain.
If you've no sympathy for human pain,
The name of human you cannot retain! .

From my point of view, all human beings on earth are connected to each other like parts of one gearbox, if an individual gear breaks down; it causes all other gears to breakdown as well. They will fail one by one and the whole gearbox will stop working eventually.

But apparently, it doesn't look like this. Why? That's only because, we cannot see every single breakdown of these gears with our eyesight, but we can see it with the sight of discernment, with logic, wisdom and eyes of insight. If we look deeply and wisely at the international capitalist society, we can see the break down of this gearbox (human society).

I can hear the crunching of the gears of this gearbox loud and clear, and I know the continuation of this breakdown will one day, totally stop the gearbox, it just takes time. And when this gearbox stops working, perhaps no one can hear nor can see it any more, because that will be the end of our life on planet earth. I hope that before the international community is completely destroyed, the world intellectuals and pioneers will wake up and do something to prevent that tragedy.

If we all thought of being human beings like Sadie expressed himself hundreds of years ago, the earth would have been a better place to live for all of us. But unfortunately many people think a poem is a dramatic way of saying things. So they look at it as an unrealistic dream and they don't act as it says. They don't want to share life and be nice to each other. They think that the Earth and it's belongings were made just for them. Of course, a virus like Corona proved to everyone that the Sadie's poetry about human beings is totally true and logical. If we don't support and cooperate with each other now, we will pay the consequences later.

If the people of the world do not unite and become strong now, as a result of separation and complete weakness, they will be destroyed one by one. A thin branch of a tree can be easily broken by hand, but when we put a large number of them together, it becomes impossible to break them by hand. Unity and solidarity equals power.

CONTROLLING THE POPULATION:

One of the goals of the community's big siblings is to be active in controlling the earth's population in every way possible. So our big brother and sister are preparing all kind of military and chemical wars to massively destroy the earth's population.

If we were supposed to control the population of some creatures by killing them, now there would be more wolves, hyenas and other predators than vegetarians because although the carnivores like wolves, hyenas and lions and other predators give birth to five or seven puppies at a time and they are not even eaten by other animals or humans. Despite that, vegetarian animals give one birth at a time and humans and carnivore animals also eat them, but the number of herbivores is still much higher than the number of carnivores.

My suggestion and solution to controlling the human population is to create social peace, prosperity, security and freedom, in which case no one will engage in raising too many children. As a result of peace, freedom, prosperity, social security, and justice, the human population will be controlled automatically. A clear example is the comparison of the fewer children of developed and relatively prosperous countries to more children of third world poor countries.

It has been proven that in any society where there is more poverty and unemployment, the level of culture and consciousness of human beings is equally low, and as a result, the number of children in their families are higher.

Conversely, the greater the well-being and comfort in a society, the higher the level of consciousness and culture of the people of that society, and the lower the number of their children.

QUESTION #5- WHAT COULD IT BE THE BEST ALTERNATIVE SYSTEM TO REPLACE CAPITALISM?

Answer #5-For the replacement of capitalism, the best alternative option would be a Social Council Democratic and Meritocracy system.

WHY AND HOW?

This new system must be hundred percent pure Socialism, run by philosophers, scientists and experts, those who take their power from people of their society. As Socrates said more then 2000 years ago in his book titled *Republic*, countries should be run by philosophers because they are spiritualist and they do not think of their own interests but they care more about their community's progress, development, welfare, social justice and freedom.

SOCRATES BIOGRAPHY

(c. 470 BCE–399 BCE)

I agree with Socrates 100% that philosophers should run the human societies.

Because I believe the philosophers logic is not politics of playing and adding people's problems, but their solution to solve people's problem is through science, logic, honesty and merit and that's exactly what human beings need.

In my perfect world, there will be no superstitious and extremist religious, no criminal and corrupt policies, and no exclusive intermediaries capitalist activities anymore. Politicians, religious leaders and capitalists have caused a great deal of scandal in the past. They have lost their chance to continue the path they have gone so far.

NOTE: In my opinion, politics means trickery and cheating

There is a proverb in the Persian language that says: *politics are dirty*. Here I am completing the proverb: *politics, money, and most religions are dirty!*

After all, in my perfect world, there would be no more Greed, Hate and Jealousy. But it will be social freedom, social human rights, social prosperity, social justice, social peace and all other social opportunities for everyone equal on earth.

Everything will be based on honesty.

WHAT IS MERITOCRACY?

A form of government where somebody's power or their position is based on their ability or achievements (from the urban dictionary).

In my definition, Meritocracy means entrusting every task to an expert in that particular job. That particular job could be working with a computer, being a president, driving a bus, building a house, mechanic, teacher, social worker, nurse and so on.

In a meritocracy system, when a job is assigned to a person, that person must be qualified to do it.

Every job in the new system should be handed over to specialists and experts based on their ability to manage that position.

The selection of the right people for each job must be done first by passing the exam and secondly, the selection of the best ones by their prior performance.

CHAPTER (3)

My Perfect World is a Social Council Democratic and Meritocracy System

FULL DETAILS AND EXPLANATION OF MY PERFECT WORLD.

The solution for solving all human problems in life is to establish a Social Council Democratic and Meritocracy system within global society.

My perfect world is a path to real happiness or a real (paradise) on earth. A global society with new world order as one united co-related human family. Life in peace; without stress or anxiety and free of chemicals; with all the necessities of life available for free and equally for everyone living on earth according to their needs. In return every one according to their ability should participate in contributing certain hours of free work for the community.

My perfect world represents a new world order philosophy with a new constitution and regulations opposing monopoly capitalism. A system, which will be in favour of 100% of the people on earth.

In the capitalist system, only one percent of people are rich and 99% are poor, but in my perfect world, every one on earth will be equally wealthy and rich with much less hours of daily work. In the new world order, social freedom, peace, justice, security, healthcare, life facilities, welfare and happiness will be available for everyone equally for free.

In the global constitution of my perfect world, there are no borders, no military, no gun makers, no wars, no slaughterhouses, no zoo, no banks, no money, no brokers, no intermediaries, no middlemen, no bureaucracy, no fake religion, no politics and no politicians, no poverty, no jails, no prisoners, no stress and no chemicals. My perfect world is a real Paradise in our lifetime on earth.

As long as my philosophy finds a majority vote in the world, I promise that these words will not be in future world dictionaries, because there will be no use for them:

> Economy, Inflation, Bank, Money, Credit cards, Stock markets, Dealers, Mediator, Seller, Buyer, Tenant, Landlord, War, Prison, Prisoner, Homeless, Poor, Poverty, Terrorist, Discrimination, Racism, Greed, Hate, Jealousy, Superstition and Politics.

In order to achieve a perfect world with the new system and new laws, human beings need solidarity, unity, desire, and a plan to build that perfect world.

So far I talked about losses and disadvantages of the capitalist system that we are currently living in. Humans on earth need an orderly efficient system with humanitarian values. A system that brings peace, security, prosperity, freedom, human dignity and social justice to its people; and eliminates poverty, corruptions, monopoly and crimes. Such a system will never exist, unless the capitalist system is completely abolished.

The planet earth we are all living on is the only habitable planet we know in this solar system. This planet can be healthy and integrated naturally around the sun and continue to live in one piece, if human beings stop destroying it. But there is no sign of peace and no guarantee this planet will continue to live for long time in the current system. In the capitalist system people consider the earth and nature as a possession that belongs to them and they can do whatever they like with them. They take everything for granted, they cut the trees, they suck the natural oil out of oil reserves, and they explode chemical and nuclear bombs on earth. Countries look at each other as the enemy and they arm themselves with nuclear warheads to prepare themselves for a big war.

A major war will not only hit humans and other creatures, but it may destroy the earth.

Every leader says god blesses my country and they don't consider that their country is still on the earth where all other countries are. Why not pray for the health of the earth? Isn't it better for humans to wish the health of the whole earth, instead of only their country? In my opinion, living in this current system has become very tedious and painful for the majority of the people of the world. It is foolish that some people live on a small planet in this universe and have armed themselves with destructive advanced weapons and inter-continental missiles and nuclear warheads against each other, instead of seeking a peaceful coexistence. The only way to save the earth and life on it, from the danger of inevitable destruction is: humans must stop hostility and violence against each other and end all battles, crime and any other aggression toward our global society.

In the order to achieve all these goals, first of all, human rights must be respected and class differences must be abolished from our society. Second, very urgently, all the religions that are superstitious and backward must be dismantled and outlawed.

Third, establish an efficient system with social welfare, prosperity, peace, freedom, security and justice for everyone equally.

I believe all of the above goals are possible to reach in my perfect world, which is based on a Social Council Democratic and Meritocracy system. I also must to say that I am one hundred percent sure this philosophy will lead humanity to a true paradise.

I am not claiming to be the first peace messenger in the world, but I hope I am not the last one. There are many war prophets existing everywhere these days, but only a few peace prophets and they are in jails or in exile. Power will never be concentrated in my perfect world, because there are no tools or devices for anyone to achieve concentration of power to them. In the new world order, all paths leading to the concentration of power are blocked. In the rest of the book I will explain how these routes are blocked.

In my perfect world every job should be handed to an honest and a decent person who is a qualified, skilled, specialist for that position. The individuals who are chosen by the people based on their abilities and merit are responsible to form the government. After the members of new government are in their position if they make any mistakes, people can question them at any time and they must answer people's questions in public.

We are all familiar with the name of socialist. Many parties in many countries call themselves socialist, but they are apparently just carrying the name of socialist and in the back door, they are controlled by capitalists, like the former Soviet Union which called themselves socialist or communist. But, capital was only in the hands of Kremlin and K.G.B and other government organizations. The ordinary people's life was below the world standard and most of them were under the poverty line. A better example of socialist society with the socialist state society is Sweden, which can be called a country governed by a socialist party. In Sweden there are also companies such as Volvo, Sub, IKIA and many others, which are managed by private companies.

Banks are a clear sign of the capitalist system and the presence of multiple banks in any country shows capitalists run the country. There are many banks in Sweden and those banks show that Sweden is capitalist as well. The name of a system does not necessarily identify the essence and reality of that system. Or in other words, we can say the characteristics of a system can be totally different from the name of that system. In fact, from the beginning of human history until today, no real social democratic system has been established in the whole world.

The efficiency and performance of one system is the result of the content of that system, not only the name of the system. The x-Soviet Union and China, who were seeking communist and socialist system, but failed and returned to the capitalism, because they did not have an efficient technique for their theory.

Why? Because the former Soviet Union and current China Communists, never eliminated money and banks from their system, which are the tools of power concentration in capitalism. The first mistake these countries made, was to keep the bank and money.

I repeat: my perfect world is not opposed to wealth, luxury life, but it is against poverty, inequality and class differences. The only way we all can live in a perfect world is, if all of us, relative to our abilities, work for our society freely for 5 to 6 hours a day, 4 days a week and 10 months a year and share the wealth on earth with each other for free. In my perfect world, there is no money, no credit cards and no class difference. My perfect world has many applicable scientific programs for welfare, peace, freedom, security and social justice for the people and their society.

In order to establish a perfect world, first, we all must be united with one global belief and one global flag. A global country with no borders, no military, no banks, no intermediaries, no gun factories and no wars. In my perfect world the main goal is to build a perfect society with social welfare, security, justice, peace, freedom and human rights available equally to everybody on earth.

In my perfect world, life will be much healthier, longer and happier, if we all come to one common point of one belief. This is possible if we have one global scientific, logical religion with a real creator; a creator that we all depend on for everything and for every second in our life. We must believe in a Creator that none of us can live without it, not even for one moment. We need to have a common belief or faith in something that our life is dependent on, at all times and in all places.

HUMANS MUST UNITE IN SOLIDARITY AND BELIEF:

The first step in building a perfect world for human beings is: to adhere to the good thoughts, good words and good deeds with universal unity and solidarity, and never to neglect these three principles. The second step is to embrace a logical, scientific, and acceptable religion by the general public belief about the creator. A religion that represents a real Creator of the earth and all of its creatures.

It is much easier, logically and scientifically for me to prove the creation of the earth and its creatures by the SUN than to prove the existence of various prophets with their invisible gods and their unrecorded miracles.

A diagram of confirmation of terrestrial life originating from the SUN

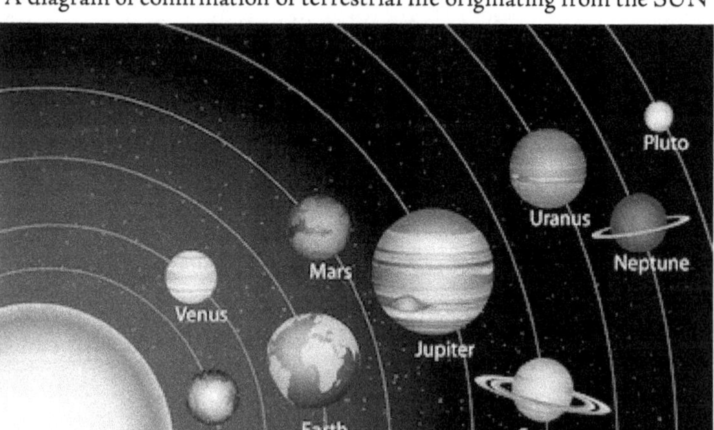

All these 9 planets are moving in the gravitational field of the SUN and they get their energy only from the SUN

One of the most scientific and logical reasons for the fact that the sun is the real creator of us is that, we can see and feel that everything about our life is completely dependent on the sun.

Being alive on earth is hundred percent dependent on the sun's energy and is not a big problem for me to prove that to anyone who has little education. But how to prove this undeniable logic for fanatics and ignorant people may be a little difficult. Anyway, there are many solutions for that problem as well, and one of the solutions is to teach and educate people who need more knowledge about the universe, nature, planets and the galaxy.

NOTE: In any case, this problem will have disappeared after a generation, when the following generation will have learned everything with the necessary training.

Religions have simple answers to all the difficult questions, and this simplicity of answering to all difficult questions makes it easy for ignorant and illiterate people to decide which path to take in their life, as a result they are attracted to religion and accept superstition stories because there is no need for much study and research.

The need for the sun's energy by all living things on earth is a common point that no one can deny, and that fact can create unity among people. No living thing is able to survive without the sun and this fact can bring us all together, united with one belief, one religion and one creator, which is the sun. This is the best idea to achieve a perfect world.

A MESSAGE TO CAPITALISTS:

The impossible assumption is not impossible, if we assume all living things will be reborn and come to this life again. What if we assume a rich person after death is reborn in a poor family? What would happen? The answer to this question is very simple. If that person still wants to accumulate wealth in his or her new life, he or she has to start to re-collecting wealth and money to become rich all over again from scratch. If we assume he or she becomes rich and wealthy, over time, when he or she has enough wealth and money they are in their old age and must prepare for retirement and death again. As a result, their life is spent on working hard to accumulate wealth with no enjoyment during different ages in their life.

If humans pass a law to establish, peace, prosperity, security, freedom and happiness to every human being as a natural and legal rights, from birth to death, the result of that law will be that no one will be worried about their future or being worried about their children's future to continue life. It will also create confidence in the society that everyone can live in peace, prosperity and freedom in this and their next life.

The ethical conclusion that can be drawn from the above hypothesis is that, if we want a prosperous life for all human beings, we will certainly have prosperous life in our next life and there will be no need to spend all our life to accumulate wealth. We no longer need to be worried for our children's future anymore. Unfortunately in the capitalist world all people are worried about their family and their children's future, that's why everyone tries to accumulate more wealth for their future and they do not like to share anything with others. But in my perfect world all the needs of life for all beings, will be equal and free, relative to their needs. From the moment a baby is born to the last moment of their life, they will be guaranteed all the necessities of life and no one needs to worry about food, home, education, health, medication and other necessities. There will be no need for anyone to be worried about paying bills or surviving in the future.

WEALTH ON EARTH:

Natural resources, products of agriculture, and the handcrafts of workers on earth are enough and perhaps more than enough for the earth's population, but because of the inequality in the distribution of wealth among people, most of the population on earth lives below the poverty line. I can confidently say that there are enough houses, apartments and other places on this planet for every one to have a shelter above their head. But, now a days there are many empty houses and many empty apartments in every city and every country that are only for rent or for sale.

No one is allowed to live in those empty houses, because these houses are named after people who just built or bought them as an investment and they live elsewhere. In the capitalist world anyone who has extra money can buy one or more houses and then lock the doors for future investment.

For example: there are many people from China or Hong Kong who buy houses in Vancouver or Los Angeles and lock the doors, just for future investment and they go back to their home country and live there. Yet, there are many homeless people in Los Angeles and in Vancouver that sleep in the streets without minimum facilities. Many others share small rooms with others in small houses.

A PICTURE OF THE POOR AND HOMELESS IN VANCOUVER

A PICTURE OF THE POOR AND HOMELESS IN LOS ANGELES

I believe there is enough food, enough furniture, enough computers, enough cars, enough doctors, enough medication and enough of other appliances on this planet for everyone in need; but all these items are stocked and controlled by a few people and those people don't know, or they don't want to know, that equality, welfare, prosperity and free life will bring more progress and happiness to their society.

In capitalist system everything is in control of one present of humans population on earth. Who gets the real benefit out of this controlling system? I believe nobody and I'll explain my reason later in this book.

Why can't we share everything with each other equally? Don't we live on one planet? Doesn't this planet belong to everyone? Isn't this planet everybody's home? Aren't we all brothers and sisters? If we look at the earth from the far in space, our home planet will certainly be smaller than a pea, but short-sighted people see the earth as an infinitely large planet, when standing on it, therefore they do evil deeds to others and they think there will be no consequences to their actions.

> NOTE: The earth is a very small but very smart planet for far-sighted and thoughtful people, and it is gigantic but stupid for short-sighted and ignorant people.

In my opinion all human beings on earth are living on one small ball compare to the huge stars in the galaxy and this little ball can be easily destroyed with pressing a button, intentionally or unintentionally. It is our human duty to prevent any possible explosion or destruction of our home planet. We are all one family living on a small planet, why do a small percentage of this family have, homes, education, medication, food, technology and everything else, but the other part of the family, which are the majority, has nothing – absolutely nothing valuable to live for, where everything is available in abundance?

The global capitalist system is divided into three classes: the rich, the middle class and the poor. The rich are the one percent capitalists and they can have what ever they need. The middle class looks like they have everything, but whatever they own, like house, car and other things, belong to the banks and they just pay the monthly instalment. The poor are the ones who often don't even have food to eat or even a shelter above their head to sleep.

Why on this small planet do some people have so much to eat that they can explode and some others don't have enough to eat and they die of starvation? Who has the right answer? Who has the right to make 99% of people to suffer and struggle all their life, just because one day a lady gave birth to them, so they must struggle to continue living all their life unless they become a part of a gang too? Why are the essential needs of human life on earth must be in control of one percent, the capitalists? Don't we know hunger can drive creatures to do anything?

I don't think any of those poor ninety nine percent want their fellow citizens to have a hard life, but most of these people work for the one percent capitalists. And most of the time they oppress their fellow citizens.

For example, when a police officer gives a taxi driver a heavy fine for a minor offence like passing a yellow light and being accused of crossing a red light, instead of giving a notice to him just to make him drive with more cautious and pay more attention to the signs, is an example of cruelty inflicted on their own class. Although the police know that his unfair fine ticket will increase the insurance of that professional driver, he still commits this injustice against his classmates. The taxi driver and the police officer are both part of the 99% of society, but in some countries the capitalist law forces the police officer to write a number of daily fines to show that he or she is an efficient police officer, and also be an income for the system.

....

Hoarding of People's Essentials

Is the hoarding of wealth of the earth in large warehouses more important than the maintenance, progress, development and evolution of the earth for future generations? If our wisdom says no, then why don't we end the greediness before the greed destroys and ends life on earth? Because greed has no mercy and no end.

How can we end this unfair system? What would be the alternative system? I am not a predictor but I know a lot about the past and history. All the evidence shows the path human life is heading in this system will end to a real hell. I believe greed is the base and root, of hate and jealousy.

The cause of all the wars, displacements, crimes, hungers, corruptions, frustrations, failures and miseries of the people of the world are due to three phenomena of greed, jealousy and hate that conquer the soul and mind of humans and control them with power. As long as these three unpleasant traits dominate human being, the world will not only never achieve peace, security, prosperity, freedom and social justice for everyone, but will ultimately lead the world to more crimes, corruption and finally complete destruction of the EARTH.

In this book, I have tried to put all the pieces of the puzzle in one frame to show what My Perfect World look likes and how it can be built.

A Perfect World without money, without intermediaries, without military, without politicians, without different religions and without class differences.

One planet. An intelligent world government run by scientists, philosophers and experts, with new world order constitution with executive guarantee.

A Perfect World for all people of the world equally, prosperous, freedom, security, and social justice. All of the above are 100% possible if all humans on Earth believe in a scientific and logical religion, which is the faith in the SUN, and the EARTH.

My goal is to preserve the Earth and dignity of human being, animals and nature.

……………………

WHAT IS THE SHORTEST PATH BETWEEN MANKIND AND HAPPINESS?

We learned in school that the shortest line between two points is a straight line. For more than 37 years I've tried to find the shortest path between mankind and real happiness; I mean a society with social prosperity, security, peace, freedom and social justice, equally for everyone.

To find out how the human race can reach social happiness, peace, justice freedom and prosperity in this life. I read many different historical books to have a better understanding about the human life in the past. I went through many different facts and questions, researching and thinking for a long time to find all the real answers.

Now, after 41 years I have to congratulate myself and the rest of the people on this world. I believe I have found the shortest path between our current state and real happiness on this world, without hurting anyone – A path to real heaven. I am sharing this new life philosophy to all the people living on this planet. This Philosophy truly promises to easily solve all social, cultural, religious corruption, and greed problems. This realistic theory will make it much easier for people to construct a perfect world (a real paradise) on this planet.

My real plan and goal in writing this book is first to save the mother earth from the danger of destruction, and my second goal is to remove all the obstacles to the progress of human beings to achieve social peace, prosperity, freedom, security and justice.

What I am offering to human kind is here in this book and you just need to read it carefully to understand my facts. I believe human happiness, peace, freedom, justice, and prosperity is based on three equations:

Human energy + time = productions

Productions ÷ to people = prosperity + peace

Peace + prosperity = happiness

In simpler language I can say; for a healthier, happier, peaceful and longer life for all of us on earth, we must all freely contribute equal work hours to our society, and in return, we must all be able to freely get everything we need in life from the society. The value of our work is far greater than the value of money. We are the ones who make everything; money is not able to make anything without us. When man invented money, it was to make his life easier and not being necessary for him to exchange some materials with other materials in the market. Instead he could buy the materials he needed in the market with the silver or gold coin he had invented. Now according to the necessity of time and the expediency of preserving and maintaining the earth and its belongings, human beings must completely destroy and eliminate money and replace this monetary system with some useful, efficient, scientific, logical, less complicated, money-less and likeable system for everyone on earth.

You may ask, what about the lazy people?

In my opinion laziness is a disease that is transmitted and spreads from society to individuals, plus, no one is born lazy. We have to be compassionate and help the sick people to pass their life in peace, prosperity, welfare and freedom. We must treat sick people with mercy and give them equal rights to pass on for one generation, until this disease is completely eradicated. This problem will be resolved over time for sure. No healthy person likes unemployment.

....

DIVISION OF PRODUCTIVE WORKERS AND NON-PRODUCTIVE WORKERS:

Throughout the earth toilers are divided into two major groups. The first category includes the industry workers, farmers, and all those who are involved in provision of social services, which are essential to the people. The second group includes the workers who are not active in any of the essential products needed by the people, like bankers, armies, arms factories, intermediaries, insurance and hundreds of other unnecessary jobs.

How many people are real useful workers and how many are useless workers in all countries on earth? Approximately 7.5 billion people live on the planet earth. A small percentage of these 7.5 billion people are active in services and production needed by people; such as doctors, teachers, nurses, sweepers, farmers, industrial workers, mechanics, cooks, hair stylists, etc. There is another large percentage of people work in unnecessary jobs supporting our current system.

The employers and employees who work every day but unfortunately this large group of working people do not contribute to any kind of essential productions needed by the people.

I see 11 unnecessary positions and jobs in human society that do not contribute to any kind of productions or services needed by people and I think these positions and jobs are unnecessary in human society.

1-Bankers and their employees.

2-Gun makers and their employees.
3-Military soldiers and commanders.
4-Insurance companies and their employees.
5-Casinos and their employees.
6- Stores and super markets and their employees.
7- Car and other dealers and their employees.
8- Religious missionaries and their affiliates.
9- Politicians and their employees.
10- Prisoners and prison guards.
11-Cigarette companies with their employees.

The total number of these people compared to whole population of the earth, reaches nearly to one billion people who do not produce any kind of materials needed by any societies. But, all of them are consumers and the owners of capital use the best products, best cars, best houses and best of everything else.

Some of these useless jobs not only don't produce any essential supplies for people, but their productions cause various cancers and other diseases in the long run, and yet they still legally sell these poisons to the public. You may be wondering how society can continue its social life without these 11 groups?

My answers to this question are as follows:

Group #1 bankers - In my perfect world, we don't need banks or bankers because in this new world order, there is no need for cash or credit cards to trade in the markets; but instead, all the essentials of the people at the time of delivery to them will be recorded on the computer and people will confirm it with their fingerprint as a receipt.

> Note: To prevent hoarding and abuse, we all must be registered in the electronic-computerized government with all our information and fingerprint. People must do all their activities by this system. In the new system everyone must be treated equally for free. Whatever people get from the society must be registered in the system with confirmation of their fingerprint or eye scan.

One example to show how the system works for a cab driver: When a cab driver starts his or her shift, they put their designated finger on the electronic scanner installed on the cab to register their shift started, and then they start work. For instance they drive for six hours and their duty is to give rides to riders for free. The only thing the riders must present to the taxi driver when he or she enter and when they leave the cab, is their ID or their fingerprint on the computer's scanner. The computer installed in the cab will register all drivers and rider activities, then the riders are free to go and the driver must look after the next ride.

The taxi drivers are able to go home after their shift by scanning their finger on the computer's scanner to end their shift. The driver goes home and he or she is able to get anything they need in life for free, they can order the things they need via computer on line and at the time of receiving their items they give a receipt to the deliver man with their fingerprint on the computer scan to register whatever they get. Every purchase or services provided to people must be registered on the government computer to prevent misuse.

Group #2 weapons factories - We won't need any gun makers because under the new world order system no one will be able to make a personal profit by making weapons, because there will be no more money and no more costumers to buy weapons, so no one will be interested in making deadly weapons or other harmful substances. Secondly, life will be without concern or poverty and the living condition will be in peace, security, welfare, freedom, justice, happiness and enjoyment, so in such a society no one will even think about harming or killing other people. There will be no reason for anybody to commit crime or murder. Besides, no one will be allowed to make or carry any harmful weapons anymore. We must also neutralize and eliminate all nuclear weapons on all over the earth.

Group #3 – military: We won't need any military or soldiers for possible wars because the entire earth will be one country under one system and one government living in peace, with no borders and no army. But, we may need one global army for researching on other stars and also for protect and prevent any kind of meteorite crash to the earth and being ready for any possible star wars.

Group #4 – insurance companies: we won't need private insurance companies because in my perfect world, everyone is insured internationally and automatically with free food, free medication, free education, free housing and every other essential need of life for free, from the first moment they are born until the last second of their life. Everybody is covered for everything for free.

Group #5- Casinos: There won't be any casinos for the purpose of making money for one or some people (casino owners), but there must be amusement centres and entertainment places for fun and enjoyment for different of ages for free, in every centre everywhere.

Group #6 - supermarkets and stores: We don't need stores or supermarkets to buy our life essentials from, because in my perfect world every product made by factories or farmers goes directly to warehouses, and people can go there to pick up whatever they need, or products can be delivered directly to their houses as they order on-line for free. But everything given to people must be registered on the computer, to avoid misuse.

Group #7- dealers :In my perfect world, we no longer need any kind of dealers because everything will be handed to people relative to their needs for free, without having any kind of intermediary.

Group #8- religions: In the new world order we don't need any man made religion. Most of the religions existing on earth are poison to human beings, because they create assassination groups, promote superstition, hypocrisy, discord between human beings, poverty, laziness, greed, hate, jealousy, selfishness, brutality, dictatorships, wars, crimes, discrimination, corruption, rape of children, anti-science and anti-progress. Most religious leaders are full of bigotry, monopolization, violence, transgressions, aggression, and other bad attributes. They have practised all these evil traits since the beginning of religion history.

> Note: Religion leaders have prevented human progress since the emergence of religion. Most of the religions on earth are about money, wealth and power; they have the best and most

expensive lands for churches, mosques, temples and synagogues everywhere. Where did they get all these money to build these religious centres? People donated them? So why is it that on cold winter nights the doors of these religious centres are closed to homeless people?

All of the religious leaders claim that their god is the real and the best god. The products of all the religion are heaven and hell, which they promise to be delivering to religious people after death. I can say with certainty 99% of all religions are good for nothing but fooling people.

The clearest example of bad behaviour among religious leaders is the current religious regime in Iran. In the last 41 years, they have made 80% of Iranian to go under the poverty line and they have led Iran to the boundary of war and destruction. They also brought the entire Middle East to great turmoil by the terrorist groups and militants trained in Iran with the nation's money, but without the permission of the nation. That religious regime is not only dangerous to the Iranian people, but they are dangerous to the whole world. The welfare, security, peace, freedom, social justice and progress of the people are no concern to them; they are even opposed to people's happiness. The only important principle for them is to export their beliefs of 1,400 years ago to other countries, however they can; by religious propaganda, by arms and force, by sending terrorists to kill the opponents of the regime, with preaching, or with an atomic bomb.

For the sake of religious law makers in Iran over the last 41 years, nearly 5 million people have been killed in war, in secret or in different protest, 7 million were self exiled to other countries and 5 million are in many different jails right now. Also, 80 million are captives inside Iran's borders by its so-called revolutionary guards of Islamic criminal regime.

Directly or indirectly by this Islamic regime many more people have been killed in Yemen, Iraq, Syria, Lebanon, Afghanistan and many other countries. More than 10 million people have been displaced from Syria, just because of the existence of a religious regime in Iran and this horrible situation still continues today.

Why? Because the invisible hands of capitalism (maybe Bilderberg group, or big brother and big sister,) are behind the regime of Iran and they want them to be in power, even if most of Iranian people don't like them and they want a regime change. What do those invisible hands want from Iran? Obviously they want oil, gas, gold and other valuable mines. Plus all these, by making the country insecure over the last 41 years, most of the geniuses and elites of Iran have fled Iran and taken refuge in colonial countries. According to the Space Magazine, 43% of NASA scientists are Iranian, including two women. (*https://iranian.com*)

> NOTE: There are millions of Iranian geniuses scattered around the world, and if all of them gathered in Iran, the Persian Empire would be revived, and this is exactly what the inhabitants at the top of the pyramid of power have no interest in. That is why they support the current terrorist regime in Iran. I believe that the more pressure there is on a race or nation, the stronger that nation will be until it gets out of control.
>
> The reason for the abundance of Iranian geniuses around the world is numerous attacks by savage, hungry and greedy tribes and that ancient land have been forcing the people to migrate for at least 2000 years. I believe that these hardships in Iran will finally end, but the shame will remain on the governments and countries that have remained silent in the face of crimes and genocide against Iranians.

With a wise and honest leader in Iran the colonial countries cannot loot Iran, that's why looters and colonial countries support the current Islamic regime to stay in power.

To save humanity, I strongly believe and recommend to every one living on this planet to stay away from religion if they want to be safe in their life. In my opinion, most religions must be eliminated from human society and all the mosques and churches and other religious centers must be shut down immediately, because throughout history religious leaders have shown they were opposed to science and community progress and they hinder the peace and freedom of human beings. They killed many scientists and many wars were started because of religious prejudice. Religious leaders only know how to brainwash youth and scare people from hell and burning hot fires. In one word I can say religions are not only unhealthy to society but are poison.

Also I must add that all religions claim that their god is the healer of all diseases and even in some cases they revive the blind and the dead, but we have seen that with the outbreak of the corona-virus all these religious centres were closed and no miracles were performed from these fake gods.

At the end of this book I will talk a little more about the details of various religions and also talk about the best belief and the creator that there is no contradiction with modern science and logic.

Group #9 politicians: In my perfect world there will be no need for politicians because, in my opinion, politics means to circumvent the truth and politicians make matters more complicated than they are. Instead of solving the problems of society, somehow they add more problems to the original problem. Politicians usually try to solve the problems with artificial solutions and they call it politics and that's exactly why everything is getting worse everyday.

They sweep the dust and dirt under the rug and they call it sweeping and they say they have cleaned the place. Here are some examples of how politician's reacts in various events:

- Instead of banning the carcinogens chemicals in tobacco, alcohol or other food companies, they just taxing those products (poison) and the owners of those companies also sell their products at a higher price to the users for covering the extra tax they have to give to government (if they pay any)?
- Instead of banning the manufacture of deadly weapons in society, they permit who wants to carry weapons.

- Instead of rooting out corruption, addiction, stealing, raping and all other crimes and social problems, they build larger prisons with higher walls and iron doors and they keep all the criminals and some innocent people together in one place with a high cost for tax payers, and they call it punishment.

There are many innocent journalists, writers, poets and artists who are suffering in prisons in every dictatorship country, and there is no one there to get them out of prison. At the same time, many criminals are free in every country and every city, going everywhere and they do what ever they like to do.

Unfortunately, many of those free criminals, hold power with lots of money and guns, and they are also in control of some countries like Iran and their army is known as terrorist groups (like the so-called Revolutionary Guards, IRGC) but the whole world is just watching these criminal terrorists like everything is normal and nothing abnormal is happening.

* SEE FOOTNOTE #6

There is no real action. Government officials have so far taken no action to prevent the consumption of sugar in various food items. We have seen and heard many times in the news that scientist and researchers have declared the results of their research on the harms and addiction of sugar consumption irreversible and equated the risk of sugar with heroin consumption. Although medical science has proven that many diseases enter the human body through sugar like obesity, diabetes, and heart diseases, have politicians banned the use of sugar in pastry and other food?

Negotiation and Compromise with the Taliban:

They set up land-mines along the road to kill innocent people and soldiers every day, but they still have so much power that the politicians of United States of America make a meeting to discus and negotiate peace with them. Isn't this policy tragic, sad and ridiculous policy of a so-called superpower country?

Is this relationship, of a country that calls itself the superpower of the world, sitting around the negotiation table to talk peace, with a bunch of deserters with guns, a wise and rational decision? Is this a normal relationship? Now the question is, how the United States of America will deal with the Islamic republic revolutionary guards, whose names are already on the terrorists list and are willing to make continental missiles and nuclear warheads? They claim their intent is to wipe Israel off the map in future and turn the White House into Husseinieh (a place of mourning for Shia Muslims).

Lets get back to the policy of politicians: A simple debtor after being imprisoned for year or two, when released from prison often becomes a professional criminal and can commit much greater crimes than before. In my opinion, politicians are capitalists themselves or they are in the service of capitalism and they are following the laws of capitalism, so they cannot solve any problems in society without the capitalists permission and they can't help it.

* SEE FOOTNOTE #7

HONESTY IS THE BEST POLICY:

In my perfect world we use the philosophy of, honesty, logic, scientifically and efficiently to solve society's problems instead of politics. In this new system we have a constitution written by philosophers, scientists, and social experts; and in the order to make it work, the majority of people must agree, care, follow, support and protect that constitution. The government members must be connected to individual people by an electronic computerized system to enforce the law and address people's needs. Scientist, technicians, experts and philosophers must be in charge of the system with merit and honesty.

Group #10- prisons and prisoners: In my perfect world there will be no prisons or prisoners, because it wouldn't be necessary to keep people behind bars with guards watching them to make sure they are not escaping. How? In my perfect world, there are no reasons for anyone to commit crimes and if there are some crazy people out there that love to do crimes like killing, raping, or harming others! Society should get rid of them with no doubt. These people needed to be kept in temporary detention before the trial.

My opinion about professional criminals and abusers of children, women, elderly people, and animals and nature is; capital punishment with fire. When a jury of 12 people fined a person guilty in a certain above cases, the society should burn them. When they come out of the court guilty, we should direct them into a great fire to show them fire is the most powerful phenomenon in the world and if someone thinks he or she is the most powerful person and they can harm anyone they like, then it shows these people they don't like to live like normal human beings so they must face the fire to find out who is more powerful, fire or them?

Fire is the only phenominon of ability that can burn and destroy filth and dirt, while not being contaminated with any of them.

It is easy to find out if there is something wrong with these people's brain, if there is no cure for this type of mental illness, the law enforcement must direct them to a great fire. I don't think there is any use to keep those kinds of people in jail and spend so much energy to keep them alive; it's just a waste of energy, time and place. That is my opinion, I think fire is a cleanser and they will be reborn fresh, healthy, clean and tidy in their next life.

Other prisoners with small cases must be educated, trained, prepared for jobs, give them a place to live, a job to work and let them be free. There are another groups of prisoners who suffer from mental or physical illnesses, but they are harmless. My perfect world will provide them with complete care in special sanatoriums so that specialists and doctors can find the cause of these diseases and the community can eradicate the generation of such illnesses.

In my perfect world, there would be no prisons and no prisoners; therefore we will save lots of energy for producing other essentials for the community. No animal species has any kind of prison for their own kind, so why should human beings have prisons for their own kind? I think my solution works better and it is easier to find and burn the root of most social problems.

Group #11- Cigarette companies: cigarette companies will not be allowed to add any chemicals into tobacco, they can make the cigarettes for the people who are addicted and who like to smoke cigarettes, but it must be with out any kind of chemicals and poison. In a free and healthy society, adding chemicals to any production must be forbidden and illegal. Natural medicines or painkillers like opium, marijuana, cocaine, and even tobacco can be grown legally anywhere, but without adding any chemicals; it will be legal and free to grow or to use, for adults. Freedom is a natural phenomenon that is born with the birth of every living thing. Also, everyone's freedom will ends where the freedom of others begins. In simpler language; the freedom of everyone is to extend so that it does not harm the freedom of others.

IS THE SUPPLY OF ESSENTIAL PRODUCTS BY FACTORIES AND THE AGRICULTURAL SECTOR EQUAL TO THE DEMAND OF THE PEOPLE?

I believe there are more then enough homes, food, cars, computers, appliances and other necessities of life for every individual people on earth. Imagine one day if all manufacturers are be able to produce 10 times more production for every individual person living on earth? For example the automobile factories can make 10 cars per person per year, house builders can make 10 houses per each person per year, computer factories make 10 computers for each person per year, food factories and farmers can produce 10 times more food per person per day and everything else become 10 times more? Some companies may already be able to do so. I know for sure, in my perfect world it is possible to do so. This is because my perfect world will reduce consumption of extra energy for non-essential products and adds to the essential products of the people's needs.

What would happen if some people have no money to buy, not even one of those products for themselves?

Does the Capitalist who is able to make these products store all the extra products in warehouses, or they will hire people to destroy the extra products, or they will make enough products for supply and demand? If the capitalists increase their production and keep them in stock, they must necessarily increase the number of warehouses, but surly the capitalist will adjust its production based on the people's demand, and then reduce the number of employees because the robots and computers also can do the job much faster and more accurately than humans do. The result of all these changes will be nothing but a growing mass of unemployed. In that case the poor people will be too many. The unemployed and hungry people will unite and they go out of the capitalists control, then this alliance will lead them to a public uprising or rebellion. Can anyone imagine what will happen?

Chaos, Anarchism, Genocide, Raping, Looting and many other horrible events that no one can imagine will happen.

HUMANS' DEPENDENCE ON THE FALSE TRADITIONS OF THE PAST;

All the problems and difficulties of human beings are that we don't separate ourselves from the proven mistakes of the past. It seems we are unable to make change in ourselves and in our society. Humans usually follow the same path in life that their parents took and taught them, and this path, no matter how wrong, is passed on to the next generation.

In my opinion, all human being are captive to the false religions, traditions, beliefs and lifestyles of past generations and their ancestors. In order to eliminate and change all these old beliefs and wrong methods of lifestyle, humans must change their mind from past to present to be able to draw a happy and brighter future for themselves and for their societies and also for the next generations.

Change, on the other hand, means entering a new life development, progress, evolution, prosperity, peace and happiness for everyone living in our great global community.

To get rid of this bondage collective servitude of belief, we must believe in a new efficient, scientific and logical system that encompasses the interests of all the people on earth. We must do that to change our destiny and to restore human dignity.

> NOTE: Unfortunatly, even though we live in the 21st century with the latest technology, we still use medieval ethics and philosophy in our daily life. Everything in the world has progressed reasonably, except the philosophy of life, human morality and virtue.

"Sometimes people don't want to hear the truth because they don't want their illusions destroyed."
– Friedrich Nietzsche

One sentence that has had much positive effect on my personal life is a sentence from the book called (Also said Zoroaster) by the German author Frederick Niche Born Oct. 15, 1844, died Aug. 25, 1900.

There are very deep and beautiful philosophical contents in that book but for me the most important and effective of them is this sentence that says: Man is something that must be overcome.

I have to admit that with only this sentence, I made many big important changes in my life. The changes were very difficult, but the results were very excellent, useful and in my favour. Nietzsche's famous sentence taught me how to overcome myself and to get rid of my wrong desires and habits, and this led me to realize more about my abilities.

A GLOBAL COUNTRY:

My perfect world will come to reality, when is established in all over the earth. One global paradise for everyone living on earth. A society run by one international electronic government, which will be controlled through merit by philosophers, scientists, technicians and experts. Their job is to serve the people of their community with honesty, knowledge and goodwill.

It is essential to have two different languages for all people living on earth. All human beings must to know two languages; one for easy international communication and the other one being their mother language. Every race with any language must teach their children the international language, alongside the mother language.

This government will be responsible to every individual living thing on planet earth. This ideal government and community will have only one international flag, which must be the earth flag. There can be different flags for different provinces for recognition of each province for different nations as well. In my perfect world, there are no borders to separate any land, nations or provinces from each other but they can have their language, their culture and traditions and their own flag. The provinces are connected to the central global government, but every province has independent executive and legal power. Everyone can travel or live wherever they like to live, with no limitation or barriers.

....

CHAPTER 4

What Do We Need To Do To Make A Perfect World?

WHAT STEPS DO WE NEED TO TAKE, AND WHEN CAN WE START?

To build a perfect world with all the facilities and conditions necessary like social prosperity, peace, freedom, security and justice for all people on the earth, we must first increase our knowledge and social awareness of this ideal society. That's why I ask you dear readers, from here and on, read this book very carefully, because this is not an ordinary book.

We all know that construction is done faster, better and easier with the help of others and teamwork. Building some great project without teamwork is almost impossible. For example building a skyscraper, or a Boeing 777, or a large aircraft carrier or a big bridge connecting two cities are impossible without teamwork.

If the above logic is accepted as a principle, we can conclude that, the more people are aligned and involved in achieving this great goal of building a perfect global community across the earth, the faster, easier, and better quality of work will be done.

In order to build a perfect world, we have to be united with great teamwork. The question is what factor or factors can shape this alliance and great global teamwork?

In my opinion, the undeniable common ground that no creature on earth can survive without, are the factors which can unite all human beings in one family. What are the commonalities of humans from all over the world?

What we all have in common is the need for air, water, fire and soil and these four elements are only available to us from the sun and the earth. We can conclude that for all living things on earth the most basic commonalities are the sun and the earth. The sun and the earth are two factors that are essential to every living thing and without them, no life will exist.

In order to achieve eternal and immortal happiness, all human being need a common religion and belief that is acceptable to science and logic. Having a common religion and belief around the globe is the most important starting point for solidarity and unity of the people and the formation of great teamwork.

By the above explanation, I conclude that building a perfect world on earth is only possible through universal unity and teamwork. To achieve this unity, requires the same understandable, logical and scientific religion for all of us. That religion must be the worship of the sun and the earth, which are common needs for all living things. My suggestion to unite the people of the world is to accept the true source from the standpoint of science and logic, and I strongly believe the creator of the earth, humans and other living things is the SUN. All living things can see it through their eyes, and feel the heat on their skin. The existence of the earth is another fact in the commonality of living beings. We are inseparable and attached to the earth forever, even after death.

Our life began from the sun and then continued on earth and it will end with them again; there is an old proverb that says "ashes to ashes, dust to dust". We all go back where we came from.

....

HERE IS MY PROPOSAL ON HOW WE CAN BUILD THIS NEW PERFECT WORLD:

A- ESTABLISHMENT OF A PARTY CALLED PERFECT WORLD.

To register and establish my perfect world, the articles of association must be based on the basic principles of this book, like good thought, good words and good deeds, worship of the sun and the earth, and respect the equality of all human beings in existence of all social rights and all benefits.

B-ADJUSTING THE PARTY'S CONSTITUTION.

After establishing the new system: A new constitution must be written by philosophers, scientist and experts, and when the new constitution is finished, it must be put to the people's vote to ratify. The new constitution must be a scientific, logical and practical which can solve and meet all the human natural needs, questions and problems; like social welfare, justice, freedom, security, peace and human dignity.

NOTE: This constitution needs to be amended every 25 years

C - REGISTER NEW MEMBERS FOR THE PARTY.

Party membership candidates must meet the following requirements.

- Minimum age of 18.
- Having no membership in any other party or political group.
- Knowledge of the party's constitution and the rules.

- Have no criminal record.

NOTE: It is noteworthy that having a criminal record from the point of view of this party is different from the capitalist system. My perfect world considers only those who are professional intruders of the earth and living beings as criminal

D- PARTY MEMBERS MUST ONLY BELIEVE IN THE SUN AND THE EARTH AS THE CREATORS AND ENDORSE THIS RELIGION.

This is a very important step for the party members to make a great and strong team for building the perfect world on earth. Having a common religion and belief will have a great impact on the unity and solidarity of all human being in the world. As a result of common belief about a creator, we will listen to each other with care, respect and love; therefore there would be no more Greed, Jealousy or Hate to cause fighting over religious differences or other things.

Our happiness must stem from the happiness of others, otherwise, that happiness is not real and will not last long. In my perfect world, no one will be born poor and no one will live poor; every individual person will be rich with equal rights and equal opportunities. That is the way we all can be happy, strong and united as one family, safe and secure, with social peace, prosperity, freedom, justice, and a much healthier, happier and longer life on planet earth.

E- REFERENDUM: WHEN THE PERFECT WORLD PARTY HAS THE MAJORITY OF PEOPLE ON ITS SIDE THE PARTY MEMBERS MUST APPLY FOR A REFERENDUM.

If the referendum favours the Perfect World's Party, the members must establish the party's favourite system with a new government.

NOTE: The party must take care of everything, like setting up an international computerized administration system and begin to register people's ID; by taking their addresses and other necessity information with their fingerprint or eye scan in this universal computer. Some people may not like to share their personal information with the new system; the question is whether the current system does not have their personal information?

F- DISTRIBUTION OF HOMES, WORKS, FOODS AND OTHER MATERIALS NEEDED TO THE PEOPLE WHO ARE REGISTERED IN THE SYSTEM.

To prevent abusing the system, no one should be allowed to get any products or any services from the system, unless they are registered with their information in the system. Also, to prevent disturbance and disorder due to any computer system crashing, everyone must have a special ID card to meet their needs and advance their activities in times of emergency.

G-THE BIG COMPANIES, FACTORIES, WAREHOUSE OWNERS AND LANDLORDS MUST GIVE UP THEIR OWNERSHIP AND THEIR INVESTMENTS TO THE NEW SYSTEM.

Everyone can keep their personal belongings, like two different houses, one in a city and one in a village and keep their cars and furniture.

The steps of changing capitalist system to the new Social Council Democratic and Meritocracy system must be done with justification, explanation and persuasion with peaceful behaviour.

NOTE: When the factory owners give up their factories to the new system, they just lose a big responsibility and as a result they wouldn't have any kind of stress or headache, but in return they will get a calm, peaceful, healthier and longer life with everything they need to enjoy life. This change is for the benefit of all 100% of people on earth. Also the factories and the company owners must know that in the new system they still can manage their companies, that they used to own, because they are more qualified than anyone else to run those successful companies or factories. The change of the capitalist system to the new Social Council Democratic and Meritocracy system must be done with absolute peace and no one should be harmed or suffer with this change.

H-EVERYONE ACCORDING TO HIS OR HER ABILITY SHOULD PARTICIPATE FOR EQUAL WORK HOURS FOR THE SOCIETY.

I am so confident and sure that in my perfect world there will be a time when working is not going to be mandatory, because a additional billion workers will be added to the labour force – they are the same people who did not have any necessary production in the capitalist system.

NOTE: Seniors, housewives, children, and sick people, do not need to work, but they are still eligible to have everything they need in life for free, exactly equal to others. Going to school and learning a field or self-educating is equivalent to working.

I- IN THE NEW SYSTEM NO ONE NEEDS TO WORK MORE THEN SIX USEFUL WORK HOURS A DAY, FOUR DAYS A WEEK, TEN MONTHS A YEAR.

Everyone in the community needs to travel and have fun, so a two-months vacation is needed for everyone and their trip to any part of the world will be free provided by the new government. But annual vacations have to be done at different times for different people.

NOTE: Everyone has the right to work in their interest field and if they need training, it must be available for them, if they are eligible to enter that field.

J-THERE WILL BE AN ELECTRONIC GLOBAL GOVERNMENT CONNECTION AVAILABLE IN EVERY CITY, COUNTY AND VILLAGE:

These services will be available all over the earth. Philosophers, technicians, scientists and experts will monitor this electronic government at all the time 24/7 and these people must be elected from every nation based on a four-years term. The new government's responsibilities are to serve people and protect every single constitutional provision.

K-EVERYONE MUST REGISTER WITH THE NEW GOVERNMENT:

In order to get services from the system for free, every one living on any society must be register their identity on the electronic government storing their fingerprints or eye scan, address and other necessary information into the system. This is to facilitate communication and getting services we need in life. Gathering people's personal information by government is to prevent possible abuse by some individuals and also to make it easier for people to communicate with their government's members and with each other.

NOTE: Personal information will be kept in secret in the computer memory and no one will have access to people's information, even if some people get accesses to these information, they can absolutely do nothing with it, because in my perfect world, no one will be able to monopolize capital or do a crime and escape the result anymore. This system will not let anyone do what ever illegal things they like to do, because we must remember our freedom will end where other people's freedom starts.

L-ESTABLISHMENT AND CONSTRUCTION OF PUBLIC SERVICE CENTERS:

Within a radius of 15 minutes walking distance in every populated area, center malls with all the facilitates must be built for people to use. These centers are connected to the central government, helping people with their needs for free.

These centers must be equipped with all kind of services like building repairmen, medical services, fire services, clinics, pharmacies, libraries, cinema, venue of the symphony orchestra, public swimming pool and sauna, entertainment center, bars and restaurants and other social services.

M- POLICE SHOULD NOT CARRY ANY GUNS OR ANY OTHER HARMFUL WEAPONS:

Police officers should not carry any guns, but they must carry a special electronic device producing a momentary shock as a response to any surprise attack or immediate danger from animals or other savage creatures.

NOTE: This device must be used in emergency times only to defend them or to defend others for security reasons.

N- ALL THE WEAPONS ON EVERY SOCIETY MUST BE DESTROYED OR NEUTRALIZED.

In my perfect world all destructive weapons must be out of order or neutralized because in the new system there is no more war nor any battles between different races, nations or different religions on earth.

NOTE: All nuclear warheads and missiles and other weapons must be destroyed or neutralized; in other words, the whole planet earth must be disarmed from any dangerous weapons.

O- WORKING HOURS OF FACTORIES AND SERVICE CENTERS:

All the factories and agricultural lands, companies and other services must work 24 hours and 7 days a week, with 3 or 4 shifts. They must always be ready and available to give services to society at any time.

NOTE: The factories or any places working with machinery should work 16 hours a day for production and keep 8 hours a day for machine maintenance, A maintenance team must be available in every factory, agricultural centers and other places needed maintenance.

P- IN MY OPINION, ALL ANIMAL SLAUGHTERHOUSES MUST BE SHUT DOWN AND HUMANS SHOULD STOP HARASSING, HUNTING AND KILLING ANIMALS:

We all know that by nature, humans are not carnivores; I am not a physician or medical expert but I know many physical illnesses originate from viruses and bacteria transmitted from animal meat to humans. If we accept the hypothesis of the transition of corona-virus from bat to Pangolin anteater and from Pangolin to humans, then this example could prove to humans that carnivores are a risk of death.

I should also add that the bat does not only feed on the blood of pangolin, but the bat feeds on the blood of all the animals available.

NOTE: Naturally some animals are able to eat the meat of other animals, because they can run after their hunt and catch them and choke them to death with their teeth and claws and eat their meat raw. Otherwise the killing of animals, the cooking of them, and the eating their flesh is a human interference with nature that does not belong to them. And this is a disturbance of the order of nature.

Most seafood is compatible with human nature.

Q- CLOSE ALL THE ZOOS ON EARTH:

If human have rights then animals, trees and nature must also have rights, and we humans must abide by them, therefore we must let the animals free back to the nature and provide places suitable to keep the sick and elderly animals for care and we must stop cutting the trees for poor reasons.

NOTE: Human must respect the privacy of animals and keep their living environment clean and tidy.

R- INTEGRATION OF ALL INDUSTRIES WITH THE SAME PRODUCTS:

To save space, time and energy and make it easier for people to use different industries, it is better for all industries to meet the best standards and offer their products to the people under the supervision of the best companies.

For example, if people all around the world think that the Mercedes car industry is the best type of car, it is better for all factories and car manufacturers work under the supervision of Mercedes to produce all kinds of cars with different colors and different sizes and present them to people.

In the same way, all other industries should be integrated to make better products with higher standards to present to the people.

S- UNIT OF MEASUREMENTS:

(The unit of weight and the unit of distance measurements in the world)

(1Pound=16 Ounces, 12 Inches=1 feet, 5280 feet= 1Mile. And 1000 Grams= 1Kilogram - 1 Centimeter= 10 millimeters, 100 Centimeters= 1Meter, 100000 centimeters or 1000 meters or 1000000 millimeters= 1 kilometer)

Given that all current different measurements governing the whole world are correct and there are no defects in them, but in My Perfect World the scale of weight measurements should be Kilogram which can be divided by 1000 grams and measurement of distances diameter, length and width is better to measure with easier standards like kilometer, meter, centimeter and millimeter which can be divided by 1000000, 100000, 1000, 100 and 10.

T- BOXING:

In my opinion, boxing is not a sport, but a brutal game in which we make two people punch each other for winning some money and we sit and watch them until one of them falls to ground and fainted.

In fact, every punch that one side hits to the opponents head, he strikes a blow to the opposite side and creates concussion. The most notably of them was Mohammad Ali Kelley, who lost control of his balance at the end of his life and he was paralyzed and he couldn't talk properly. Due to lack of money in My Perfect World and given the savagery and violence used in boxing match which is very harmful to the players, it should be completely banned.

U- SOCIAL EQUALITY OF RIGHTS OF MEN AND WOMEN AND THE DIFFERENCE BETWEEN JOBS AND THEIR RESPONSIBILITIES:

In my perfect world, women's rights are all equal to men's, but women's work and responsibilities must be different than men's. Due to women's physical delicacy and weakness their responsibilities should be lighter than men's.

Note: When a woman is pregnant, two months before delivery and up to two years after delivery, she dose not have to work voluntarily. In fact, work out of the house is not mandatory for mothers.

V- RELATIONSHIPS BETWEEN HUMANS:

In My Perfect World, love and emotional relationship between people in society are completely self-related, as long as it is not against personal and community's health, freedom, peace, justice and happiness.

Note: Forced relations between individuals are completely illegal.

W- TO MAINTAIN THE GLORY AND GREATNESS OF OUR COMMUNITY WE MUST HONOR AND HAVE SPECIAL RESPECT FOR:

Mothers and Fathers, Teachers and Professors, Artists and Philosophers, Doctors and Nurses, scientists and Inventors, Farmers and Industrialists, workers and toilers. Maintain special respect for those who make life possible and easier for all of us and move society towards progress, development and evolution it is necessary.

X- THE POSITION OF MEDIA IN MY PERFECT WORLD:

Due to social freedom and the right to freedom of expression for society, all media such as television, radio, newspapers, magazines or virtual world, must be free to say their opinion and what ever is happening in their community. Also they have a right to send their reporters to where the incident and news taking place.

Note: In my Perfect world, broadcasting any false and unreliable news on radio, television, newspapers, magazines or virtual world is crime, and the reporter, executive or individual must appear in court to answer to the judges.

Y- ARTISTS:

All artists, such as poets, writers, singers, actors, sculptors, musicians and other artists should have a steady job doing production work or social services, along with their artwork.

Z- ZERO TOLERANCE:

My Perfect World has zero tolerance with the crime, corruption and violation of the rights of others, nature and animals , such as bullying, raping, the children, women and harming elderly.

…………………

STARTING FROM ONE POINT:

This new Social Council Democratic and Meritocracy system has to start from one country to begin with.

Before this new system is established all around the world, it must establish and start from one country to be tested and developed. All the rules for establishing this new system in one country are the same as establishing it all over the world. The only difference is, this new system has no money or any other kind of currency, so when it is established in all other countries, everything on earth will belong to everyone else in other parts of the earth. But when the new system begins in only one country, for imports and exports, the government of that country has to give (export) some valuable things to get (import) goods of equivalent value from another country.

NOTE: When people are travelling in a different country, the Government prepares and provides all travel needs for their citizens, for free. Also, until my perfect world is only in one independent country, the composition of the army and intelligence service for national defense and counter-espionage operation will be maintained.

Family and society:

In my perfect world, everyone must pay more attention to their family and their society's culture and health, because there is a direct relationship between families, community, culture, ethics and health and happiness. If all families in one society are perfectly healthy and they have no problems like poverty or sickness, addiction, illiteracy, violence or any other problems, it shows that community is fine and they are healthy with good culture and ethics, and vice-versa. If most families in one community are illiterate, addicted, unemployed and poor, that community is unhealthy and have no culture to support their background. Those communities are usually lost to different addictions like alcohol, cigarettes gambling and other drugs, and usually they have no money, and live with difficulty. Or, they have a lot of money through illegal means, all of which are spent on addictions. Those communities are not healthy or cultured at all. A normal family in a society must be in full health, education, cleanliness, prosperity, security, peace, freedom and happiness to be in a good condition. Moral teaching should replace immoral teaching, and moral education is possible when all human needs are met.

> NOTE: The relationship between human culture and health is directly related to their economic situation. For example: If we assume that home and food is economics and assume reading books and brushing out teeth is culture, it is so obvious that a person who has no bread to eat certainly does not brush and does not have any feeling to read a book. In order for a society to be considered healthy and cultured, that society must be accompanied by social prosperity, healthcare, security, social justice, freedom, and happiness, without any kind of addiction.

Birth:

Everything starts with the birth of a baby. To have a healthy, secure, educated and prosperous society, the first things required are a healthy, prosperous, secure and educated couple. To make a healthy baby, a couple must take a children training course and pass an exam before deciding to have a child. The couples wanting to have children must pass a course to learn how to raise a child and then they must upgrade themselves with new learning, as the baby grows older. People must be responsible for their children's behaviour, If a young man goes in the street and shoot many other people and the end kill himself too, the parents, and all people who were somehow related to the growth and upbringing of that young man, must be investigated about the raising and educating that child since he or she was a baby and if they were the blame, they must pay the consequence. In the mother's pregnancy, if the baby is diagnosed as incomplete or defective in the womb, the medical council must have a meeting to decide on immediate abortion, because a healthy community needs healthy children. We don't want to bring an unhealthy child into this world and hire so many people to give care to that child and also make those unhealthy children suffer all their life. To believe the truth of this statement, it is enough to look at the sanatoriums that take care of mentally disabled children and adults. After a healthy baby is born all the necessary things must be done to promote healthy growth of the child.

NOTE: Abortion is legal in my perfect world, provided it is performed at a time diagnosed by doctors and obstetricians. Also, circumcisions of children under 18, boys or girls, is forbidden. Anyone who wants to have that operation on themselves can do so after the age of 18.

Education:

Children are better off with uniforms with the same opportunity through kindergarten, elementary and high school. Education through to a high school diploma must be obligated for everyone. After finishing high school, anyone who wants to go to university must be able to do so, if they can pass the university entrance exams. Those students who do not intend to continue their studies at the university after completing high school, and instead are interested in physical, agricultural, technical and industrial work, must complete the courses of their interest.

NOTE: All teaching places from kindergarten to university must have a gym, theater, amusement room, restaurant and health clinic with all other important facilities.

Housing:

Housing for different classes in different area must be no problem. Two examples: If a doctor or an engineer wants their house in the area where all the doctors and engineers are living, it shouldn't be any problem. If a publisher wants to live around other publishers, poets, writers and journalists, there shouldn't be any problem. But, the quality of the highly educated people's houses will be no different then the ordinary workers houses.

In my perfect world, no one has a higher life class quality than others; if some people like to continue and get their bachelor or masters degree that just depends on their personal ability and interest. It's up to them to do what they want to do and who they want to be in their life but that doesn't mean they must have better life quality than a simple factory worker or farmer. In addition, in my perfect world, people's life standard will be at the highest level of standards compared to capitalist and communist and all other systems we have seen so far.

> Note: The only things can make someone different and higher status than others is what they do for their community. For example when someone gives more services to the community or creates an invention to make life easier for everybody or doing some kind of arts to amaze others; these better practices and behaviours in society raise their reputation and their eternal fame will be the best reward for them.

In my perfect world when anyone does good things for their society, they can make their name stand apart from others in a higher position with what they do, and I think that is much greater value than money and wealth.

The community may want to make a statue of these people to commemorate future generation.

A little explanation: For the last 41 years that I talk to people about my philosophy, some people have asked me if there is no money and no wealth, then what can motivate people to be active and productive? My answer to this question is very simple.

The motivation of the people working in the capitalist system is to earn some money for living expenses and possibly saving some for the hard rainy days or a short vacation. So the motivation for people to work in the capitalist system is just to continue living and nothing else.

But in my perfect world, the motivation for people to work and produce is not only to live free of the slavery life, but the first natural motivation of people is movement and physical activity and second motivation is to participate in the production of essential products of our society, which we all are consuming.

As a child no one ever thinks about making money while playing with friends, but they are looking for excellence in terms of personality and reputation. My last answer to them is that we were not born with money to continue living with money.

••••••••••••••••••••

CHAPTER 5

Details About The Religions

The ignorance and need of early humans to justify natural interactions motivated the emergence of religion, and the religion immortalized human stupidity. The duty of religion was to justify natural factors and frighten people out of hell by a supernatural agent, which they call God.

In appearance, most religions have been created for the proper education of moral and good behaviour of human beings. They were supposed to come and teach us the idea of Good thoughts, Good words and Good deeds, or at least people think that way. But the aura of holiness created around the religious leaders, separated them completely from the ordinary people. So nowadays these religious leaders do not care about other values on earth, except money, wealth, power, lust, fame and corruption; or to breed terrorists to physically eliminate their opponents.

Religion is a major problem of our society within the capitalist system; therefore the truth of all these religions and where they came from must be clear to everyone.

GENESIS OF RELIGION

Sometime after the beginning of the Ice Age a group of monkeys took refuge in some caves to survive from the cold and they were forced to eat meat instead of vegetables and fruits because all the vegetables and fruits were buried under the snow and ice. That was the beginning of human carnivores history. Due to the extreme cold of the earth and plants and trees covered by snow and ice, those monkeys had no choice but to eat other animal's meat to survive. That great change in the lives of those monkeys or we can say, early humans put them on the path to becoming today's modern human.

How?

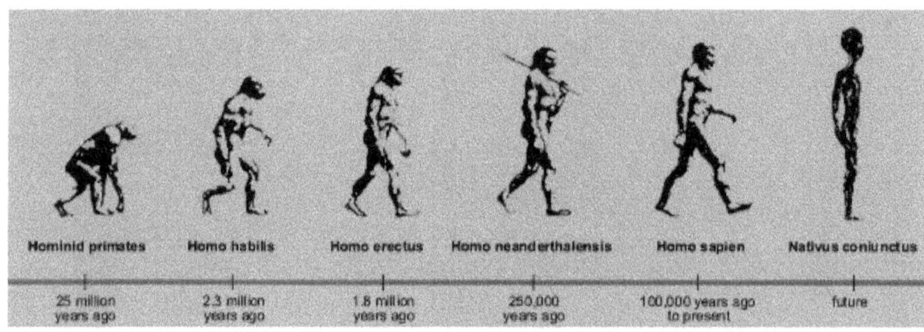

That lifestyle change, made them to learn how to hunt with a team. For hunting other animals, they had to learn the teamwork, how to hunt together, and how to make hunting tools like spears or an axe or etc. As a result of these changes, overtime their brain and forehead grew and got bigger.

Due to the lack of using their legs and hands to climb trees and jumping from one branch to another branch, as they were sheltered from the cold air into the caves, over time early humans got out of bending mode and they stood up straight.

Therefore, it can be concluded that our current form of human beings and our way of thinking is due to the need to continue the life of those monkeys or Neanderthals from millions of years ago.

As their brain grew bigger by thinking how to make tools for hunting, and thinking of how to make life easier in cold weather, they were getting wiser and smarter everyday. As they struggled to survive, their intelligence increased and the more they became aware of their surroundings and environment, a big questions was growing in their head? Who created the sun, the earth, the moon and all other things? Who create all the creatures living on earth? Who created all the stars?

Who is the real creator? Is the earth flat? How does the day change to night? Is the sun turning around the earth or vice versa?

(SEE FOOTNOTE 8)

They had no knowledge about anything; how do earthquakes, flooding, lightning, fire in the forests happen? How does it rain and how do other natural factors happen? They were terrified of all kinds of natural interactions.

As a result of the fear of natural interactions, many questions came up in their brain one by one. They attributed these natural factors to the anger of nature. They came to a conclusion that possibly an animal or a human must be sacrificed to end the anger of nature.

Idolatry:

JEROBOAM'S IDOLATRY
1 Kings 12 : 25-33.
GOLDEN TEXT :—Keep yourselves from idols.
1 John 5 : 21.

Theses beliefs led them to make gods formed from rocks, wood or mud, which we know as rocky idols. For different natural incidents they made different idols and they worshipped them and sacrificed their children or animals to these rocky idols when natural disasters happened. When nature was calm again, they were thinking that, the peace was due to their sacrifice. Abraham so called "Prophet of Arabs", who wanted to sacrifice his son (cut his neck with a butcher knife) for his god, but then he changed his mine because of revelation from his god. Then his god commanded him to cut the head of a sheep instead of his son, and Abraham obeyed his god's order and cut a head of a sheep and Muslims call that day Eid Ghorban which means Holy scarify day.

Every year in that day, Muslims sacrifice many sheep all over the Muslim world, especially in Mecca, Saudi Arabia, where and when

Muslims go to pray to their god. I recently heard a news in the virtual world that the Crown prince of Saudi Arabia Ben Salman has banned the killing of animals on that day; an action that if it's true is a surprise and admirable.

Anyway: lets go back to the topic of idolatry. Over time some lazy and deceitful people, became interfaces between rocky idols and early humans, and they were called the clergy. These clergies made places to keep people's idols and the name of those houses were, god's house. People kept their rocky idols in these houses and went there to worship their idols whenever the time was for praying.

Of course, people had to pay the clergy to look after their rocky idols. One of the old existing rocky idols or god's house is still in Mecca, Saudi Arabia. In Mohammad's time there were many rocky idols in that house and Allah was one them, which belonged to Mohammad's father. It was the biggest rocky idol in that cubic shaped house and that is exactly why they call it Allah o Akbar that means Allah is great.

When Mohammad came to power, he closed the doors of that cubic house and said there is only one god and that is Allah and I am his prophet; therefore everyone must believe and accept Allah as a god and creator of everything and pray to Allah only, otherwise they will be beheaded.

Even today, on the flag of Saudi Arabia is written "there is only one god and that is Allah, and Mohammad is his prophet." Below the script, there is a picture of a sword and that means, if you don't believe Allah is the only god and Mohammad is his prophet, you will be beheaded.

In Islam, if a man from a different religion wants to be Muslim, he must let a Muslim man cut and remove part of the skin of his penis (circumcision, the old Jewish tradition) and if he ever dares to get out of Islam, he will loose his head by Islamic law.

From 1400 years ago, until now, people go to that cube house to pray to one rocky idol called Allah. Islam is an example of idolatry. Every year Muslims go there and they turn 7 times around that house and then they throw stones at their fictional Satan.

In Persian language there is a proverb that says, *people who throw stones at the devil when they are in Mecca, they call the Devil when they return home*. That means they are not enemies of the Devil, but they are close friends, they do the ceremony of Haj only to pretend they are a real Muslim and that they hate Satan, and they are good people and they never commit any sin. Such tricks and pretence of being good are found in most religions.

They also kill many sheep for sacrifice for Allah and the carcass of many of these sheep are buried in mass graves. In short, ignorance, fear and curiosity was the first motivation to create religion. Then religion kept the ignorance and fear alive until now.

....

WHAT OR WHO IS THE REAL CREATOR?

In a very short sentence, I can say all the religions were born out of human fear and ignorance and they continued the same traditional path to this day. That's why most current religious leaders disagree with education, scientific phenomena and logic, until now. If religious leaders believed in science, knowledge and logic, they would finish university before becoming clergy. But today, all religious leaders without a study and awareness of any knowledge want all scientists and scholars in the world to follow them

I don't want to talk about the beginning of the universe and how everything has been made, because first of all that field is not in my specialty and secondly, because it has noting to do with subject of my book, but for awareness of where all living things on earth came from, we need to know other philosophers' point of view in this regard.

Where did the universe and our planet sun and planet earth come from? How did life start on earth?

For awareness of where all living things on earth came from, we need to know other points of view in this regard. Where did the universe and our sun and earth come from? How did life start on earth?

There are many theories about the birth of the universe. One of them is The Big Bang. There are many other theories, and many superstitions, which don't have logical and scientific basis.

Astronomers say our universe was born about 13.7 billion years ago in a massive expansion that blew space up like a gigantic balloon. They say that the universe is still expanding even now, at an ever-accelerating rate.

10 MIND-BLOWING THEORIES ABOUT THE UNIVERSE AND REALITY

From List Verse https://listverse.com/2013/04/15/10-mind-blowing-theories-about-the-universe-and-reality/

10 Big Freeze

The "Big Freeze" is a scientific theory of the end of the universe. Though it doesn't entail gigantic tubs of ice cream drowning everyone, it does spell disaster for all.

According to this theory, the universe has a fixed amount of energy in it, and as this energy runs out the universe slows down. In other words, there is a slow loss of heat, because the movement of energy particles produces heat. There is also a slowdown in movement, and supposedly, everything would eventually come to a halt. It brings to mind the lines by T. S. Eliot: "This is the way the world ends: not with a bang but with a whimper."

9- Solipsism

Solipsism is a philosophical theory, which states that nothing can be verified except the existence of one's own mind. This seems silly at first; and who, after all, would wish to deny that the world around them exists? The only problem is that it's impossible to verify the existence of anything except your own consciousness.

Don't believe it? Take a moment to remember all the plausible dreams you've ever had in your life. Couldn't it be possible that what you see around you is nothing but an incredibly elaborate dream? But we have friends and family whose existence we can verify, simply by touching them, right? Wrong. People on LSD sometimes report seeing (and touching) the most convincing hallucinations—yet we don't assume their illusions are real.

So what can we verify? Well, not even the chicken drumstick we had for dinner, nor the keyboards at our fingers; only our own thoughts can be proven by each one of us to exist. Have fun sleeping tonight!

8- *Idealism*

Idealism: is the belief that all things exist as an idea in the mind—or more specifically, as an idea in someone's mind. George Berkeley, a famous idealist philosopher, found that his views were dismissed as idiotic by some of his peers. It's said that one of his opponents closed his eyes, kicked a stone, and stated: "I refute it thus."

The point was that if the stone really existed only in the man's mind, he should not have been able to kick it with his eyes closed. Berkeley's refutation of this was a bit troublesome, especially in modern eyes. He stated that there existed an all-powerful and omnipresent God, who perceived everyone and everything simultaneously. Plausible or not? You decide.

7- Plato and the Logos

Everyone has heard of Plato. He is the most famous philosopher—and like all philosophers, he definitely had something to say about reality. Plato claimed that in addition to the world we're all familiar with, there exists another world of perfect "forms." All the things we see around us here are merely shadows; imitations of the real thing.

By studying philosophy, we hope to catch a glimpse of the originals. To add to this bombshell, Plato, being a monist, tells us everything is made out of a single substance. This means (according to his view), diamonds, gold, and dog poo are composed of the same basic substance arranged in different ways—and according to modern science, this theory may not be too far from the truth.

6- Presentism

Time is something we take for granted: if we consider time for a moment, we normally divide it simply into the past, the present, and the future. "Presentist" philosophers, however, argue that there is neither a past nor a future; only the present exists.

In other words, your last birthday does not exist and every word in this book ceases to exist after you look at it—until you look back at it again. The future does not exist, as time cannot be both behind and ahead, according to Saint Augustine. Or in the words of the great scholar of Buddhism, Fyodor Shcherbatskoy, "Everything past is unreal, everything future is unreal, everything imagined, absent, mental ...is unreal... Ultimately, real is only the present moment of physical efficiency."

5- Eternalism

Eternalism presents a sharp contrast to presentism. This philosophical theory postulates that time actually has many layers, and could perhaps be compared with a sponge cake (unlike time, sponge cakes do not divide philosophers). All layers exist simultaneously, but the layer seen by a particular observer depends on where he is standing.

So dinosaurs, World War II and Lady Gaga all exist at the same time but can only be viewed from a certain point. According to this view, the future is hopelessly deterministic and free will appears to be an illusion.

4- Brain in the Vat

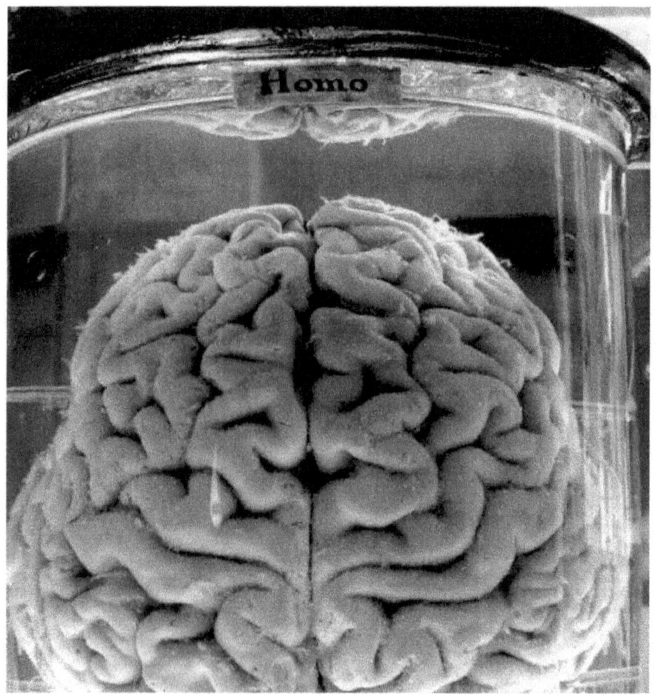

The "Brain in the vat" thought-experiment is a problem encountered by philosophers and scientists who propose (like most people) that the external world is independently verifiable.

So what's the problem? Let's imagine for a moment that we are merely brains in vats, with our perceptions being manipulated by aliens or evil scientists. How could we possibly know? And how could we disprove the possibility of this situation actually being the case for us right now?

Brain-in-vat is a modern spin on Descartes' Evil Demon problem; it makes the same point—that we can't prove the existence of anything but our consciousness—but employs slightly different thought-experiments. And if this sounds like the Matrix, that's because the Matrix was based on this very scenario. Unfortunately, we don't have any red pills.

3- Multiverse Theory

Anyone who hasn't been living under a rock for the past 10 years will have at least heard of the multiverse, or parallel universe, theory. Parallel worlds are said to be very much like ours, with only minor (or in some cases, major) differences. According to the theory, there are an infinite number of these universes.

So, what's the implication for us? Well, in one parallel universe, you've already been killed by dinosaurs and now lie eight feet under (because that's how they do things, there). In another, you're a powerful dictator with the morals of a North Korean Saddam Hussein. In yet another, you were never even born—you get the picture.

2- *Fictional Realism*

The most exciting implication of the Multiverse Theory? Superman is real. Okay, so some of you might be able to come up with slightly more exciting ideas—but let's stick with Superman. Logically, if there are an infinite number of universes, then there must be quite a few which contain real-life versions of our favourite fictional characters.

1- *PHENOMENALISM*

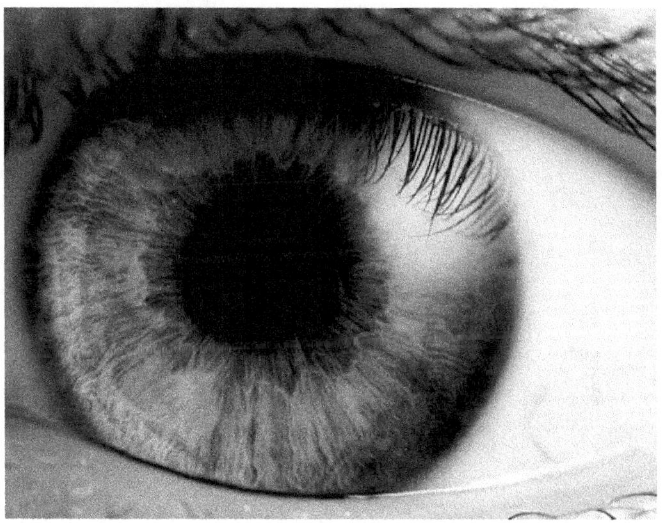

Ever wonders what happens to things behind your back? Philosophers have studied this problem intently, and some have reached a simple conclusion: they vanish. Well—not exactly. Some philosophers, known, as "phenomena lists" believe things only exist insofar as they are perceived. In other words, your cheese sandwich only exists so long as you are aware of its existence. So, trees that fall in forests with no one around to hear them; they don't. No perception, no existence. That's phenomenalism in a nutshell.

- LISTVERSE.COM

....

My personal belief in the emergence of the universe is close to Big freeze #(10) and Plato and the logos #(7), and my theory is based on Albert Einstein's formula E=MC2.

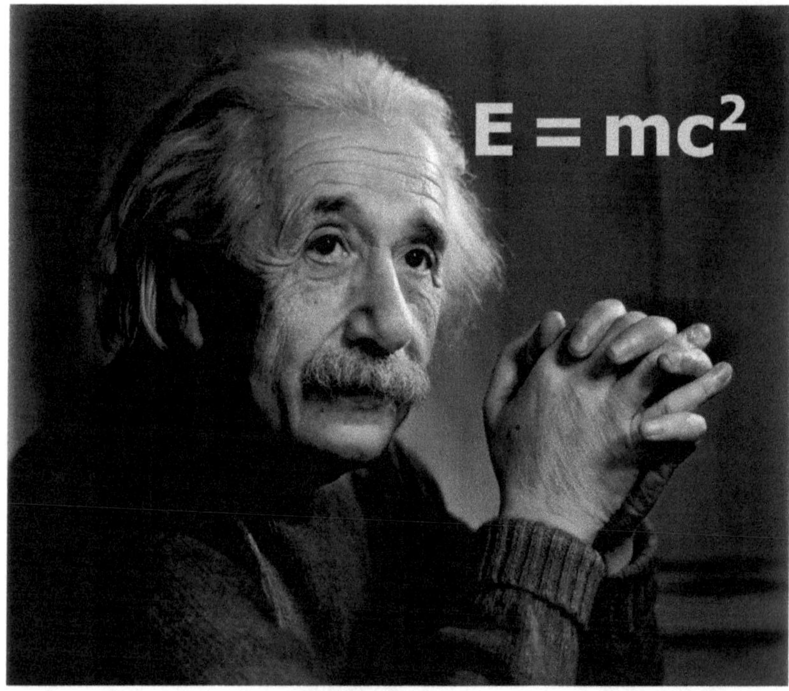

E=MC^2 is a familiar equation developed by German born physicist Albert Einstein (BORN: MARCH 14, 1879, DIED APRIL 18, 1955) to express the theory of special relativity. It states mass and energy is the same physical entity and can be changed onto each other. This finding is what implies that gravity can bend light. This formula also calculates the amount of released or consumed energy during a nuclear reaction. It was the rest energy formula that helped create the first atomic bomb, and Einstein is given credit for writing a letter to then-President Franklin Roosevelt encouraging him to find uranium for making nuclear weapons during the Second World War.

In simple words, energy is released when an object is moving at the speed of light. As I said before, my goal in this book is nothing to do with proving the emergence of the universe, but before talking about the sun and the earth, two important bodies to all living creatures, I would like to give a brief overview of the formation of galaxies.

Space suspended gases, which rotate at the speed of light around an axis, become extremity large and hot planet, and over time, small planets separate from it and revolve around the axes of the same parent planet.

Energy was never born and never dies, but in different interactions, it comes to different shapes and forms, with chemical and physical changes. All the smaller stars separated from larger stars and are rotating around the one they were separated from. All stars in space are made up of gases moving together at the speed of light around one axis.

Before these planets become perfectly shaped like an egg, some smaller stars or meteorite separated from them. They always rotate around the mother star, where they came from. The best example is our own sun and its 8 + 1 planets.

Perhaps our sun has been made by colliding spacious thermal gases in space, or has been separated from a greater star and is rotating around its axis. Earth is one of the nine planets separated from the sun and therefore rotates around the sun. The moon has been separated from the earth and that is why it rotates around the earth.

The earth and eight other planets have been separated from the sun, therefore all these planets are rotating around the sun with different speed and distance from the sun and each other. Also, all the elements of earth and other 8 planets are the same elements that exist in the sun. I don't want to talk about the universe or even other planets in our solar system, but my specific discussion is about the sun and the earth, two important and essential bodies for our existence and life on earth.

Specifications of the sun and the earth:

The sun is made up mostly of hydrogen, helium, oxygen, carbon, neon, nitrogen, magnesium, iron, and silicon. The size of the sun is 864,400 miles (1,391,000 kilometres) across. This is about 109 times the diameter of the earth. The sun weighs is about 333,000 times as much as the earth. It is so large that about 1,300,000-planet earth can fit inside of it.

There are nine planets in the solar system, Mercury, Venus, EARTH, Mars, Jupiter, Saturn, Uranus, Neptune and Pluto. They all have been separated from the SUN at different times and they are rotating around the sun at different distances from the sun. All nine planets rotate in the same direction as the sun rotates around itself.

For example: One year on Mercury is only 88 days and one year on Uranus is 31,000 days, and one year on neptune is 165 years

In my opinion, once upon a time, most of the planets in our solar system had life and living things lived on them, but after the central fiery core of these planets turned off, the planets became cold and frozen. All the gases and liquids around the planet became cold, compressed and accumulated on those planets as solid ice. On some other planets such as Venus or Mercury, life may arise in the future

Gradual formation of the earth:

About 4.543 billion years ago, the earth separated from the sun and was thrown circling around its own axis and turning around the sun ever since. The moon also has been separated from the earth and it turns around the earth axis.

When the planet earth separated from the sun, the whole planet was fiery for a long time, before the outer layer of earth became stiff and cold. Due to the gradual cooling of the earth, the gases in the space around the earth flooded into liquid and filled the pits of the earth. It took a long time for the water and other liquids on earth to cool down.

Evolution on earth:

THE MODERN THEORY OF THE DESCENT OF MAN.

Bacteria arise at a certain temperature and the first cells were born from bacteria. It took about 3.5 billion years for single cells to emerge from the bacteria.

Life evolution on earth moved from bacteria to single cell, from single cell to multi cellular, from multi cellular to fishes, from fishes to amphibians, from amphibians to birds and reptiles, and then to livestock, from livestock to apes (monkeys) and finely to early humans (Neanderthal).

Neanderthals are an extinct species or subspecies of archaic humans, who lived within Eurasia from circa 400,000 until 40,000 years ago.

- WIKIPEDIA.

....

About the living organism evolution, I have the same belief as Charles Darwin Born: February 12/1809 Died: April/19/1882. He was a British naturalist who proposed the theory of biological evolution by natural selection. Darwin defined evolution as "descent with modification," the idea that species change over time, give rise to new species, and share a common ancestor.

The mechanism that Darwin proposed for evolution is natural selection. Because resources are limited in nature,

> organisms with heritable traits that favour survival and reproduction will tend to leave more offspring than their peers, causing their traits to increase in frequency over generations.
>
> Natural selection causes populations to become adapted, or increasingly well suited, to their environments over time. Natural selection depends on the environment and requires existing heritable variation in a group.
>
> – KHANACADEMY.ORG

••

Based on evolution there is no invisible god who made the earth and its belongings in six days and who ordered resting on the seventh day. Another thing that the abrahamic religious have put in the head of human being as is that all human beings came from Adam and Eve. If this is the case, we are all brothers and sisters. The contradiction of this statement is that Muslim leaders say that all men are illegitimate to all women. If the origin of all humans is from Adam and Eve, than it can be concluded that one daughter and one son of Adam and Eve had sex and created the next generation, and so on. From the above we can conclude that all the stories of the Abrahamic religious leaders are all false. So, we must find out about the real creators.

Where does the real energy come from and who is the real creator?

Obviously, our energy comes from the sun, which is solar (light) or heat energy. Through the sun, we are able to produce different kinds of energy and these allows machines and even living things to move around and be able to do things.

We use a lot of stored energy without really thinking where it comes from. We get food from the supermarket, petrol from the service station, and electricity through power lines. But where does the energy in these things come from, in the first place?

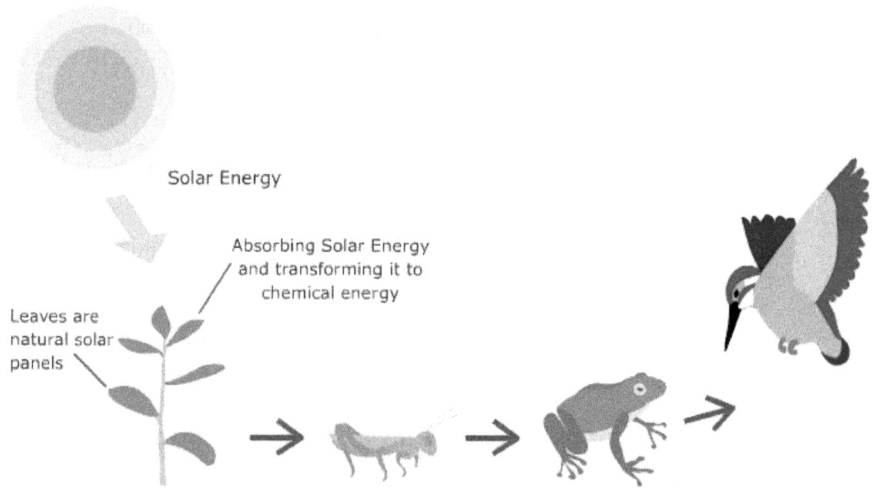
Solar Energy
Absorbing Solar Energy and transforming it to chemical energy
Leaves are natural solar panels

Plant is eaten by grasshoper is eaten by frog is eaten by bird.
Stored chemical energy is transferred from the plant to the grasshopper, to the frog, to the bird, enabling each in turn to function as a living organism.

Green Plants store the sun's energy and through a process called photosynthesis create fruits and other nutrients. Animals, which eat these plants, use most of the energy for their bodily activities and store the rest.

Some animals eat plants, grasses and fruits that grow in direct sunlight, and carnivores eat the animals that are vegetarian, so carnivores are also indirectly fed by solar energy.

Most of our electricity comes from power stations, which burn coal to produce steam. This steam is then used to turn turbo generators, which produce electricity for the cities. The petrol we use in our cars is produced by the distillation of crude oil. We use natural gas for heating.

Coal, oil, and natural gases are called fossil fuels because they were formed from plant and animal remains. Most of the earth's energy comes from the sun.

The famous relativity equation of Albert Einstein means that energy is equal to mass travelling at the speed of light. In essence, it states that there is an equivalence between mass and energy.

The result is that, everything comes from energy and energy is all from the sun. If there was no sun, there wouldn't be any energy and therefore life would not be sustained on earth any more. The conclusion can be drawn from the above logic, that the sun is the first and the earth is the second important body in this universe for us, and no other astronomical bodies are more important to us than sun and earth, because everything we have in life, directly or indirectly, comes from the sun and the earth. So we can conclude that, the sun is the real creator of the earth and all creatures on the earth.

CREATOR AND CREATURE:

Certainly there was a beginning to the existence of this universe and unlimited stars and planets. That beginning could be started from another gigantic sun, which all these stars and planets were in the heart of that sun and they separated by a big explosion, or by a tiny particle according to modern astronomer's theory, the Big Bang.

However, as I said before, this book is not about the creation of the universe, stars and other planets, but we are looking for truth of where and how the earth and its creatures came into being. We know the earth rotates around the sun, and the reason for this rotation around the sun is from the attraction of the sun that holds the earth and all other eight planets in its orbit. From this simple explanation it can be concluded that the earth has been separated from the same sun that shines on us every day. So far, we can conclude that the sun could be separated from a bigger sun or came from big bang theory, or from compressed gases that rotate around an axis at the speed of light so we can say for sure that the earth is separated from the sun.

How living things on earth came into being is related to the interactions that have taken place on earth throughout its life span.

In a nutshell, the earth has been separated from the sun billions of years ago; we all know no living things can continue living on earth, not even for one moment, without the sun. The sun and the earth, these two bodies, provide water, air, energy, and home for us all the time. The earth will have no life without the sun and the living things cannot live without either the sun or the earth.

From the scientific and logical point of view, god is what we cannot live without it, even for one second. So we can say that we cannot continue to live even for a moment without the sun and the earth. With that logic we conclude that the sun is the creator of the earth and all-living things on it. In order to unite people and have a perfect world, we need one religion for all over the earth. We must accept the reality that the sun is our undeniable creator and we all should pray to him for appreciation instead of all those false gods.

The sun provides life for all living things on the earth. If there is the need for praise or worship to any creator or god who created the earth and its living creatures, surely it must be for the sun to signify that all of our existence is first dependant on the sun, which is our great father; secondly to the earth which is our great mother.

If human beings in this 21th century, forbid all false religions and regularly worship the sun and the earth as the origin and beginning of our life, we will reach the knowledge and intelligence needed to discover the scientific realities of our current world and we will all have a much better life on earth. We can like many things in life, but true love must be reserved for the sun and the earth only, because we are never alone with them. Nothing should be more sacred to living beings than the sun and earth.

> Note: In the order to have peace, justice, prosperity, freedom, happiness and love for each other, we all need to have one belief, one religion, and one god, that can bring us all together united as one global family and great teamwork.

What can be the most acceptable religion to everyone on earth? What other phenomenon but the sun can be the common denominator of all living things on earth, through which we can establish...

Peace, freedom, justice, security, prosperity, happiness and long life? After cloudy and rainy days, when the sun shines on the earth and makes nature bright and makes the birds sing, doesn't it bring smiles on human faces and makes them happy? Is it not the sun that brings all these miracles and beauty to us?

Perhaps because of the repeat of all these miracles and the beauties of the sun and earth, we humans regard it as ordinary and do not care or value the sun, with it's radiance, generosity, and beauty of nature that are the reason for the existence of life on earth, and humans take all these for granted. So instead of worshipping the sun and the earth, they worship many other different invisible, powerless and false gods in churches, mosques synagogues and other religious centres. All these gods together are not capable of even one small change or miracle in human daily life.

I've heard many stories of miracles happened by many different prophets; thousand of years ago, but no one has recorded a miracle since the historical events were recorded in the world. In short, I can say, it is better for human beings to research, study and think about the sun's abilities and the benefits that have endless effects on our life; then maybe they will care more about the sun and honours it.

All living things have one thing in common, and that is their need for the sun and the earth, because we are all living on earth and getting our food and energy from the sun. In my opinion, in this endless galaxies, nothing can be more important to all living things on this planet, than the sun and the earth, so I am very honoured to be the first person in the history of human beings, to invite humans to accept and believe the sun as the real creator of the earth and its creatures.

I cannot do any miracle to prove that the sun is our real creator, but my message is verifiable through science and logic and this book will be testimony to my claim. So, my suggestion about one alternative religion to all-existing religions is: Worship the SUN as a great father and worship the EARTH as a great mother. So I conclude that, undoubtedly the survival of all living beings on earth depends entirely on the sun and the earth.

Humans must remove all useless, unnecessary and harmful religions out of their brain and replace it with the most real, logical, scientific, peaceful and approvable new religion, which can bring alliance, correlation, freedom, justice, love, peace, prosperity, happiness and long life to all of us.

In this endless universe, the earth and the sun are the only objects that deserve our reverence, worship and respect; because they create air, fire, water, food and our existence depends hundred percent on these two planets.

With one united religious belief, we will be one family and we care much more for each other as part of one family and we will never be separated or be against each other, because of conflicts over religion.

Note: Those who oppose the theory of unity and solidarity of the people of the world are either completely ignorant or indifferent to the well being of social peace, freedom, security, welfare and justice, equally for everyone. In either case, their opposition does not really matter. Because for a good and efficient philosophy, even if the entire population of the earth opposed it, that philosophy will still remain a good and efficient.

To achieve the perfect world on earth: All of us human beings must believe in a single religion with two creators, which would be the sun and the earth. Even though the earth is the sun's daughter and she has been separated from the sun, but if the earth didn't exist, no living creature was alive in this solar system. Therefore, I can strongly say, our creators are; the sun (great father), and the earth (great mother). They are our great parents, because they are the cause of our creation and we cannot live a single second without them, and we will never be separated from these planets even after death.

Many religious leaders say that there is only one god and that god is invisible. But, I am saying we have two gods and these two gods are visible to everyone living on earth, we can see, touch, and feel them every day in our life, they are the (sun and the earth). They created us, so I am asking everyone on earth to respect and have appreciation for these two bodies, because they are the real source of our life.

I do not want to disrespect any one, but at the same time I can not hide and imprison my thoughts with the fact that if any pioneering intellectuals are still suspicious of the capabilities and creativity of the sun and the earth and they are still worshipping some nonsense, powerless imaginary idols, I doubt the wisdom of those people that they can not see the facts as they are.

I believe following in any other religion is misguidance, ignorance and ungrateful of the sun and the earth. The interest of human beings in a common belief will be in the care and love of fellow human beings and share the possibilities of life with each other equally.

At that point we can claim a perfect world has been deployed on earth.

••

My Last Words

* Maybe if I wanted to talk about all the details of my thoughts in this book, I could add at least 100 more pages. But I am not interested in exaggeration. I believe that those who are supposed to understand what I am saying will be able to do so with the current number of pages, and if they aren't meant to understand even a thousand more pages wouldn't be enough.
* When the wisdom, knowledge, and goodness become worthless in a society, ignorance and filth become valuable and their leaders lead that society to misery, destruction, and nothingness.
* For me the worst insult to this philosophy, which I consider the perfect world, is for someone to say that, this is the same theory of communist system in China or in the former Soviet Union, in Venezuela, in Cuba or in North Korea. I really think it's unfair to compare such a beautiful, efficient and universal theory with the failed methods and theory of others.
* This book and its contents are mostly about my personal dreams, beliefs and imaginations, which were born in my mind 42 years ago. I have spent all these years researching, thinking and analyzing how to create a complete and an efficient philosophy to run the human society with all its necessary questions and answers. In all the terms of this book, I have tried to avoid all the details about other subjects to make the book as short as possible, to get to the main topic of the book, which starts from Chapter 3, about my proposed solution to resolve

social, religious, cultural and class differences problems among human beings.

* My personal prediction for the future of this book in a short time is that the majority of the people of the world will agree with my theory. But it is not far-fetched to know that there are always those who oppose everything. Those people are divided into two groups: conscious and ignorant. Some of these two groups are honest and others are biased.

NOTE: Worst case scenario, in the current systems of the world, when a benevolent genius emerges, all the biased ignorant and professional criminals unite to eliminate him or her.

In any case I believe in the next 50 years at most, the majority of human being on earth will be in agreement with my perfect world. *This book will be evidence in history, and future generations judge whether its contents is right or wrong, efficient or useless.

Nothing in the world can change truth:

* If all people on earth agree with a misguided and irrational philosophy, that philosophy will still be wrong and irrational, and vice versa, if all the people of the world disagree with a rational and correct philosophy, that philosophy would still be rational and correct.
* Ignorant in Persian language is NADAN, and from any direction you read NADAN it still reads NADAN. This means that looking at ignorant from any angle is still ignorant. Also, there is another proverb in Persian that goes: "never approach a donky from behind, a cow from the front, or an ignorant person from any direction." Ignorant people are dangerous from any direction you could approach from.
* In my opinion, the earth is a planet of greatness and intelligence with countless capabilities that have lived for billions of years and with the help of sun's energy has created all kinds of

living and inanimate creatures on itself, therefore in order to preserve the earth, we human must do our best.

* A perfect mother first must reach to a perfect physical and intellectual maturity in order to give birth to other perfect beings. The result of the above analysis is, that the earth is the mother of all living things on herself and if she has given life to all living beings, it's because she first could breathe and have a life herself before giving life to other beings.
* I believe the earth is female and the sun is male, because the sun is fertilizing the earth with its light and energy, and the earth gives birth to various living things. I also believe that Mother Earth monitors all its creatures and she is able to see and hear us all. She can reward for our good deeds and punish for our bad deeds at the right time and right place.
* I believe after death it is even possible for the earth to create filthy and wicked people in the next life in the form of degraded animals. The thoughts of every creature in this life can shape their next life.

Damage and destruction to the earth:

* The damage and destruction that humans does to the earth and nature, no other creatures are able to do so. Capitalists cut down trees and destroy forests to make lumber to make buildings and furniture to sell. They destroy all natural, historical and recreational resources to build luxury offices and residential buildings for sale. By using fossil fuels and producing greenhouse gases, they changed the earth's climate and have taken nature out of the ordinary.

Those who do not think of anything but their own interest:

* Those who cut the diamond from the diamond mines and exchange them with dollars in the worlds of jewellery markets or those who pull oil out of the ground by millions of barrels a day, just for more dollars; do they ever think that oil could be

the blood of the mother earth or the diamond mines could be the brain of the mother earth?

* How about if one day scientists come to the conclusion, and they can prove, that the earth is a big living creature and has a heart, brain, eyes, ears, blood, and lot more organs that we can not even imagine. Then what can humans do to repair all the bodily damage they have done to the earth? Can they return all the oil back to those underground oil reservoirs that they pulled out the oil in the first place? Can they return all the diamonds to where they cut them? I think humans are the most dangerous creatures to planet earth and other animals, because they are more intelligent than other beings, therefore they are able to make fireworks. If capitalists continue to destroy the planet earth for their immediate benefits, the consequences will be the short life and complete destruction of the earth and its creatures.
* I wrote this book with the belief that if we humans do not strive for the progress, development and evolution of this world, no other creature from other planet will do this for us.
* I ask you, dear reader, to think what is the sin, guilt or fault of the new generation that are not able to enjoy the healthy life on earth? Or what is the sin of a child who is born in a poor family that they have to continue to live poor all their life?
* Why any family has to be poor in the first place? And that makes their children to be poor as well. I don't say why happiness is inherited? Because happiness is a good and necessary phenomenon for every one especially the children. But my question is why misery should be inherited? Happiness must be inherited from every society to their people, everything for every child on this planet, equally; because we must think of every child as our own child and all children and every individual on this planet deserves to have the same opportunity as others.
* Why misery and happiness must be inherited? Some children inherit happiness and some others inherit misfortune? Why

don't we do something about this unfair situation? Why can't we make sure all children born today are insured of having food, house, education, medication and freedom and every other needs for living, equally, like every one else?

* I am taking advantage of my human rights and freedom of expression (article19) and publishing my beliefs (My Perfect World). I had to censor myself on some cases in this book, because I believe in some parts of the capitalist world no one is allowed to say whatever they like to say, otherwise their book will never be published and they may lose their life before publishing any books, but I live in a free country like Canada and I hope I don't have to censor myself anymore before publishing my book.
* I don't believe that everyone must or should understand this philosophy in my lifetime; because not everyone can have the same imagination and the same dream at the same time. But, I know for sure, one day in future, sooner or later this philosophy will be many people's dream and they will make it come into action and it will come true.
* I must say the capitalism will come to an end, one day soon or later because first of all every game has an end and secondly, capitalism is covering only small percentage of people's interest and will keep the majority of people out with no interest, benefits or opportunities. It is very likely that with the continuation of this system, we will reach to more social violence because of greed, jealousy and hate, and the result will be more crime and corruption.
* As time goes by, human social status becomes more dangerous, because, everything is under the control of a few people and nothing is left for the majority, that will make the society unbalanced and it will put lots of pressure on the majority and that will bring them to a common pain and anger, and that common pain will eventually brings them together and they will be united. The result can be a blind rebellion; revolution or anarchy and then no one will be able to control the destruction

nor to stop it. But my perfect world system will be a cure for these social pains – a healing drug to treat this ancient and destructive diseases, once and for all.

* My perfect world will cure all social-philosophical, cultural, religious problems of the world. My new world order covers every individual peoples interest living on earth and it promises, social peace, freedom, security, welfare (prosperity), justice, with long, healthy and happy life equally for everyone.
* I have never had a tendency towards idolatry and individualism in my life. But the philosophy of rationalism and the worship of the Sun and Earth are part of my life.
* In my perfect world no one will be able to commit crime in one country and escape to another country; because in this new world order, the whole planet earth would be only one country and no matter where the criminals are living, communities will recognize them immediately. In that case the crime rates will eventually decrease to zero.
* Please do not judge my book before reading it yourself, with accuracy.
* I am using my freedom of speech to complain and criticize the current existing capitalist, communist and even so-called socialist systems, which exist on this planet right now, and so far they have already shown that none of them are practical or useful to their community.
* I welcome your literary criticism and suggestions, and will work hard to fix the deficiencies in the contents of this book.
* I am the author and responsible for my philosophy.
* PageMaster Publishing is the responsible of the proofreading, correction, editing and finely set this book.
* The errors that come from other sites in this book are the responsibility of those sites themselves.
* If you, dear reader, have a review of this book please leave comments, I will try and be happy to respond to your criticisms, suggestions or to your possible encouragement.
* Thanks for taking the time to read this book.

* I am not the first man on this world to talk about peace, prosperity, security, justice, freedom and happiness, but I hope I will not be the last one. If you agree with my philosophy and want to live in a perfect world, make sure to vote for it and support my philosophy.
* In short, the cause of all corruptions, crimes, insecurities, wars, miseries, and all other deficiencies in the world are due to tactless, dogmatic, selfish, greedy, and evil-minded big siblings sitting at the top of the power pyramid, and their criminal mercenary political dwarfs running smaller countries.
* Have a good life.
* I hope one day, human beings will reach my perfect world.

....

For publishing this book one man, Dale of PageMaster, helped me with challenge, proofreading, editing and essay, even though he doesn't agree with all I say. Now I am here to appreciate his efforts, Thanks Dale.

NOTE: From January 2021, another Pagemaster employee, Teddy Edwards, joined us to finish this book. Therefore, I have to thank Teddy for helping us deliver this 42 month ship in the turbulent sea cruise to the final destination. Thank you, Teddy.

} The End {

Footnotes:

Footnote #1 – (Because the British had made an oil refinery in southern of Iran with a contract of something like much more than half of the profit was going to British partners and small portion to the Iranian side) The British net income from Iranian & British oil company was $40 million dollars a month and probably a few million dollars the share of Iranian side of the contract.

Footnote #2 – Can you imagine a religious book from 1400 years ago, written by someone who admits to his god that he was an illiterate and he didn't know how to write and read, can be taught at schools and universities as a book that has to educate scientists, philosophers, engineers and doctors for human beings? My answer to this question is absolutely no.

Footnote # 3 – The general and main policy of the Islamic regime of Iran is defined based on physical elimination of human beings and the founder of this kind of thinking in Iran was a Mullah named Navab Safavi, someone who managed several important assassinations. Former regime officials executed that man, but Ayatollah Khomeini confirmed all his actions and his name is placed on some streets and a subway station in Iran by the Islamic regime.

Footnote #4 – In January 334 B.C.E, The king of Macedonia: Alexander, invaded Persia and began a series of campaigns that lasted ten years. He conquered Persia but the Persian culture conquered him. He married the Persian Princess Roxana and ordered all his generals and 10,000 of his soldiers to follow suit in a mass Persian wedding.

THE SELEUCID EMPIRE

Seleucid Dynasty was established by one of Alexander's generals in (311-129 BC). After Alexander's conquest, Persia fell under a foreign occupying force.

His name was Seleucids and he started the Seleucid dynasty in (311-129 BC). His dynasty lasted for 182 years and at that time all their children were born in Iran for almost three generations so they learned Persian language and culture. As a result their children had no interest in their parent's language and culture anymore and they called themselves Persian and they didn't want anything to do with their background. In the last year of the Seleucid dynasty rule, some people from north-east of Iran called Parthian started an uprising and they overthrew the rest of Alexander's solders off Iran and they established the Ashkanian Dynasty in (247 BC- CE 228).

Mehrdad was the name of the leader of Parthians who were living on the northeast side of Iran plateau. They reclaimed Iranian soil from Alexander's old commanders.

They started the Ashkanian dynasty in (247BC- CE 228) and they ruled Persian Empire for 475 years and they were at war with Rome most of the time.

PERSIAN PARTHIAN EMPIRE HYPERLINK "http://www.persepolis.nu/timeline.htm"

The Parthians (Ashkanian), a tribal kingdom from north-eastern Persia of the coastal areas broke the Macedonian dynasty, gradually defeated the Greek Seleucids and consolidated their control over all of Persia and they remained true to the spirit and culture of Persia, and did their best to make positive contributions.

PERSIAN SASSANID EMPIRE HYPERLINK "http://
Then Sasanian dynasty started their Empire in (224-651) and they were in power for 427 years until the Arab Invasion in 651AD and Arabs were ruling directly or indirectly for 295 years.

The Sassanid Persians (Descendants of Sassan) coexisted with the Roman Empire, and there were many great battles between them. Many of the victories of Persians is carved in stone. They were proud of their Persian heritage, and they wanted to reestablish the borders of the Old Persian Empire.

Note: Except for Alexander, who invaded Persia 336 BC in retaliation of the burning of Athens by Xerxes in (480-479 BCE) Iran has always been in trouble with a bunch of hungry, savage and ignorant attackers, those who had no particular enmity with the Iranians, but they attacked Iran only for wealth. Iran has rich soil for agriculture, good water and great weather so most Persian people of those days were farmers and they liked to work on their land and live in peace, but they always had attackers from everywhere, so Iranians had to defend themselves, their family and their home country, as well as farming. That made them have many different problems and that's why they lagged behind in technology, science, progress and development of the world. But instead they became a very strong nation and throughout the history they have learned four important principles with their enemies.

1-Being patient
2-Using their collective wisdom against their common enemy.
3- Compromise with the enemy to keep the cost of living low.
4-Being opportunistic and recognizing the perfect time to destroy the enemy.

The collective wisdom of a society is formed when the people of that community are in pain or a common problem, such as war or flood or earthquake. The collective wisdom function of a society is the same thoughts, speeches and deeds of the people of that society at the same time. What I mean by collective wisdom is, when every person's wisdom in one society works on one specific goal at the same time.

....

ARAB CONQUEST OF PERSIA (651-819)
THE DARK AND BRUTAL ARAB CALIPHATE ERA

The history of Persians after the Arab conquest can be summarized in three words: oppression, misery and massacre. The Arabs invaded Persia not only for its reputed wealth, but to bring into the faith new converts and to impose Islam as the new state religion.

The next attacker to Iran was Arabs from Saudi Arabia. Before the invasion of Iran or the Persian Empire, the Arabs lived in the tents and their main occupation was selling and buying goods, camel grazing and different tribes fighting each other, killing and looting. They didn't have significant land for agriculture. Before Arabs entered the territory of Iran they were serenading one of the Sassanian capitals, and they promised Iranians that Mohammad's new religion is a peaceful idea and everyone is equal to others and so on.

At that time many Iranian farmers who were living outside the city walls (castle) weren't happy with the last king of Sassanian dynasty, (Yazdgerd III) therefore they joined with the Arabs troops to open Iran's gate. The number of those farmers was about 55,000. The Arabs stayed in Iran almost 200 years after the occupation of Iran. During that time they burned and destroyed many Persian poetry and historical books, they also broke down many historical buildings (monuments). They took Iranian ladies to their country as slaves or to sell them or for their sexual use. They committed countless crimes while they were in Iran. But eventually the Iranians were able to kick them out of the country after a few centuries.

Some time after the liberation from the Arab invaders, another invasion of Iran by Genghis Khan Temujin the Mongol in 1219-1221 happened.

He committed many crimes and destructions in a short time, but after a while Genghis left Iran to invade other countries so Iranians were free again.

Amir Timur Gurkani (Lang) titled (Timor Lang) led the next invasion of Iran, he attacked Iran and he also did many crimes, looting and destroying. He left Iran after awhile to invade other countries.

Safavid Empier, which was the Monarchy system. They were the ones who brought Shia to Iran.

After the Safavid Dynasty period, there were other attacks to Iran, but since it is not the subject of my book I refrain from mentioning them.

Islamists and the entire Mullah, have taken Iranian people captive since 1979. Now it's time for all Iranian's enemies to leave Iran as soon as possible, because the Iranian tolerance is over. For Iranian people, the culture and the soil of the country are more important than Islam or Quran or any other religion.

Unfortunately, most Westerns and Eastern politicians without any clear thinking supports this Islamic criminal, deceitful regime; only because of their own economic interests. Their theory seems to be to loot a country and make the youth flee away from their homeland and go to the colonial countries for doing cheap labour requires a corrupt dictator, deceitful, criminal and delusional leader to rule that country. Iran is a country known for its hospitality and honesty but unfortunately, Iranian farmers have always had to fight the uninvited and unwanted attackers throughout the history of their country. So a country with all this number of alien attacks, progress is either slow or sometimes completely stopped.

As a rich country, Iran has historically defended itself against hungry savage invaders at all the time.

LIST OF MONARCHS OF PERSIA FROM WIKIPEDIA

Cyrus the Great Empire (559 BC to 530 BC)

Persian Empire at its greatest territorial extent, under the rule of Emperor Darius I (522 BC to 486 BC)

This article lists the monarchs of Persia (Iran) from the establishment of the Median Empire by Medes around 705 BC until the deposition of the Pahlavi dynasty in 1979. "https://en.wikipedia.org/wiki/Median_Empire"

Earlier monarchs in the area of modern-day Iran are listed in:

List of rulers of the pre-Achaemenid kingdoms of Iran

MINOR DYNASTIES AND VASSAL MONARCHS CAN BE FOUND IN:

List of rulers of Parthian sub-kingdoms
Median Empire (678–549 BC)
Achaemenid Empire (559–334/327 BC)
Macedonian Empire (336–306 BC)
Seleucid Empire (311–129 BC)
Parthian Empire (247 BC – CE 228)
Sasanian Empire (224–651)
Islamic dynasties of Iran
"https://en.wikipedia.org/wiki/List_of_monarchs_of_Persia"
Dabuyid Kingdom (642–760)
Rashidun Caliphate (642–661)
Umayyad Caliphate (661–750)
Abbasid Caliphate (750–946)
Samanid Empire (819–999)
Saffarid Kingdom (861–1003)
Ghurid Kingdom (879–1215)
Buyid Kingdom (934–1062)
Ziyarid Kingdom (928–1043)
Seljuk Empire (1029–1194)
Khwarazmian Empire (1153–1220)
Mongol Empire (1220–1256)
Ilkhanate and successor kingdoms (1256–1501)
Ilkhanate (1256–1357)
Sarbadars (1332–1386)
Chupanids (1335–1357)
Jalayirids (1335–1432)
Injuids (1335–1357)
Muzaffarids (1314–1393)
Kara Koyunlu (1375–1468)
Aq Koyunlu (1378–1497)
Timurid Empire (1370–1507)
Safavid Empire (1501–1736)

Afsharid Empire (1736–1796)
Zand Kingdom (1751–1794)
Qajar Empire (1794–1925)
Pahlavi Empire (1925–1979)
Republic Islamic (1979-present day)

Footnote #5 – With a simple calculation we can figure how thirsty the capitalists are for Oil, Gold, Land, Money and Power and it looks like they will never be satisfied and the greed has no end. Even if one day, they took over and owned the whole world, all countries, all the lands and all the wealth on earth, they would still want more and more.

> Note: As they become rich every day, they need more wealth, money, land and weapons, and more and at the same time the majority of people become poorer and the class differential increases everyday. This is the game of capitalism. It is called greed and it is a rich man's game. Even if they try to be sociable with others and let other people play their game, it doesn't matter who plays the game better, the profits still go to the rich man's pocket (the capitalist), the rest of the people end up with almost nothing.

Footnote #6 – The old and worn-out leader of this terrorist system has been talking about the enemy for the last 41 years while he himself is the biggest enemy of Iran and Iranians. Recently this so-called world Shiite leader has a new illusion and he has spoken about a Ghost enemy. Before it was the United States and Israel and now the Ghost has been added – another hypothetical enemy. .

The rudeness of this old man has reached such a level that although he ordered the killing of more than 4,800 people on the streets of Iran in November 2019 just in 3 days, now he sheds crocodile tears for George Floyd and condemns killing, and wants to name a street in Iran after him. Isn't it ridiculous?

When Khomeini died, cleric Rafsanjani in parliament asked Khamenei to succeed the Supreme leader, he said that there must be bloodshed for the people possibly that I become their leader. I think this was the only truth he confessed. He also said I don't deserve to be a leader. But in any case, after the positive vote of the assembly of so-called experts, and with many coquettes and apologies he accepted the leadership. Now he is 81 years old and he has been in power for the last 31 years, and he has not made any positive move for Iran or Inanians so far, but he still refuses to give up the seat of power.

THIS IS THE PICTURE OF OLD ALIBABA AND THE 4000 THIEVES OF BAGHDAD

As a teenager, I read some stories about Alibaba and the forty thieves of Baghdad and I saw cartoons of that fictional character as well; with my kids, but now the real Alibaba is 81 years old and his thieves are 4,000 and they are in Tehran instead of being in Baghdad. They are looting, killing and destroying that old country, it seems that Iran is his father's legacy. This Alibaba is the supreme leader of Republic Islamic of Iran who has drawn his sword, and obviously wants to fight with Iranians and the whole world with one hand.

He is so fanatic that he wishes to bring humans to a lifestyle back 1,400 years. But at the same time he use iPhone, he use Mercedes and BMW, and the best and highest technology for himself and his family and nothing for Iranians Except death. Recently, he used the pfizer vaccine for himself and his family, but banned the import of American and British vaccines into Iran

Footnote #7 –

A BRIEF LOOK AT THE WORLD POLITICAL LEADERS

Politicians and leaders from around the world fit well within the climate, culture, traditions and way of thinking of the people of their own country.

Apart from the individual personality of politicians, a general definition of them can be provided.

For example:

British Politicians:

Their appearances are often very organized, with combed hair, tidy and polite. There are other politicians in this country who are very disorganized, with unkempt hair as if they had just woke up hungover, and very rude. But both groups are very sneaky in politics, and have insidious ideas for other countries, for their own political lusts and personal gain. They only think of the interests of the very near future, never about long-term consequences their policies may have in the world. From a philosophical and meritocrical point of view, they can not see beyond the tip of their noses.

Russia:

Due to the blistering cold of Russia, its politicians are very violent, power-hungry and materialistic. When they come to absolute power to lead their country and bring welfare, happiness, prosperity, and justice to their community, they forget that they are also human. They violate human morality and dignity, altruism and interaction with others, and they sacrifice everything for their own political desires and lusts.

Chinese politicians:

Chinese politicians have all been enslaved to their 75 year-old political mindset, and do not accept any effective new or up-to-date ideas that could work better than their old political and wrong philosophical system. They are not even willing to listen to that new philosophy, or even think about it. In China, anyone who wants to say something against the philosophy of the country's politicians is sentenced to prison, or sent to labor camps, or death. I however say that everything changes over time, and philosophy can be one of those things. Nothing is one hundred percent forever. Although their main philosophy is communism, or at least socialism, we see that they have surpassed all the capitalists' countries of the world in wealth, and are willing to do anything to keep it that way. I think the coronaviruses was created in a chemical laboratory in Wuhan city for the same purpose. For a monopoly in wealth and power.

American politicians:

American politicians are similar to British and European politicians, but with only 243 years of experience governing their country.

Because of their newness, American politicians are more subordinate to the British and Europe than other types of politicians. They always react to actions of other countries, and in fact consider themselves the gendarme of the entire world. They intervene in Third World countries with the help of British and Europe, removing the elected leaders of the people and replacing them with corrupt, criminal monsters. They think they are one of the best and most powerful superpower countries, but they are far from being the best. If they do not take action to change, or improve their beliefs and become less selfish, their power will not last long.

However, in the current global capitalist system, we have reached a critical juncture. The world's three great superpowers, the United States, Russia, and China, are spending all the energy and resources available on earth to become more capitalist. They should instead spend it all for the welfare of the people. They accumulate capital for political power, for no other reason than their own political lusts . In general, these politicians have forgotten that their main responsibility is to serve welfare, security, justice and freedom for the people.

For example:

When an irresponsible person in Iran allows the Chinese to enter the country to build some factories to make BITCOIN, and they spend so much of the country's electricity on their equipment that makes an electricity shortage for ordinary people. Electricity otherwise meant for the every day life of the people, who then must spend nights in the dark, days without their electrical devices.

Another example: Someone irresponsible with their power has allowed Chinese fishermen to enter the Persian Gulf. These fishermen have a giant fishing vessel, and they use it to plunder all the fish from that sea, sweeping the sea floor. What does that mean? There is a proverb in Persian: *Where has the cat's shame gone, when the lid is off the pot?*

This proverb is about a wildcat that enters the kitchen of a house, and sees a pot without a lid. Maybe there's a big piece of meat in the pot, and he takes it away. It is a mockery of the sort of opportunistic , uninvited people who come to your house and put whatever valuables into their pockets and they leave.

Now I ask these Chinese fisherman: can't you catch as much as you can eat? Without drying out the sea, or destroying the natural ecosystem of the earth? As for those who are making BITCOIN In Iran, as I have said before in my book, money doesn't bring happiness, prosperous, welfare, freedom or justice. It promotes corruption, crime and unemployment. It hinders human well-being, happiness, and peace.

What do you need the currency for? Is the currency you are making going to make anything by itself without human energy? Or by making this virtual money, or you are producing more corruption, crimes, and poverty?

Did you know this action of yours in a foreign country is against human dignity.

Iranian Politicians:

I have no interest in talking about the current regime in Iran. They do not deserve to be in my book. But for the sake of my country and the people of my country, who have been captured in the clutches of a thousand-headed historical dragon, I'm forced to say a few things about them. The current corrupt and criminal politicians of Iran are opposite to all other countries. They bear no resemblance to the culture, civilization, history, or traditions of Iranians, they do not even resemble Iran's climate. They're awkward patches that the big brother and mafia of capitalism prepared for Iranians. I have already explained this enough in my book, which I do not see the need to repeat.

These chosen corrupt and criminal monsters have not come to power for the welfare and comfort of the Iranian people, but they want to spread their own beliefs all over the world. that's why the stench of their beliefs pervades all over the world. They won't stop before they've spread them all around the world, destroying the earth in the end of their hollow philosophy. First they want to remove Israel from the face of the Earth in another 20 years, but before doing that, they don't have the logic to ask themselves where the Jews lived before Islam? Now they are spending all Iranian wealth on this goal. The second stage of their philosophy is to lead the whole world with Islamic religion, (Shiite type,) and that goal must also be done with the wealth of the Iranian people. I think there is no need for additional explanation, you can guess the rest of the story.

A short talk with the world's politicians who claim human rights , democracy and freedom

I don't have much to say about the leaders of Russia, China and other dictatorial countries, because they have no claim to democracy and freedom. They do whatever they like, using any means to silence their opponents. They think they are always right. These politicians never think about the whole planet as one country that belongs to all human beings. I mean, when they hide their nuclear waste in the ground of another country, it damages the whole earth, not just one country. It seems they either don't know this important point or they have misunderstood themselves.

These people may not know that when they return to this life after death, they might be a child in one of the low income families with no political power, under the pressure of poverty.

In my opinion, it is not an art for a person to have a position, power, and wealth, and then to use it to be a dictator against their people. The art is to have absolute power but to also be kind and fair to the people of the community.

Dictatorship and coercions are a disease that is inherited to some people from childhood.

Coercive politicians who like to throw people in glass jar and control or play with them, are the people who have suffered a lot of mental and physical injuries at their childhood.

Now about the political leaders of countries that claim democracy, human rights and freedom.

You who claim freedom, democracy and human rights, do you really believe in what you say? If your answer is yes and you believe what you are saying, than why does your political behaviour contradict your speech so much?

For example, if you are a supporter of human rights, freedom of expression and democracy, then why do you make repression equipment in your country's factories and sell it to dictatorial countries to suppress their own people who protest for human rights, freedom and democracy? Why are you rioting for your own interests in other third world countries? Why do you compete to plunder the third world countries? Why do you always put the interest of your country before other countries? Are you, or people in your nation, different then human? Why do you always ask your God to only protect your country? Isn't your country part of the planet earth?

Why do you want the third world countries as your colony? Why not consider peace and co existence, instead of building weapons like intercontinental ballistic missiles and nuclear weapons? If you allow your country to have nuclear warhead, why don't you let other countries build bombs as well? And many other whys.

I think we should all join hands and unite to build this world for all, not just for small minority of one country and one percent of population.

CRITICISM OF FORMER PRESIDENT OF THE UNITED STATES

I have lots of things to talk about Politicians, Religious, the big Capitalists, Intellectuals and Elites of the international communities, so much that I would need to write another book. But for now, I want to talk about one former president of a prominent country, someone who was in a position of power for 8 years, during which he caused a lot of damage on the world.

I heard he recently published a book. I don't know exactly what that book is about, and I really have no time and no interest of reading that book, because for me the most important factor that determines someone's character is their actions in life, and the rest is extra.

Mr. Barack Hussein Obama

In 2009, the Iranian people took to the streets to protest against election fraud. The regime of the Islamic Republic cowardly targeted the hearts and brains of the demonstrators with its mercenary snipers. People in the streets of Iran were killed, thousands were imprisoned and tortured to death. Neda Agha Sultan was the symbol of them all. People were chanting slogans, "*Obama Obama*," either with them, or with us. In Persian language when we read *Obama* separately (*o ba ma*)it means "he with us." That's why people made the above slogan.

The demonstrators wanted to know if Obama was with them, or with the Islamic regime? At the same time, Obama had not heard the Iranian demand, and sent 1.7 billion USD along with a love letter to the bloodthirsty leader of the Islamic regime. He turned his back on the Iranian demonstrators. I don't know exactly why Obama sent that amount of money to Islamic Leader, I can only guess. This is what I think:

A year later, in 2010, the Arab Spring started in Tunisia.Later, the movement continued in Egypt, and then , Libya. When Arab Spring arrived in Syria in 2011, the face of the movement suddenly changed to bloody repression from all sides. The Quds Force, one branch of the Islamic Republic revolutionary guards under the command of Qassem Soleimani, was the one that carried out the massacre in Syria. With assistance from ISIS, the Syrian army, Hezbollah of Lebanon, and the Russian Air Force (among other terrorist groups,) they killed more then 500,000 innocent young Syrians. These Syrians demonstrated only for freedom and an easier life. They displaced tens of millions of people from their homes in deserts and other countries. I think everyone has heard of and seen those crimes on TV and online, and there is no need for my additional explanation. In one case where Bashar al-Assad dropped chemical bombs on the Syrian people, Obama gave Bashar al-Assad an ultimatum, that *this is our red line and if you do it again, then you will face the consequences*. But Bashar al Assad hit the Syrian people with chemical bombs again. And Obama, the president of the strongest country in the world, did nothing. Absolutely no reaction at all. I think Bashar knew Obama was not a man of action. My question to Mr. Obama is: *What did you mean by asking Bashar al- Assad, not to use chemical bombs?* Did you mean Bashar al Assad could still kill people with bullets, tanks, grenades, swords and knives? I think the order came from the above (big brother and big sister) that you shouldn't do anything about that. You chose to listen to them and not do anything.

What about the 1.7 billion dollars you sent to Islamic regime?

Perhaps it was a prepayment on the massacre of the Syrian people to stop the Arab Spring uprising on behalf of your bosses. You followed in the footsteps of your partisan; Jimmy Carter went 41 years ago to Iran to support Ayatollah Khomeini's devestation of natural resources, looting of the national wealth, and killing of young genius Iranian people. The massacre that took place in Syria, Iran,

Libya, Iraq and the entire Middle East during your 8 year presidency was the highest massacre in the last half-century. That Syrian civil war took place during the eight years of your presidency. The Syrian people were massacred while you were sitting in your comfortable White House chair, watching them kill the children, women and every patriot who had a painful life. When people were coming to visit the White House, you appeared in a very nice suit and tie. You spoke to people and their children nicely, you joked with them with your artificial smile. You were pretending to be cool, that you were a real liberal, and that anyone can approach you, no problem. My second question to you is; apart from race, is there another difference between Syrian children and American children? If you do not make any different between children around the world, then why did you have fun with American children, and at the same time, watching the killing of Syrian children? And you watch misery of others by the repressive forces in Syria and you didn't do anything to rescue them? I do not know exactly how many millions of American votes you entered the white house. But from the point of view of meritocracy, you didn't deserve that 8 year presidency. The time was gold, and you wasted 8 years of humanity's time. Most killings in the Middle East took place during your 8 years as president. You, Jimmy Carter, and many of your fellow democrats in the United States (among many other countries) do not qualify to even lead a small village, never mind a country with more then 300 million people. Of course I know the capitalists prefer the people like you to be president, the one who listen to big brother and big sister and have no will or power of their own. Presidents like you must get order from above capitalist's leaders. You were just a broker. If I don't want to say a puppet of the big capitalists in the White House, just like the presidents of Iran who are the agent of the leader of the Islamic republic (The presidents of the Islamic Republic are all agents of the Supreme leader, and leader uses them like napkin and throw them in the trash after consumption) .

Basically, politically and religiously, employees are made up of two distinct classes: the wealthy and less wealthy and it should be noted that there is no poor class among politicians. Now, if the wealthy rich of the politicians become leader or presidents, they usually try not to be accountable to others and they go their own way in politics. But when the less-wealthy class of politicians or religious reaches the leadership or the presidency through elections or selections, they must take orders from the wealthy rich (capitalists) only. They have no power or ability to do anything of their own will. If somebody like Obama does not want to follow the orders from his siblings, they can easily oust him from the presidential palace in 3 seconds, even if he has majority of the people's votes, like Richard Nixon. He was in White House from January 20/1969 to August/09/1974. They kicked him out of the palace. But when the very rich men from the capitalist class come to leadership and presidency, they do not take orders from the above, from big brother and big sister. For instance Mr. Donald J Trump, who was very rich already before he was a politician. He became the president, and entered the White House, and didn't want to take any order from the big siblings.

When a rich person like Mr. Donald J Trump becomes president and wants to go in opposite direction of the corporations rule, and do not want to listen or take any orders from any of them. Suddenly all the propaganda machines of capitalism start to work against him. Exactly what they did with Trump in the last 4 years, or what they did to the former king of Iran Mohammad Reza Pahlavi in 1979. All the big corporations in Europe opposed Donald Trump, because Trump was going different direction from them. Even China wanted to confuse and disable Trump because they lost their business with Americans just because of his presidency. So by creating the Corona virus and exported to America and other parts of the world, just to show Trump's inefficiency in the face of such crises. So everything went hand in hand to get Trump out of White House and even if they could not get him out of the White House in their way, they would have surely try to kill him with a sniper rifle like they did it to John Fitzgerald Kennedy.

In Short, people think that if they vote for poorer politicians into presidency, they will serve the people more, but this is not true, because a president who is not rich enough must take orders from the rich class (Capitalists). In addition, a less-rich president can be easily bought with a bribe. I saw a picture of Obama bent to his knees to kiss the hand of the King of Saudi Arabia. What does that mean? What does he want to prove with his humiliating act?

My last word with BARAK HUSSEIN OBAMA

In the end I hope you are not offended by my words and criticism because I have nothing against you personally. What I said about you is the opinion of at least 95% of the Iranian people, and if you don't believe me, you can check statistics. My only intention is to save and rebuild the earth, to make a comfortable life for all living beings.

I believe that in order to create and build a new world order, the foundations and infrastructure must be built and prepared. Constructive criticism of each other can also help to build a healthy, prosperous, free and just society.

I must add that you dance well, you are well dressed and well spoken, but you cannot be a good leader for any communities.

Footnote#8

Human ignorance of natural factors continued until 400 years ago in the sixteenth century when Galileo, an Italian astronomer, discovered that the Earth revolved around the Sun, not the Sun around the Earth. But Catholic religious leader pope Urban VIII opposed him. Inquisition leaders accused him of apostasy. The story of Galileo was as follows.

"In questions of science, the authority of
a thousand is not worth the humble
reasoning of a single individual."

Born: February 15/ 1564, Pisa, Italy

Died: January 8/1642, Arcetri, near Florence.

Italian natural philosopher, astronomer and mathematician who made fundamental contributions to the sciences of motion, astronomy and strength of materials.

Galileo invented an early type of thermometer. Although he did not invent the telescope, he made significant improvements to it that enabled astronomical observation.

Galileo influenced scientists for decades to come, not least in his willingness to stand up to the church to defend his finding. His improvements to the telescope led to advances in the field of astronomy. Isaac Newton later expended on Galileo's work when coming up with his own theories.

In any case if I want to shorten Galileo's history, Galileo used his hand-made telescope to conclude that the Earth revolves around the sun.

But Galileo's scientific proof that the earth revolves around the sun was contrary to the claims of the religions, especially the Catholic religion in Italy in the sixteen-century. The result of this opposition was a church dispute with Galileo, who summoned him to an inquisition and eventually charged him with apostasy.

Since Galileo's scientific discovery was very logical and undeniable, the pope decided to negotiate the issue with him. So the inquisition offered Galileo a deal. The inquisition suggested to Galileo that if he dropped his claim in a public speech, the court would drop his charge. According to historical accounts, Galileo accepted the offer, but when law enforcement officers took Galileo to a high place overlooking the people to speak for them, Galileo defended all his scientific claims despite the Inquisition's request. So the enforcement officers took him back to the detention center and harassed him. The condemnation, which forced the astronomer and physicist to recant his discoveries, led to Galileo's house arrest for eight years before his death in 1642 at the age of 77.

NOTE:

Unfortunately, I have to say that religious people in this 21st century who still do not want to accept the scientific results of Galileo and other scientists and researchers are a great obstacle to progress, freedoms, prosperity, peace, security and human social justice.

WHY?

Why should we be strangers to each other?
Being from one planet but displaced.
Why are we displaced people.
Are we homeless people?
We all think of gold, money and wealth accumulation .
But we don't value the soil of the earth.
Why do we worship gold and other material?
Are we merchants?
Why should brother be enmity with a brother?
Why should the place of braves be under the soil or in prisons?
Why should anyone who does good be hanged on a stick?
Why are we ungrateful people?
Unless we are false worshipers?
One day we cheer for someone bad to bring him to the highest position of humanity.
The next day we shout death to a good person to crush him under our feet.
Why did we take falsehood instead of right?
What happened with wises?
That we chose idiots.
Why do we worship traitorous people?
Have we people gone crazy and lost our way?
Once open a time we were ahead of knowledge.
We were followers of morality and human dignity.
But today we are exhausted in this world.
To philosophy, human rights and the truth we remnants of the world.
Why should it be so?
Hostility and religions is intertwined.
Why are we in hurry in our choice?
Why are we in such hurry in life?
Where are we going?
Don't we want to enjoy the route too?
I think the demon is gone in the spirit of the world.
The intellect and intelligence are gone from our head.
Why are we sleeping in blood and misery of the world?

Are we neglected sleep in world?
Get up, brave ones, dear ones.
That the land of the world has become miserable.
Burn the dirt off this tired planet.
Which are here only to destroy the earth.
Uprooting any coercion, poverty injustice and wars.
Which is no other choice for the human rights.
Cleanse the world of filth.
Release the body from the shroud.
Tell the narrators to return.
To repeat the world history.
Tell people about the past.
That the history of the earth has become alien. Tell them about Ali Sine,
Cyrus the great and Asho Zoroaster.
Tell us about the good men and women of the world.
Tell the braves to find a solution to all these problems on earth.
Build oppression to fight the demon.
Tell the singers to be ready to sing the anthem of Meheregan.
There is celebration in this last war.
Lack of traitors awaits.
The time of ignorant is over.
Ahura of the world is rebellious.
Gone are the days of idolatry.
Human rich the age of principle and righteousness.
All morality returns to the world.
Benefits of the goodness, against the badness.
That will come to seek good from evil.
Teach dignity to the people of the world.
Whether the right wins or not.
The earth shouldn't rotate around but for the good deeds.
This is the last word from me.
It is time for the judgment of the righteous on earth.

Poet: .... Adam Wiseman
Place composed: .... Edmonton
Date composed: 30/January/2021

About the author

Back in 1995 I published a Persian poetry book containing 34 poems titled *Warning*, mostly about Iranian Social Political and Religious Issues. So this is my second book, but it is my first book in English. This book is about the losses of the capitalist system and its politicians and religions and also about my proposed new world order called my perfect world.

My name is Ahmad and my last name is Yousefi, but none of them are my favourite nor can determine my DNA, because Ahmad is an Arabic name and I am Persian, and as I can remember, when I was a child our family name was changed by my father once and who knows how many other times that has been changed before I was born.

Note: Since Ayatollah Khomeini and his followers took power in Iran, I was in active opposition to the regime and incarcerated for 14 months as a political prisoner. For security reasons I have had to use a few different names so I could continue my political activities without putting my family and myself at risk.

I also published my first book under my artistic chosen name, Ahura Tehrani, The meaning of Ahura comes from the Sun, and Tehrani comes from Tehran and it is the city where I was born. The name of Ahura has been mentioned in several places in my poems. Some people who heard my poems have called me Ahura, so I chose it as an artistic name. I picked this artistic name when I was acting in Centennial Theatre in North Vancouver, in December 29th 1994. I also used it when publishing my first poetry book.

Twenty-eight years ago when my ex-wife was pregnant with a boy, we wanted to name him Adam. That child suffocated in the mother's womb due to the negligence of the nurse, so I chose Adam as my third global name. I used that name, Adam Wiseman, to publish this book. Adam in Persian means human, and everyone knows the meaning of Wiseman, so I don't need to explain.

My most philosophical responsibility ends with publication of this book.

I did not translate my poetry book because the rhymes disappear when poems are translated, and also it's not my job. I am not a university professor, nor a professional English author, or one who spoke English from the childhood. My goal in writing this book is to express my dream of a better life for all living things on Earth, before I die. I tried to use my best ability to communicate this new philosophy in simple words, to make sure every one, in any class, or age will understand it.

I believe this book belongs to all people living on Earth and for this reason I am publishing it in English and I urge people to read it once meticulously. If any of you dear readers find any misspelling or any other mistakes on this book, please let me know with your comments on my website, which I will make it available to everyone when it is available to myself. I will correct them as soon as I can. I appreciate your attention, and your review.

Thank you all.

Adam Wiseman.

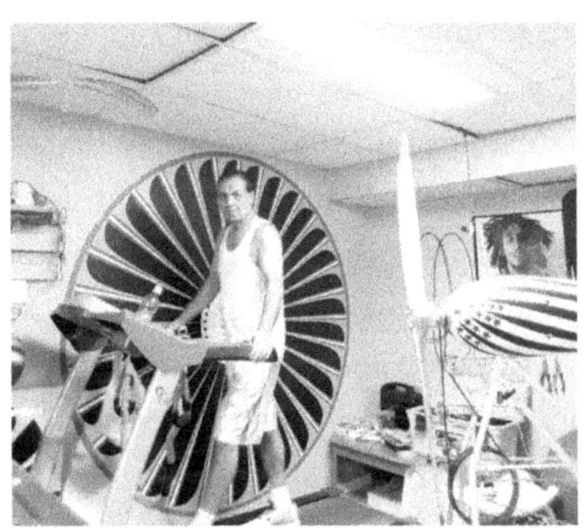

The book was finished on: March 21, 2021
Place: Edmonton, Alberta, Canada
Author: Adam Wiseman

THANKS AND GOODBYE TO THE READER OF THIS BOOK:

After thanking you dear reader, for taking the time to read this book to the end, I would like to take the opportunity to say goodbye to you with a few words.

If you agree with me on the topics of this book, it means that we are on the same front and the same trench and we are fighting for the same goal. Therefore I say lets get together to achieve this sacred goal. We need a billion wise and mature people from all over the world to be able to change this situation and to start building a perfect world. Your literary criticisms and opinion will help me to solve the possible small or big mistakes of this book.

Please do not forget about review.

Best

Adam

adamwiseman.ca

WARNING

Ahura Tehrani

1995

www.ingramcontent.com/pod-product-compliance
Lightning Source LLC
Chambersburg PA
CBHW052029090426
42739CB00010B/1840
* 9 7 8 1 6 1 2 4 4 8 5 7 2 *

www.ingramcontent.com/pod-product-compliance
Lightning Source LLC
Chambersburg PA
CBHW052030090426
42739CB00010B/1852

* 9 7 8 1 7 7 3 5 4 2 9 8 0 *

هُشدار

سروده هایی از

تهرانی

هُشدار

اهورا تهرانی

ISBN 91-630-3462-X

هشدار

اهورا تهرانی

ناشر: شاعر

چاپ اول: بهار ۱۳۷۴

چاپ و صحافی: چاپ آرش، استکهلم

مرکز پخش:
Music & Film Tehran
Tensta Centrum
Tenstagången 19A
163 64 Spånga-SWEDEN

فهرست

تقدیم به دخترم ماندانا

بعد از اینکه تو پا به جهان هستی گذاردی در فکر آن بودم تا هدیه‌ای به تو بدهم که با گذشت زمان آن را فراموش نکنی و ارزنده نیز باشد تا این که بعد از مدت‌ها این هدیه را برای تو یافتم. آری چه هدیه‌ای با ارزش‌تر و فراموش ناشدنی‌تر از تقدیم احساس پدر به فرزند خود، از این رو تصمیم گرفتم سروده هایم را که آکنده از احساسات قلبی و تجربیات سی و چند سالهٔ عمرم می‌باشد به چاپ برسانم و آن‌ها را در یک مجموعه به عنوان هدیهٔ تولدت به تو تقدیم کنم. امیدوارم مورد قبول واقع شود و آن را هرگز فراموش نکنی. از تو می‌خواهم که فراموش نکنی که پدرت یک ایرانیست و از زمانی که خود را شناخته برای رسیدن به آزادی خود و کشورش لحظه‌ای آسوده خاطر نبوده و این مجموعه نیز بیانگر این ادعا می‌باشد. باشد که تو نیز برای آزادی خود و بشریت تلاش کنی و ادامهٔ این راه را به فرزندانت نیز آموزش دهی. و این ادامه تنها از طریق تحقیق و مطالعات در مورد اقوام مختلف بشری امکان‌پذیر می‌باشد. این شناخت را اول از خود آغاز کن و بعد در مورد نژاد و اصلیت خود و با تاریخ اقوام مختلف بشری ادامه بده، و گذشتن تو از این مرحله باعث شناخت نسبی تو از جهان و بشریت خواهد بود و آنگاه

می‌توانی ادعا کنی که یک آزادیخواه جهان‌وطنی هستی. در هر زمان و هر مکان از تو می‌خواهم این سه اصل را در زندگی‌ات به کار ببندی که هم نیک‌نام باقی بمانی و هم این‌که در زمان حیاتت با وجدانی آسوده زندگی کنی. و آن سه اصل از این قرار هستند:

پندار نیک گفتار نیک کردار نیک

این‌ها سه اصل زرتشت فیلسوف بزرگ ایران می‌باشد که تقریباً در هزارهٔ قبل از میلاد مسیح می‌زیسته، تحقیق در مورد این بزرگ‌مرد تاریخ ایران را نیز به تو توصیه می‌کنم. با آرزوی سلامتی و سعادت و موفقیت برای تو

پدرت ۱۹۹۴

سخنی با خوانندهٔ این کتاب

با درود به همهٔ آزاداندیشان و همهٔ آن‌هایی که در راه آزادی بشر جان خود را فدا کرده‌اند و با سپاس از هموطنان عزیز که با خریدن یک کتاب قدمی در راه پیشرفت فرهنگ برمی‌دارند چرا که با این کارِ خود نویسنده را تشویق به ادامهٔ راه خود می‌کنید.

به عقیدهٔ من نویسندگان به دو دستهٔ بزرگ تقسیم می‌شوند:

دستهٔ اول آن‌هایی هستند که برای حکومت‌ها می‌نویسند و بازتاب نظرات و عقاید حاکمینند و دستهٔ دوم نویسندگانی که دردها و کمبودهای اجتماعی مردم را می‌نویسند و قلمشان شمشیر و بدنشان سپر حوادث است. دستهٔ اول از طریق حاکمین، هم تأمین مالی می‌شوند و هم تأمین جانی. دستهٔ دوم هیچ پشتوانه‌ای بجز مردم و عقیدهٔ خویش ندارند و به این سبب اگر مردم هم از آن‌ها حمایت مادی و معنوی نکنند در کوتاه مدت قلمشان از حرکت باز می‌ایستد و اگر هم بنویسند به این امید است که شاید روزی مردم او را بفهمند و آثارش را به چاپ برسانند. ولی متأسفانه در گذشتهٔ جامعهٔ ما نویسندگان آزاداندیشی که فقر مادی داشتند اگر دارای عقیده‌ای بودند، جدا از معتقدات حاکمان، اکثراً ناشناس باقی می‌ماندند و عقیده شان

نیز با آن‌ها به خاک سپرده می‌شد ولی بعد از انقلاب ۱۹۷۹ توجه مردم به نویسندگان مردمی بیشتر شده و از آن‌ها حمایت و پشتیبانی مادی و معنوی می‌کنند. عقاید گوناگون شمع‌های یک جامعه می‌باشند و هرچه تعدادشان بیشتر باشد نور آزادی و آگاهی در جامعه تابنده‌تر خواهد بود و برعکس هرچه این عقاید کمتر باشند تاریکی و جهل و در نتیجه حکومت‌های زور در جامعه پایدارتر خواهند شد و باز هم به عقیدۀ من هیچگونه تغییر و تحول و دگرگونی اجتماعی، بدون انقلاب فرهنگی که همانا بالا بردن سطح آگاهی مردم نسبت به مسائل تاریخی و اجتماعی و سیاسی زادگاه خویش و جهان می‌باشد نمی‌تواند ضامن آزادی جامعۀ بشری باشد.

من نیز به عنوان یک انسان مسئول نسبت به جامعۀ بشری بخصوص کشورم و مردم ایران، نظر و عقیدۀ خود را در مورد چگونگی کسب آزادی و پیشرفت در راه ابر انسان شدن را، در سال‌های بعد از انقلاب به روی کاغذ آوردم تا اینکه احساس کردم چاپ و انتشار آن ضروریست. البته یک سالی می‌شود که این ضرورت احساس شده ولی به خاطر مشکلات مادی قادر به چاپ و نشر آن نبودم تا این که این مشکل را با پیدا کردن کاری حل نمودم و خوشوقتم که امروز می‌توانم این کتاب را در اختیار شما هموطن عزیز قرار دهم و این یکی از مجموعه‌هایم می‌باشد که موفق به چاپ آن شدم. لازم به توضیح است که تمامی این مطالب در اوقات بیکاری تهیه و تنظیم شده و من یک نویسندۀ حرفه‌ای نیستم چرا که اصولاً حرفه‌ای بودن و یا شدن نیازمند به پشتوانۀ مادی و معنوی می‌باشد.

این سروده‌ها و یا اشعار تابع نظم و قوانین شعری شناخته شدۀ امروزی نیست به این خاطر که من قوانین شعری را قوانینی دست

و پاگیر یافته‌ام که برای ادامهٔ بیان منظور شاعر موانعی ایجاد می‌کنند و من برای این که بتوانم منظور خود را تماماً به صورت ابیات بیان کرده باشم مجبور به سنت‌شکنی شدم و سعی کرده‌ام که معنی را فدای وزن و قافیه نکنم و البته تا آنجا که ممکن بوده حتی با صرف وقت و تحمل چندین ماه روی یک شعر سعی در قافیه‌سازی نیز کرده‌ام که اساس و پایهٔ شعر سنتی در هم نریزد مثلاً در غزل قانون چنین است که غزل باید حدیث عشق و عشقبازی زنان باشد. تعداد ابیات آن نباید بیشتر از پانزده و کمتر از هفت باشد و لی اینجانب این قانون و سنت غزل را در اشعار خود شکسته‌ام و از این سَبک برای مطرح کردن مشکلات اجتماعی و فرهنگی و سیاسی مردم نیز استفاده کرده‌ام و به تعداد ابیاتش نیز توجهی نکرده‌ام چون مطلبی را که می‌خواستم بگویم در چنین محدوده‌ای نمی‌گنجید و در سَبک‌های دیگر نیز تنها از قوانین خود پیروی کرده‌ام و معتقد به این هستم که گاه سنت‌شکنی موجب پیشرفت انسان می‌گردد.

به هرحال من با کمال میل برای شنیدن پیشنهادات و انتقادات و احیاناً تشویق شما عزیزان حاضر هستم تا بتوانم ثابت‌قدم‌تر از پیش به راه خود ادامه دهم. نکتهٔ دیگر که فکر می‌کنم برای خواننده دارای اهمیت می‌باشد این است که من این مجموعه اشعار را فقط برای این که شعری گفته باشم تهیه نکرده و منظوری برای این که شاعر نامیده شوم ندارم بلکه هر یک از این اشعار به مناسبتی خاص گفته شده که در مورد بعضی از آن‌ها که برای خواننده مناسبتش معلوم نیست در صورت لزوم توضیح داده شده و اگر آن‌ها را به صورت مقاله و یا کتاب معمولی ننوشته‌ام به این خاطر بوده که اولاً نفوذ کلام شعر در مردم و بخصوص ما ایرانیان بیشتر است و دوم این که گاهاً یک سرودهٔ

بیست بیتی به اندازهٔ یک کتاب دویست صفحه‌ای می‌تواند معنی و مفهوم داشته باشد. با توجه به این که یک کتاب معمولی بعضی‌ها را زودتر خسته می‌کند و حال آن که یک سرودهٔ کوتاه انسان را به وَجد می‌آورد.

در آخر، بار دیگر از شما هموطن گرامی سپاسگزاری می‌کنم که برای خواندن این مجموعه وقت گرانبهای خود را صرف می‌کنید.

با امید به این که مورد قبول واقع شود.

شعرم به گوش جان شنو

در گفتن احساس خود، منطق به فرمان است.
ای حامی شعر و ادب، این شعر نیست آیینه است.
مقصودم از شعر و ادب،
جان حقیقت گفتن است.
گویم ز عدل و عشق و کین
هر تشنه آبی خوردن است.
جان کلام فارس را
بی آب و تاب گفتن است.
آنی شهیدش می کنم، آنی به پا می دارمش
حرف و کلامی را که صد جا گفتن است.
ابزار من فکر و قلم
نیشش به جوهر روشن است.
سازم سخن ها دلنشین
کز شهد گل شیرین تر است
ای حامی شعر و ادب
جان کلامم با تو است.
شعرم به گوش جان شنو!
کین راز عشق برتر است.
چون گوش کردی شعر من
انجام ضدش خفتن است.
آزادی از آزادگی
بی راهه بر حق رفتن است.
دردا حقیقت را چه سود؟
نشکفتنش پژمردن است.

باری چنین گفتارمت
فولاد کین از آهن است.
مقصودم از شعر و ادب
جان حقیقت گفتن است.
هر مصرعش را دشمنی
از نیش ماری بدتر است.
دارم به کندو انگبین
چون زور و زوبین و زَر است.
خواهم که بخشایش کنم
هرکس که جانش را غم است.
ای شاعر اهل ادب
شعرت به درد و غم بس است.
پیمانه را باور کنید
ساقی به ساغر زنده است.
ای جاهلان بی خِرَد
این جنگ نیست، اندیشه است.
اندیشه نزد شاعران
ابزار نیست، گنجینه است.
من در پی شهرت نی ام!
رسم دلیران گفتن است.
هر آنچه از عقلِ بشر،
آید که باید گفتن است.
مقصودم از شعر و ادب
بی جنگ و دعوا گفتن است.

۵ آوریل ۱۹۹۲

سرباز عشق

پندار و کردار و گفتار نیک را پذیرفتمی
باری به هر جهت را نپذیرفتمی.
سرباز عشقم و جانم به کف!
و تو را مقصدی بی‌بها نپذیرفتمی.
همواره صد هزار بار گفتمت
که تو را ذلت بندگی نپذیرفتمی.
تو هرچه مرا گویی پذیرفتمی
طوقت به گردن حق را نپذیرفتمی.
به ساز دلت خوانمت آنچه را که می‌خواهی
سازی به جنگ محبت را نپذیرفتمی.
جانم فدای تو گردد، اگر خطا گویم
روزی به ظلمت شب را نپذیرفتمی.
در جنگ شجاعم و جنگاورانم آرزوست
اما، نبردِ مقابل به حق را نپذیرفتمی.
دریای بی‌کرانم و موجی به سوی عشق
دجال روسیاه زمان را، نپذیرفتمی.
آیم ز کورهٔ عشق و مقصد به سوی بهشت
آنی جهنمیان را به همره خویش نپذیرفتمی.
آنان که خائنین زمین و زمان باشند

هرگز به درگه دادش، نپذیرفتمی.
هر کس که بشر را، سِتَم روا دارد
وجود پِلشتَش را به روی زمین نپذیرفتمی.
من شاخه‌ای بر گَردن مرداب غفلتم
اما پلید قَسَم خورده را نپذیرفتمی.
اینک زمان نَبَرد است در راه نیک
سَدّی برابر خورشید را نپذیرفتمی.
لشگری سازمش ز جمع انسان‌ها
که به بیماری و ذلتش را نپذیرفتمی.
بعد از آن چنان که شد عنوان
بنده‌ای به غیر بندهٔ حق را نپذیرفتمی.
بعد از آنکه جان گُلستان شد
هرزه‌ای عَلَف به باغ برین را نپذیرفتمی.
آن زمان است که خالقَش گوید
حق چنین است و غیر از اینش نپذیرفتمی.

جمعه ۴ آوریل ۱۹۹۲

بگو یاران

چه شد بر ما؟ چه شد ما را؟
چه شد آزادی ما را؟
چه شد ثروت؟ چه شد هستی؟
چه شد کاشانهٔ ما را؟
چه شد اشعار آزادی؟ چه شد ایثار و جانبازی؟
چه شد آگاهی ما را؟
چه شد فریاد غُرنده؟ چه شد شمشیر برنده؟
چه شد مردانگی و غیرَت ما را؟
چه شد رستم؟ چه شد کاوه؟ چه شد فردوسی و حافظ؟
چه شد افسانهٔ ما را؟
چه شد آداب و سُنّت؟ چه شد آئین ملت؟
چه شد تاریخ و فرهنگ، قدمت ما را؟
چرا گریان؟ چرا نالان؟
چه شد خوشحالی ما را؟
بگو یاران بگو ایران بگو آنان!
بخوان با ما!
بیایید گرد هم آییم که تا روشن کنیم راز نهان را!
بیابیم راه بهزیستن، در اسرار زمان را!
بگیریم نور خورشید و بتابیم این جهان را!
ببخشیم افتخار، خاک وطن را!

۱۹۸۹

یکی بود یکی نبود

یکی بود یکی نبود
یک روز و روزگاری بود
آفتابی بود، مَهتابی بود
درخت و سبزه زاری بود
یک شهر با صفایی بود
دنیای بی ریایی بود
دلها همه با هم بودند
دست ها همه تو هم بودند
غُصه ها مال هم بودند
همه به فکر هم بودند

روزی یه باد سرد وزید
سرماشو بر همه گزید
باد اومد صفا رو برد
ریشهٔ عشق و کَند و خورد
همه از هم جدا شدند
آدم ها بی وفا شدند
دختره ضد مادرش
پدر علیه دخترش
یارو به جنگ همسرش
یار علیه یاورش
خلاصه غوغایی به پا
دست علیه پیکرش

سیاهی مهتاب رو گرفت
ماه به جنگ دشمنش
تاریکی عالم رو گرفت
نور به جنگ دیدنش
چاره برای کس نبود
دید، بجز هوس نبود

فردای اون روز که دمید
وقتی زمین خورشید و دید
مردمی که جدا بودند
همه توی رویا بودند
یکباره از خواب پریدند
وقتیکه خورشید رو دیدند
نور به چشمشون تابید
انگاری که خواب می دیدند
معجزه ای رخ داده بود
منتظر نور نبودند
روز قیامت شده بود
خورشیدی که بالا می رفت
بالا و بالاتر می رفت
آدما رو صدا می کرد
صدایی بی صدا می کرد
می گفت بیایین آی آدما
ای پدرها، ای مادرها
می گفت قیامت نشده

زمانه آخر نشده
می گفت بازهم با هم باشین
پُشت همو داشته باشین
می گفت اگر من نبودم دل هاتونو روشن کنید
با دوستی و عشق و صفا خونه هاتونو گرم کنید
می گفت که اتحاد خوبه
دشمنو از بین می بره
می گفت که خوب بودن خوبه
بهشت روی این زمینه
بهشتتون خوب بودنه
خوبی و یک رنگ بودنه
می گفت با هم رفیق باشین
باهم و متحد باشین
رفیقی رسم موندنه
که غیر از این مرگتونه
هرچی که هست مال شماست
تابش من رو به شماست
زمین به زیر پاتونه
دور تا دورش خونتونه
فقط باید یاد بگیرین
چه جوری لذّت ببرین
شادی ها رو شریک باشین
غم ها رو از بین ببرین

۱۹۸۸

بی اعتنا

هرکه را عشق ورزیدم، خَصم جانم شد
هر که را بی اعتنا، همدم و یارم شد
هرکه را آموختم، مُدعی بر حَق شد
هرکه را آزمودم، اندرونش زرد شد
هرچه خوبی می کنم، بدتر نصیبم می شود
هرچه بدتر می کنم، نیکی نَصیبم می شود
حیرتم از سّر و قانون خدا!
این چه جور است و کدام است این بقا.

اگوست ۱۹۸۷

سنگ

اگر خواهی که سفت و سخت باشی
اگر خواهی که مثل سنگ باشی
اگر خواهی که مثل گُل بمانی
اگر خواهی بهاران را ببینی
اگر خواهی که یارانت بدانند
تو هم ایمان و عقل و نَفس داری
ریاضت پیشهٔ راه خودت کن
که درویشان ریاضت پیشه بودند.

مارچ ۱۹۸۷

نوروز

فصل بهار وگل و بلبل رسید — روزی چو نوروز به ایران رسید
پیک رهایی ز زمستان سرد — از ره خورشید و گُلستان رسید
بوی گُل و سبزه و لطف نسیم — عید عزیــزان به عزیزان رسید
حاصل برف ویخ وسرمای سرد — در گُل یاس و گُل سُمبل رسید
نغمهٔ مـــرغان بهاری به مـا — بانگ زنند فصل بهـاران رسید
سـاز و دُهُـل از در و دیـوار شهر — بر من و تو، بر همه یاران رسید
شـادی و تبـریک صمیمـانه ام — پَر زده از من به عزیزان رسید
با دلـی غُـربت زده از دوریت — بوسهٔ من بر لب خندان رسید.

مارچ ۱۹۸۴

پرواز

مرغ دلم با تو به پرواز رفت
قصهٔ عشقم به سرآغاز رفت
رفت به آنجا که دگر دید نیست
مقصدش عشقی که سرانجام نیست
رفت به بالاتر از عرش خدا
تا دهدش آگهی عشق ما
رفت که تا بانگ زند این سرود
عشق منو و تو به نهایت دِرود

۱۹۸۹

راز

آنکه مرا بر تو فرا خوانده است / معنی هستی به جهان داده است
خواند مرا بر سر آن کوه نور / تا دهدم قصهٔ آن قوم کور
راز چنان بود و چنین شد بیان / آنچه عیان است به همان است نهان
گفته زیاد است و سخن ناتمام / هرچه که گویم رقمیست در رقام
راه دراز است در این راستی / مرد بخواهد نکند کاستی
هرچه که هست درخلأ و در زمین / مُلک تواند، گر که تو خواهی چنین
هر که تو را زور کند زور باش / آنکه نکو داندت، او نیک باش
گر تو بخواهی به عدالت رسی / عدل که باید بکنی هر کسی
ملک حسادت نتوان کِشت کرد / آنچه که هست بایدش آباد کرد
حاصل ماندن به فسادی رسد / هجر و تحرک به تکامل رسد
تفرقهٔ قوم، در این مُلک دین / دین همین است و همان و همین
مذهب اگر باعث سُستی شده / علتش آن است که هزاران شده
منطق اگر ریشهٔ مذهب شود / فکر بَشَر واحده روشن شود
پول و زر و سیم و طلا، جملگی / علت ظلمند و ستم، بَردگی
رسم تکامل نه همان است که این / آنچه تو بینی و کنی اینچنین
سُنّت اگر راه عقب رفتن است / عکس چنین راه همان بدعت است.

۱۹۸۹

هر آن کس

هر آنکس که افتاد به دام هَوس　　کند عقل و ایمان درون قَفَس
هر آنکس شود فاتح نَفس خویش　　رِسَد سَهل وآسان به آمیال خویش
هر آنکس بَرَد پی به آغاز خویش　　دَهَد تابشی ره به انجام خویش
هر آنکس که باشد به دنبال عقل　　هدف گرددش بر فنا ظُلم جَهل
هر آنکس که منطق شود راه او　　به روز قیامت شود حق نگهدار او
هر آنکس که وجدان شود عدل او　　به حق است کهِ انسان شود نام او
هر آنکس شَرَف را کُند آرزو　　ره راستین بایدش جستجو
هر آنکس خدا را کُند جستجو　　به قلب زمین وعده دیدار او
هرآنکس که نیک است پندارو کرداراو　　به فرمان یزدان ملائک نگهدار او
هرآنکس که نیکی در او راه یافت　　به پیکار شیطان و زشتی شتافت
هر آنکس خیانت کُند بر وطن　　کِشَد پوششی بر بَدَن از کَفَن
هر آنکس که از قافله باز ماند　　به دامی چو گُرگان صحرا فِتاد
هر آنکس که بیگانه شد با خدا　　کُند حیله با آدمی در خِفا
اگر ملتی را چنین عاقبت گرددش　　به عقل و شعورش چنان بایدش

دسامبر ۱۹۹۱

هشدار

بیایید آدما
ای مردم دنیا
بیا ای برزه گر
ای روستایی
تو ای زحمتکش و دانشجوی ثانی
بیایید رنگ ها
ای زردپوستان
سپیدان
ای سیاهان
تو ای قوم یهود و قوم عیسی
تو ای زرتشتی
ای بودا پرستان
مسلمانان
بیایید تا یکی باشیم
یکی واحد
یکی آزاد

یکی در صُلح
یکی انسان
یکی پر قدرت و قادر!
ز نفرت کینه‌توزی و شقاوت،
گُل نمی روید.
زمین بایر نمی گردد.
ز خونریزی و بمباران
تکامل سر نمی گیرد.
گُلی در خون نمی روید.
طبیعت مظهر عشق است.
زراعت حاصل کشت است.
زمان تنگ است و بس تاریک.
هدف کوتاه و بس نزدیک
زمان در سیر تغییر است.
بشر قادر به تقدیر است.
بشر در مجمعی واحد
بشر در عالمی عالم!
به قرن بیست‌ویک وارد شود دنیای ماشینی،
من از دنیای ماشینی،
من از جنگ اتم، افسانه می گویم.
من از نابودی انسان،
من از دوزخ در این عالم سُخن گویم.
تو ای انسان
تو ای والای مخلوقات
تو ای عالم
تو ای دانا به دنیا

تو ای حاکم به تقدیر
من از صلح بشر، علم بشر،
ماندن در این عالم سُخن گویم.
من از یگانگی،
آزادی از شیطان سُخن گویم.
از این خونریزی و نادانی و غفلت بپرهیزید.
زمین را، مادر جاندار هستی را نرنجانید.
زمین جاندار و آگاه است.
زمین سیاهِ‌ای بیدار و هوشیار است.
زمین معبود خود، خورشید را همواره دوّار است.
زمین آرامشی معمول می‌خواهد.
بشر آسایشی بی زور می‌خواهد.
توقف در زمان جایز نمی‌باشد.
زِ مُردن جُز عَدَم حاصل نمی‌گردد.
ز بمباران بپرهیزید.
دقایق را نلرزانید.
طبیعت را نرنجانید.
زمینی!
ای بشر!
دریاب مادر را!
همان مبدأ
همان مقصد
همین معبود را.
مَیفشان شعلهٔ خَشمَش.
مزن آتش بر این پیکر.
قَسَم بر شعلهٔ آتشفشانش،

قَسَم بر سیل و طوفانش،
قَسَم بر آب‌ها و کوه‌های بی‌کرانش،
مَزَن آتش بر این پیکر،
مَکُش آزاده‌ای دیگر.
دقایق را نلرزانید،
طبیعت را نرجانید.

اگوست ۱۹۹۱

محور

آه این تنهاییم، افسرده جان مـــی سازدم
هرچه گـــویم آدمی را، از زمین از مادرم،
همچنـان او ساز نادانی به گوشـــم می زند
با چماق جاهلیت ضربه بر جان و روانم می زند
گویمش از گمرهی بر راه واهی می روی
همچنان آبی کـــه بر مرداب جانی می روی
مـــــرکز هر کهکشانی محوری را بایدش
گرنه هـــــر سیاره ای نابود و فانی بایدش
د رطبیعت هرچه باشد گرد نظمی در بقاست
همچوخورشید و زمین بر گرد هم در انتهاست
این جدایی عاقبت ما را به بی جا می برد
هر سر بی محوری را رو به ســـودا می برد
ما همه همجنس و خـــویش و همرهیم
با زمـــان و با زمین و زندگانی در رهیم
پس چرا هـــــر کس به تنهایی رود؟
کـــــاروانی را به کیش خـــود بَـــرَد
این همه دین ســـــتایش بهر کیست؟
جنگ و خونریزی و مُردن بهر چیست؟

ارتش و سـربـاز رزمی بر کجـاست ؟
نیزه و بُمب افکن و بُمب اَتُم بَرمرگ کیست؟

این زمین یک کشـور پهناور است
جملگی یک محور و یک پیکر است

علت پیدایش مـا او بُـوَد
هر چه هست در او، بر او ، از او بود

پس بیایید مرزها را بَر کَنیم
کشوری واحد بر او احیا کُنـیم

گرد او گردیم ستایش او کُنیم
همچـو مادر مهر او بر دل کنـیم

تفرقه از دل زُداییم یک شویم
یـار و یـاور همدل و همـره شویم

تـا زمین بر نعمتش افـزون شود
تا بهشت آدمـی بر پا شـود

بیا آدم تـو یـار بی‌کسان باش
به یـاران و نجیبان مهـربان بـاش

۱۹۹۲/۴/۱۴

با یاوه گویان

گفت با من همدمی خاموشیت با یاوه گویان بهر چیست؟
گفتمش با یاوه گویان ارزش گفتار نیست
گفت این حرف و سخنها را مداوا بایدش
گفتمش حرّاف بسیار است مخاطب را به سر حق بایدش
گفت این بی آبرویان آبرویت می برند
گفتمش آبی به رونیست روی خود را می برند
گفت در هر حال شمشیری بِکش حرفی بزن
گفتمش شمشیر بهرجنگ بامردان بود، نی بَهر زن
گفت ابله را به جای خود نشاندن کار کیست؟
گفتمش ای دوست جواب ابلهان خاموشیست
گفت شاید این وقایع سهل و آسان نگذرد
گفتم او را بر سر اولاد آدم هرچه آید بُگذرد.

۱۹۹۳/۵/۲۷

انسان تا وقتی که نیکی مـی‌کند انتظار نیکویی نیز دارد، حال این انتـظار ممکن است از مردم باشد یا از آفریدگار.
من توقعی بجز نیکویی از دیگران و یا آفریدگارم نداشتم، چون جز این نمی‌کردم. که ناگهان فرزندم را که چند روزی بود انتظار تـولدش را مـی‌کشیدم، از دست دادم و او دنیای ما را نا دیده ترک کرد و دیـده از جهـان فـرو بسـت. ضـربـه‌ای فـرامـوش نشدنی بر من و همسرم وارد شده بود. در همان روزها دوستی به من پیشنهاد کرد و گفت شعری به نام اشک مرد بنویس. با اینکه او اشک مرا ندیده بود ولی انگار دردم را درک می‌کرد. پیشنهاد او در من اثر کرد و روزی این سروده را که مملو از درد و خشم و فریاد یک پدر داغدیده بود به روی کاغذ آوردم.

اشک مرد

باز دردی در کمین است بر زمین
اشک مردان گوهر است و انگبین

گر تو نوزادی ز کف دادی چنین
پس طبیعت پُر ز دَرد است و ز کین

چون گُل مردان حق پژمرده گشت
عاقبت دنیای گُل افسانه گشت

گر چنین باشد نظام روزگار
پس هزاران مرگ باد بر کردگار

چون به تاریکی رسد دنیای عشق
عاشقان را دَرد باید مرگ عشق

این بلا از آن تاریکی بُود
نی ز خورشید و فروزانی بُود

ای خدای ظالمین و مرتدین
خَنجر عشقم به زَهر است در کمین

باشد آن روزی که روز ما شود
دشنهٔ کینَم به جان غم شود

ما گذشتیم آنچه را بر ما شدی
وای بر حالت که خصم ما شدی

هر چه نیرو در توان داری بتاز
هر مُصیبت بهر ما داری بساز

این مصیبت ها به جان ایمان دهد
قُدرتی چون رُستم دستان دهد

روزگار غم به پایان می رسد
نوبت پیروزی نیکان و خوبان می رسد

جسم اهریمن به آتش می کشیم
روح او را خط بطلان می کَشیم

مُزد دَجالان جانی در عزاست
اجر هر کس را به کردارش سزاست

عاشقان محتاج حق اند در جهان
همچودرویشی به در خویش و نهان

گر تو نوزادی ز کف دادی چنین
پس طبیعت پُر ز درد است و غمین

بر اَبر انسان شدن سبقت رواست
بر بشر خَصم و قصاوت نارواست

بانگ من بر جمع انسان ها از اوست
کُل هستی یا از آن است یا بر اوست

هر که بر او زی کند از آن اوست
آنچه آبادش کُند جانان اوست

هر که وجدانش اهورایش شود
هرچه دارد خوش گوارایش شود

این زمین میدان سبقت درفضاست
چون بشر نیکی کند یزدان پاکش راسزاست

باز دردی در کمین است برزمین
اشک مردان گوهر است و انگبین

چون به مادر غُصه ای دادی چنین
پس فراوان درد باشد بر زمین

۱۹۹۲/۴/۲۵

در همان زمان‌هایی که در داغ از دست دادن فرزند خود می‌سوختم مشکلات دیگر اجتماعی نیز مزید آن درد شده بود و احساس می‌کردم که نیرویی برای بیان احساسات خود ندارم البته می‌دانستم که آن مشکلات رفع خواهد شد و باید همت و زمان در رفع آن‌ها به کار بست و تا خاتمهٔ کامل مشکلات خود تصمیم به سکوت گرفتم و چنین گفتم

سکوت

مهر سکوتم بر دهان
اشک دریغم در روان
خون جگر آتشفشان
بر سوگ آدم اَخترم

چون مشعلی روشن شدم
نوری به هر مَحفل شدم
خورشید تابان بر زمان
بر آدم و حوّا شدم

پیغام صلح و جنگ را
اخطار بر کردار را
بر عاقلین و جاهلان
فریاد بر انسان شدم

اما به جای اجر نیک
یا سعی برکردار نیک
از کشور و کاشانه ام
آواره در دنیا شدم

گویی که جمع حاضرین
پندارشان از من به دین
در بین این نابخردان
دیوانه یا اغوا شدم

اینک به صبرم قانع ام
در فکر یک کاشانه ام
تا جان بَعدی در تَنم
از گفتنم ارضاع شدم

۱۹۹۲/۵/۹

چرا

چرا باید به هم بیگانه باشیم
ز یک کشور ولی آواره باشیم
چرا ما مردم از آواره گانیم
مگر ما ملتی بی خانمانیم؟
همش فکر زَر و سیم و طلاییم
ولی خاک وطن را بی بهاییم
چرا ما زَر پرستیم
مگر ما تاجر هستیم؟
چرا باید برادر با برادر خصم باشد؟
چرا جای دلیران وطن در زیر خاک و بَند باشد؟
امیری چون تقی خان را به رگ بازیم
وزیری مثل خائن خان نوری را دگر سازیم
چرا هر کس که نیکوکار گردد
سرش بالای چوب دار گردد
چرا ما مردمی حق ناسپاسیم
مگر ما ملتی باطل پرستیم؟

زمانی برمصدق کف زنیم هورا فرستیم
دمی چند بر هویدا کارت تبریک می‌فرستیم
زمانی که مصدق‌ها به تبعید و به زنجیرند
هویداها حکومت می‌کنند و دست تقدیرند
چرا ما اهل حق را ناسپاسیم
مگر ما ملتی خائن پرستیم؟
چرا قربانیان ما همه از خادمینند
ولی دولتمداران جملگی از خائنینند
چرا باطل به جای حق گرفتیم
چه شد دانا که ما اَبلَه گرفتیم
چرا ما مردمی خائن پرستیم
مگر ما ملتی دیوانه هستیم؟
زمانی ما ز عالم پیش بودیم
مُرید مذهب و آیین و کیشِ خویش بودیم
ولی امروزه از واماندگان این جهانیم
به علم و دین و آیینِ زمان جا ماندگان این جهانیم
چرا باید چنین باشد؟
که خَصم و دین اَجین باشد
زمانی شاه رهبر بُود روزی خمینی
گهی آمریکایی گه انگلیسی
چرا در انتخاب خود عجولیم
مگر ما ملتی بی بند و باریم؟
زمانی پیرو زرتشت بودیم
ز قدرت چون عقاب و شیر بودیم
ولی با حمله‌ای از سوی تازی
مسلمان گشته و روبَه صفت در حقه‌بازی

چرا از جّد خود یکجا بریدیم
مگر از اصل خود خیری ندیدیم؟
مگر ما کاسه از آش داغتر هستیم؟
که دین اجنبی را می پرستیم
مگر فرهنگ ما عیبش چه بوده؟
که فرهنگ عرب دل را ربوده
مگر جز جنگ و خونریزی و مردن بهره ای داشت؟
مگر جز صَلب اطمینان مردم حاصلی داشت؟
چرا ما مردمی خودناشناسیم
مگر ما ملتی افسانه هستیم؟
گمانم دیو در روح وطن رفته
که عقل و هوشمان یکجا ز سر رفته!

چرا در خون و نکبت خفته ایی ایران
مگر در خواب غفلت مانده ایی ایران
بپا خیزید دلیران ای عزیزان
که نکبت زار گشته خاک ایران
بروبید نکبت از این جان خسته
که جز ویرانیش چادر نَبَسته
ز ریشه بر کَنید هر هرزه ای را
که جز این حق نباشد چاره ای را
بسوزانید خائن را به ایران
برویانید خادم را به ایمان
وطن را از کثافت پاک سازید
بدن را از کَفَن آزاد سازید
به نقالان بگویید باز گردند

که تاریخ وطن را ساز گردند
به مردم باز گویید از گذشته
که تاریخ وطن بیگانه گشته
به آن‌ها از ابوسینا بگویید
ز وَصف کاوه و رُستم بگویید
بگویید تا دلیران چاره سازند
برای جنگ با دیو سِتَم ارابه سازند
بگویید مُطربان آماده باشند
سرود مهرگان را خوانده باشند
که در این جنگ جشنی برقرار است
عَدَم بر خائنین در انتظار است
زمان جاهلان پایان گرفته
اهورای وطن عُصیان گرفته
گذشت آن روزگار بُت‌پَرَستی
رِسَد دوران اصل و حق‌پَرَستی
همی زرتشت بازآید به ایران
به سود نیک خویان ضد رندان
همو آید که نیک از بد بجوید
اصالت را به ایران بازگوید
چه حق پیروز گردد یا نگردد
زمین جز این به کام نیک کرداران نگردد
کلام آخر از من این چنین است
زمان حُکم نیکان بر زمین است.

۲۳ جولای ۱۹۹۲

سرگذشت آدم

بنده نامم آدم است و شهره بر تهرانی ام
غربتی گشتم ولی آزاده و ایرانی ام
کسب و کارم صنعت و هرکاره ام
صدهزار افسوس، چون دور از وطن بیکاره ام
روزگاری من به این دنیا شدم
چند سالی که گذشت بر نیک و بد دانا شدم
خواستم من هم به نیکی چون اَبَر انسان شوم
پیرو حق و حقیقت همره نیکان شوم
این چنین بر خویشتن پیمان شدم
بردهٔ حق، رو به ایمان، فاتح نَفسَم شدم
در زمان نوجوانی مشکلاتم بیش بود
از تُهی دستی و جهل جاهلان، قلبم اجین با نیش بود
انقلابی سر گرفت و من در آن ویران شدم
همچو کاهی در هوا حیران شدم
اولش پنداشتم این گردباد حق بود
انقلابی پر ثَمَر از جانب ایزد بود
چون چنین پندارم از آن باد بود
جسم و روحم جانب ایثار بود.
با گذشتی چند، از آن حادثه آگه شدم

از خطای خویش در راهی خطا گریان شدم
جسم و روح و عقل را از آن بلا بیرون شدم
مانعی بر راه آن باد بلا از جان شدم
جسم من یک ذره کاهی بود در آن باد سخت
برگ وزنی نیست بر روی درخت
چونکه بادی بَر کَنَد از پایه تخت شاه را
آدمی چون من چگونه سَد توان باشد ره آن باد را
ملتی چون عکس رهبر توی ماه و موی او را لای قرآن دیده است
سفرۀ عقل و ذکاوت را ز سر برچیده است
چون صدای حق و آزادی به گوشی می‌رسید
دسته‌ای چوب و چماق و اسلحه بر دادخواهی می‌رسید
ملتی گر خُفته باشد ذلتش بی‌انتهاست
رهبری چون رَذل باشد ملتش را بی‌بهاست
این چنین بود وصف من در آن زمان
انتخاب راه آزادی و حق در این جهان
چند ماهی که گذشت من راهی زندان شدم
دور از کاشانه و آزادی و خویشان شدم
قصه‌ای بی‌انتها در وصف آن زندان کم است
هرچه هست زَجر و ستَم از آدمی بر آدم است
جُرم من آزادگی از ظُلم و بیداد زمان
خواندن چندین کتاب فَلسفی از این و آن
زور بازوی جوانی در تَنَم بازنده بود
چونکه یک تَن را به صد، یارای جنگیدن نبود
چند ماهی کنج زندان ماندم و تنها شدم.
از غم و تنهایی مردان حق آگه شدم
بگذریم یک سال و اَندی در گذشت

نسبتش با فَهم من، یک چند قَرن از سر گذشت
آنچنانکه منطقی بر جُرم من حاضر نبود
خَصم را راهی بجز آزادیم از کُنج آن زندان نبود
بار دیگر چون کبوتر باد از بالم گذشت
فکر دوری از وطن در جان و امیالم گذشت
چون اگر بار دگر در بند طوفان می‌شدم
قطره‌ای در سیل و طوفان خُرد و ویران می‌شدم
این چنین بر عَزم خود راسخ شدم
راهی خاکی بجز ایران شدم
حال دهسالی از آن دوران گذشت
آن غرور نوجوانی رفت دیگر برنگشت
حاصل ده سال غربت شعر و اندرز من است
کول‌بار تجربه آکنده بر پَند من است
ثروت من هرچه هست غیر از زَر است
خاک عالم بر سر پُر جوهر است.

۱۹۹۲/۷/۲۵

عزا

بیا ای هموطن تا در عزای کشوری ویران بگرییم
به حال بچه و پیرزن و بیوه زنان با هم بگرییم
بیایید تا سیه بر تن بپوشیم
به حال شیرمردان به خون خفته بگرییم.
دلیران یک به یک اعدام گشتند
به حال آن جوانمردان بی همتا بگرییم
زنان در زیر چادر لانه کردند
به حال ماه در ابر سیه پنهان بگرییم
برای قتل حق لشکر بسیج است
به حال حق پرستان جدا از هم بگرییم
گروهی گرم عیاشی و کیفَند
به حال سرخوشان بی‌غم و بی رگ بگرییم
گروهی فکر دارایی و مالند

به حال فقر دانایی آن‌ها هم بگرییم.
هنرمندان همه گُمنام گشتند
برای نام ایران در هنر باید بگرییم
همه فرهنگ و آثار قدیمی در حراجند
به حال قدمت و تاریخ ایران بر فنا باید بگرییم
همه دارایی ایران به یغما می‌برند دزدان و دجالان
به حال ملتی بی‌چاره و بی‌خانمان باید بگرییم
گروهی دزد و دجال سیه پوش، خانه در خاک وطن کردند
به حال ملتی آواره و غربت زده، باید بگرییم
چنان گویی که تار عنکبوتی بر گُلستان است
به حال باغ و باغبان و گلش، باید بگرییم.

۱۹۹۲/۱۲/۵

بهار

بهار آمد بهار آمد
زمستان رفت و خُرَم شد
چمن سبزید و گُل رویید
خبر آمد خبر آمد
عمو نوروزمان پیروز
به بارش نُقل و شیرینی
چه خوش آمد، چه خوش آمد
بساط کینه جارو شد
عِناد و دشمنی رفت و
وفا آمد، وفا آمد
حاجی فیروز چه خوشحاله
گل شادی شکفت بر لب
صفا آمد، صفا آمد
دل عاشق دگرگون شد
کشاورزان چه دلشادند
مبارک باد این نوروز و هر روزت

چه با صلح و صفا آمد
بهارِ سبز و ناز آمد
قناری نغمه خوان آمد
که نوروز از سَفَر آمد
چو پیکی خوش خبر آمد
برای تهنیت آمد
که بوی زندگی آمد
دل انسان به رَحم آمد
محبت، دوستی، مهر و صفا آمد
چه خندان، بی ریا آمد
که فصل رقص و ساز آمد
که خندیدن به بار آمد
شراب و شعر و نان آمد
که عشقی تازه تر آمد
که فصل کشت و کار آمد
که عیدی خوش ز سالی پر ثمر آمد

جمعه ۵ مارچ، ۱۹۹۳

آزادی آدم

لحظهٔ آزادی آدم همان بَدو تولد بود
همان یک لحظهٔ اول همان آغاز رُستن بود
سپس آزادی آدم به دست مادرش افتاد
برای اینکه مادرمالک ومسئول آدم بود
پس از چندی پدر اُستاد آدم شد
و او فرمانده و آقای آدم بود
چنین از عمر آدم در جهان بگذشت
ولی او همچنان در خواب شیرین بود
زمان کسب آگاهی نمایان شد
و آدم پیرو آموزگاران بود
و بعداز سال ها آدم ز دانش نور اَفضَل شد
ولی در بند تشریفات بی جا بود
زمان کار و کوشش، کسب ثروت شد
و آدم بردهٔ سیم و زر و ماشین و آهن بود

خلاصه حرف استقلال آدم در میان آمد
سخن از انتخاب زوج آدم بود
و آدم مستقل از قوم و خویشان شد
و زوج و همسرش از نوع حوّا بود
در این قسمت فریبی سهم آدم شد
و آن سیب بزرگ و سرخ شهوت بود
از آن پس آخرین ته ماندهٔ آزادی آدم
به روی آب یا باد بیابان بود
و آدم پیر گشت و پشت او خم شد
ولی او همچنان جویای آزادی در عالم بود
و آنی مرگ بر جانش فرود آمد
و این آغاز آزادی آدم بود.

دو شنبه ۱۹۹۳/۶/۱۴

زن

شنیدم که زن عاجز از غم شده
دلش خون ز مَرد و ز عالم شده

شنیدم که زن در سِتَم غوطه است
گرفتار زور و ملامت شده

شنیدم که مردی جدا گشته ازهمسرش
و هم خانهٔ ننگ و شهوت شده

شنیدم که مردی زنش را کُتَک می زند
و او بهر هم خانه اش مَرد جنگی شده

سئوال است برای من و مردم روزگار
چرا نام نیکوی زن طعمهٔ زور و ثروت شده

مگر زن دلیل تـــــولد نبود
که اینگونه نامش مُکدّر شده

مگر زن نگهبان شب های کودک نبود
که آن کودک اکنون دلیری ز مردان شده

مگر پهلوان مادرت زن نبود
که اکنون زنت کمتر از زن شده

مگرعلت عشق مردان همان زن نبود
که اینک دلیلی برای تنفر شده

کجا رفته آن مهر و عشق و صفا
که جایش دروغ و دو رنگی شده

چرا زور بازو در این روزگار
دلیل کُتک خوردن زن شده

چرا دست ناز و نوازش برای زنان
مبدل به شلاق و تهدید و سیلی شده

چرا جای الفاظ شیرین عشق
سخن های بی معنی وفحش و نفرین شده

چرا جای گُل های سُرخ و بَنَفش
نصیب زنان خار پُر کین شده

نه مرد آن است که با زن زور گوید
که اینگونه مردانگی خُشک بی بو شده

به عشقش بنازید و از دَردَش آگه شوید
که زن عاشق دَرک مردان شده

نیاز زنان را بجویید با عشق خویش
که رفع نیاز زنان واجب از حَق شده

مُحبت نثار زن خود کُنید
که زن جانثار مُحبت شده

به رویش بخندید و شادش کُنید
که زن خسته از کینه و غم شده

به گفتار و کردارتان نیک ورزی کُنید
که دوران زور و سِتَم طی شده

ببارید باران گُل بر زنان
که او مادر کودکی بَرتَر از گُل شده

به زن ها مقامی چو مادر دهید
که زن مادر سربداران شِده

حقوق زنان را به وجدان رعایت کُنید
که حَق تولد بر انسان برابر شده

به پاس زن نیک شادی کُنید
که آن نیک زن باعث سرفرازی شده

و ای حوا تو هم یک نیک زن باش
که آدم دلش کاسهٔ خون شده

۱۹۹۳/۶/۲۶

کلاه سیاست

سیاستمداران لَندَن کلاهدوز ایران شدند
همه عاشق ثروت و نَفت ایران شدند
شب و روز در فکر ایران و در کوششند
که گویی همه جان نثاران ایران شدند
زمانی کلاه توتون، بهر دربار ناصر شده
و روزی کلاه بر سر پهلوی، شاه ایران شدند
و روزی که شاه پشت به ارباب کرد
به عنوان هیتلرکُشی، وارد خاک ایران شدند
زمان محمدرضا شرکتی ساختند
و مسئول آن شرکت و نفت ایران شدند
و میهن پرستی به‌نام مصدق، طلسم چپاول شکست
وآن ها کلاه برسرکودتاچی شده، وارد خاک ایران شدند
زمان انقلاب آغاز گشت و جنبشی رُخ داد
و آنها کلاه خدا گشته و بر سر ملت ما شدند
و این آخرین طرح آنهاست تا این زمان
که عمامه، تاج سر خائنین جماران شدند
ولی جای هیچگونه شک یا که تردید نیست
که این دیوها ظاهراً شکل آدم شدند

چنین است که هر دوره‌ای عده‌ای
گرفتار این دیو هفت سر شدند
دریغا که این غفلت از مردم ما بُوَد
که دُزدان دریا سیاستگزاران ایران شدند
جدایی ز کیش و ز فرهنگ باعث شده
که ته ماندهٔ تازیان، خاردر چشم ایران شدند
و نادان به تاریخ و علم وطن بودن است
که غارتگران سرور کشور ما شدند
و آنها که از دین کلاهی گُشاد بهر ما دوختند
همان خُبرگانند که ویرانگرخاک ایران شدند
کلاه سیاست سر بی سیاست رود
چنین است که رِندان، کلَاهدوز ایران شدند
و آغاز این ضعف در ریشهٔ جَهل ماست
که عمامه داران سوار من و ما شدند
بیا هموطن چاره‌ای بهر فردا کنیم
که این کهنه کاران مهیا به فردای ایران شدند

۱۹۹۳/۶/۲۹

زندگی

زندگی یعنی تنفس، زندگی یعنی تکامل، زندگی یعنی حقیقت،
زندگی یعنی یه عادت،

زندگی فقط زمین نیست.
زندگی یعنی زمانه، زندگی یعنی ستاره، زندگی یعنی یه عالم،
زندگی یعنی یه عادت،

زندگی فقط سکون نیست.
زندگی یعنی تحرک، زندگی یعنی تکامل، زندگی یعنی حقیقت،
زندگی یعنی یه عادت،

زندگی فقط سحر نیست.
زندگی یعنی دمیدن، زندگی یعنی شکفتن، زندگی یعنی سپیده،
زندگی یعنی یه عادت،

زندگی فقط خدا نیست.
زندگی یعنی خودیّت، زندگی یعنی تنفس، زندگی یعنی حقیقت،
زندگی یعنی یه عادت،

زندگی به گندگی نیست.
زندگی یعنی یه سلول، زندگی یعنی تفکر، زندگی یعنی حقیقت،
زندگی یعنی یه عادت،

زندگی به سرد شدن نیست.
زندگی یعنی حرارت، زندگی یعنی تحرک، زندگی یعنی تکامل،
زندگی یعنی یه عادت،

زندگی فقط بدل نیست.
زندگی یعنی اصالت، زندگی یعنی درستی، زندگی یعنی حقیقت،
زندگی یعنی یه عادت،

زندگی به ابتدا نیست.
زندگی یعنی ادامه، زندگی یعنی مشقت، زندگی یعنی تکامل،
زندگی یعنی یه عادت،

زندگی به حرف زدن نیست.
زندگی یعنی شهادت، زندگی یعنی به پندار، زندگی یعنی به کردار،
زندگی یه عادت،

زندگی فقط منم نیست.
زندگی یعنی جماعت، زندگی یعنی یه عالم، زندگی یعنی یه دنیا،
زندگی یعنی یه عادت،

زندگی فقط ریا نیست.
زندگی یعنی صداقت، زندگی یعنی رفاقت، زندگی یعنی تحمل،
زندگی یعنی درستی، زندگی یعنی یه عادت،

زندگی همه‌اش هوس نیست.
زندگی یعنی اراده، زندگی یعنی ریاضت، زندگی یعنی تحمل،
زندگی یعنی یه عادت،

زندگی همه‌اش رقم نیست.
زندگی یعنی الفبا، زندگی یعنی معما، زندگی یعنی زراعت،
زندگی یعنی تجارت، زندگی یعنی یه عادت،

زندگی فقط گذر نیست.
زندگی یعنی گذرگاه، زندگی یعنی تماشا، زندگی یعنی سیاحت،
زندگی یعنی یه عادت،

زندگی به قتل و خون نیست.
زندگی یعنی عدالت، زندگی یعنی تَرَحم، زندگی یعنی عبادت،
زندگی یعنی یه عادت،

زندگی به سیم و زر نیست.
زندگی یعنی اصالت، زندگی یعنی ارادت، زندگی یعنی یه کلبه،
زندگی یعنی یه عادت،

زندگی به های و هوی نیست.
زندگی یعنی ظرافت، زندگی یعنی لطافت، زندگی یعنی تواضع،
زندگی یعنی تحمل، زندگی یعنی یه عادت.

۱۹۸۳

شکایت

مردم ایران ز یکدیگر شکایت می‌کنند
یکدگر را شرمسار و خُرد و رسوا می‌کنن
چون کسی همراه باشد نیک‌ورزی می‌کنند
وای بر روزی که ضد شد هرچه بد شد می‌کنند
هرکه می‌گوید که من از دیگری بَرتَر بُوم
یا که میگوید رژیم بعد من رهبر بُوم
عده‌ای هم ادعای پادشاهی می‌کنند
یا اگر شاهی نشد، قصد وزیری می‌کنند
یک طرف از من بدی گوید ومن از دیگری
فارس با رشتی رَجَز خواند و لُر با آذری
این رَجَزخوانی ز یکدیگر خودش سُنَت شده
یکدگر را خار کردن عامل عزّت شده
به هر جا محفلی یا مَنبری هست
برای غیبت از پیغمبری هست
توپنداری که بدگویی ز مردم امر حق است
غیابت کردن از غایب نماز ظهر وعصر است
تمام سازمان‌های سیاسی با وطن بیگانه هستند
چرا؟ چون با چپ وراست وعرب، وابسته هستند
نیست حتی یک جماعت یا گروهی مستقل
تاطرفداری کند از سنت و فرهنگ خود با جان و دل
سازمان‌های چپی داریم و راست
یک گروه هم با عرب، نَه چپ، نَه راست
حزب چپ با داس وچکش صحنه سازی می‌کند
یا برای استالین افسانه سازی می‌کند

سمت دیگر نوکران غرب هرجا حاضرند
انگلیس یا آمریکا فرقی ندارد هردوتا را چاکرند
عده‌ای هم حزب‌الله‌اند و حاکم بر وطن
باعث بدبختی و آوارگی بر مرد و زن
این جماعت غافل از فرهنگ و استقلال خویش
می زنند با تیشه نابخردی بر ریشهٔ اقوام خویش
نقش مردم در میان حاضرین روشن بود
پله‌ای بالا رونده بهر رِندان بر سر قدرت بود
هرکه از این پله بالا رفت تا مقصود خویش
کرد ویران نردبان را بهر استحکام خویش
لیک افسوس و هزار افسوس بر این حاکمان
چون خیانت می کنند براعتماد ملت و آزادگان
دل انسان پریشان می شود بر حال این ملت
که محکوم و اسیرند زیر بار اینهمه ذلت
ز روشنفکرمان تا کارگر یا مردم عامی
همه دل مرده‌ایم و شرمسار کوس بدنامی
چرا این پیشگامان رهایی این چنین‌اند
که درتفسیر اوضاع جهان واماندگان وآخرینند
چرا هر کس به یک سازی به رقص است
مگر پرچم برای دست شخص است
از این بدگویی و تهمت به یکدیگر بپرهیزید
خودی را ضد خویشان بر ناینگیزید
از این تهمت زدنها جزضرر چیزی نصیب ما نمیگردد
که همچون تُف به سوی باد جُز بر ما نمی گردد
نگویید سرنوشت ما به دست انگلیس است
که این مطلب بسی خوش بر مذاق انگلیس است
به امید نجات از سوی این و آن نباشید
کسی در فکرتان نیست، اگر خویشان نباشید

رهایی از غُل و زنجیر کار انقلاب است
و آن وابسته بر بیداری مردم ز خواب است
ولی منظور من از انقلاب آتش زدن نیست
برادر کشتن و ویرانی و پَرپَر زدن نیست
برای انقلاب آموزش فرهنگ می باید
برای کسب آزادی جدا از ننگ می باید
خلاصه ای برادر، خواهرم هوشیار باشید
برای انقلابی تازه تر بیدار باشید
بیایید دست ها را حلقه سازیم
که نیرویی اهورا وار سازیم
سلاح عشق و آگاهی بسازیم
مُصیبت را به ایران چاره سازیم.

مارچ ۱۹۹۳

تا کی

به من تاکی، به خود تا کی، به ما تا کی؟
دروغ و تهـــمت و بی حرمتی تا کی؟
خصومت تا چه حد، بغض و غـــرض تا کی؟
به غـربت مـاندن و آوارگی تا کی؟
بگو ای هموطـن، با میهنت تا کـی؟
به فرهنگت، بتاریخت، به فرزندان خود تا کی؟
خرابی تا کجا، ویرانگـــری تا کی؟
برادر کشتن و غـارتگری تا کی؟
تعصب بهر چی، یک دندگی تا کی؟
تماشـــای جهان از روی بینی بی هدف تا کی؟
ببخشید، قصد من، قصد اهانت نیست
ولی ایـــن من منم‌های دروغیـن وکهن تا کی؟
سیاسیون، مُصرند بـــر خطای خویش
خطـــا روی خطا، سـر خوردگی تا کی؟
هموطن، ای پیشـــگام راه آزادی
بـــه دنبال رهـــایی، در بیابان عرب تا کی؟
بیـا و ذره‌ای در فـــکر ایـــران باش
به خـــط شـــرق و غرب و تازیان تا کی؟
زمـــانی دور از رسم ابر انسان جدا گشتیم
به راه دیـــگران رفتن، ز خود غافل شدن تاکی؟
از این ایسم‌های گوناگون برای ما چه حاصل شد؟
به هر بادی دگرگشتن، مرید حزب باد و بادیان تا کی؟

تو ای شاعر، تو ای انسان روشنفکر
سکوتت بهر چیست؟ خاموشیت تا کی؟
در ایران شیخ بی‌ریشی و در خارج مبارز
سرت در زیر برف و تن به خارج، مثل کبک تا کی؟
سر از چادر برون آرید و ذلت را رها سازید
زبونی و حقارت، ترس از این پست فطرتان تا کی؟
شما یک ملتی را پشت خود تا مرز نابودی کشاندید
به دنبال شما، کور و کر و لال و ملنگ تا کی؟
نگاهی بر مزار این دلیران کن
کفن بر پیکر آزادگان تا کی؟
و ای وابستگان پول و قدرت
تملق از برای لقمه نان تا کی؟
دو رنگی تا کجا، نا مردمی تا کی؟
خیانت بر زمین و زندگان تا کی؟
به این خوش باش، عمرت جاودان باشد
فرار از دست مظلومان در بند و ستم تاکی؟
خداوندا، ز صبرت جان به لب گشتم
صبوری تا چه حد؟ بیداد با آزادگان تاکی؟

فوریه ۱۹۹۴

مرگ

چون مرگ بما رسید کار اجل است
این رسم زمانه بوده و در گذر است
چون لحظهٔ عمر ما به پایان برسد
دارو و حکیم و روضه خوان بی ثمر است
گر من زمیان زندگان رفتم و نابود شدم
اشک تو و لبخند تو در کالبدم بی اثر است
آن کس که پس از مردن ما شیون و فریاد کند
از رسم طبیعت و جهان بی خبر است
افسوس که ما مرده پرستیم و گرفتار خرافات
چون مرده برای جانشینی و حسد بی خطر است
ای کاش که در حیاتمان ارزش ما ارج نهند
لاکن که پس از مرگ، بد و نیک جهان در کفن است
هرکس که برای زندگی تن به حقارت بدهد
ازخوک کثافتر و از گربه و سگ پست تر است
مرگ در ره آزادی و نیکی و شرف خوش باشد
آن کس که برای شرفش مرد نکونام تر است
ای دوست بیا و زندگی را به غنیمت شمریم
هر لحظهٔ عمر ما گرانبهاتر از سیم و زر است

ژانویه ۱۹۹۴

خلایق هر چه لایق

بگفتا پیر دیری
به هر دانا و غیری
به پیر و طفل نوزاد
به انسان های آزاد
بگفت با مردم عام
به هر خوشنام و بد نام
بگفت از داد و بیداد
ز خاموشی و فریاد
از آن دولتمداران
وطن دزدان و رندان
ز جلاد و قصاوت
ز بدبختی و ذلت
ز اشک مادر پیر
ز فرزندان در گیر
از آن سرمایه داران
ز بازار گدایان
بگفت با تخم و ریشه
به گندمزار و بیشه
به گلزار شقایق
خلایق هر چه لایق

بگفتا از خدایان
ز مذهب ها و ادیان
ز ابطال و خرافات
ز سنت ها و عادات
بگفت ازجهل و جاهل
از آن مردان کاهل
از آن افکار بی بی
و آن جنگ صلیبی
بگفت از حق و باطل
طناب دار قاتل
از آن باطل پرستان
حقیر و زیر دستان
از آنانی که دولا
شدند مزدور ملا
ز کلاشی و رندی
از آن ملای هندی
همان شیخ ریاکار
جنایتکار و مکار
بگفت با خلق وخالق
خلایق هر چه لایق

بگفت با شاه شاهان — سران و تاجداران
بــه آن بالانشـینان — به قصـر و خوش نشینان
اگـر خود کامه گشتی — ز خود بیگانه گشتی
ز خلق خود گذشتی — شدی استاد زشتی
اگر کشتی پسر را — برنجاندی پدر را
پدر را سر بریدی — یتیمان را ندیدی
اگرزندان به جای خانه سازی — وکاخت برسر ویرانه سازی
نکردی باوطن عدل و مساوات — نترسیدی ز ایام مجازات
چو تختت واژگون شد — تبارت سرنگون شد
رمیدی از حقــایق — خلایق هر چه لایــق

بگفت آن پیر بُرنا — به بیمـار و توانا
به هرکس در چپ وراست — و یا خط عرب هاست
به آن احزاب پرگو — ولی کم کار و پر رو
به آنانی که خوابند — گرفتــار ســـرابند
بگفت با هر که آگاه — و هر کس ناخودآگاه
اگر زشتی سرشتی — کتاب غم نوشتی
شدی پاییچ مردم — برای جذب مردم
ز ارزش ها گذشتی — روابط را گُسستی
اگر رفتی به مرداب — فرو رفتی به گرداب
شــدی سوراخ قایق — خلایق هر چه لایــق

بگفت با مردم نیک
به انسان های هوشیار
به آن چشمان بینا
ز عشق و نور ایمان
ز قانون و عدالت
بگفت از کشت وصنعت
بگفت از مسکن و نان
که خود سازنده هستند
بگفتا حق آن است
هر آنکس نیک و لایق

رفیق و یار و نزدیک
به وجدان های بیدار
به روشنفکر و دانا
بهارِ سبز و باران
ز آزادی ملت
ز کار و رنج و زحمت
به صنعت کار و دهقان
ولی بی خانه هستند
که خود با کاروان است
خلایق هر چه لایق

۱۹۹۴/۶/۵

ستارهٔ من

آمد ستارهٔ من، از آسمان هفتم
تبدیل شد به انسان، آمد میان مردم
درجستجوی من بود، در دشت و کوه و صحرا
مأیوس از گذشته، امید او به فردا
یابنده شد زمانی در کشوری غریبه
همخانه شد به جانم، با قلب و روح و دیده
اینک سعادت من، افسانه شد به دنیا
با او شدم منور، آتش برای سرما
نام زمینی او نسرین، گُل بهار است
عشق و محبت او جاوید و ماندگار است
این افتخار من بود، تا با ستاره باشم
با دلبری چو نسرین، با یک شراره باشم
امید و آرزویم، در تندرستی اوست
اهداف من ز دنیا، در خنده های با اوست
ای ایزد توانا، همراه و حافظش باش
در زیر چتر عشقت، خورشید و سایه اش باش
او را به من روان کن، کز دوریش ملولم
بی جسم او در عالم، از دیده زار و کورم

پیام

ای هموطنان شعر پیام است
هر مصرع آن، جان کلام است
منظور من از گفتن ابیات، غزل نیست
نام من و اَحسنت شما، مَدِّ نظر نیست
منظور پیام است و سرافرازی ایران
مقصود زمین است و براندازی شیطان
ای هموطن از خواب بپا خیز که خورشید دمیده
دوران جنایات سلاطین به سرانجام رسیده
باید که دگربار خدا گشته و ماشیم
از بند منمهای فریبنده رها شیم

باید که بپا خیزیم — از فتنه بپرهیزیم
باید که یکی گشتن — از تفرقه برگشتن
باید که چنان باشیم — از کینه برین باشیم
باید که عمل کردن — از ترس حذر کردن
باید که سخن گفتن — از مهر وصفا گفتن
باید که نکو بودن — پایانگر غم بودن
باید که درو کردن — از هرزه برون کردن
باید که چنان باشیم — آذر گه جان باشیم
باید که چنان بودن — پابند شرف بودن
باید که چنان کردن — بر وعده عمل کردن
باید که به نیکویی — نی از همه بدگویی
باید که چنان باید — ذلت به عدم باید
باید که چنین باشد — غیرش ره کین باشد
چون راه دگر رفتن — دور از ره حق گشتن

چون برده صفت بودن
در مذهب شَر بودن

چون مصلحت اندیشی
درنکبت و شر پیشی

دیگر چه توقع داشت
باید به جزا پنداشت

دیگر ز بشر دوری
گوش، حلقه به مزدوری

دیگر زرت حاصل شد
صبر از همه فارغ شد

دیگر درِ بازی نیست
درمحکه قاضی نیست

ای اشرف مخلوقات
ای سَروَر موجودات

ای پادشه عالم
ای سلسلهٔ آدم

ای مجری و سازنده
ای مخرب و کوبنده

ای آنکه توانایی
سازنده و دانایی

گوشت به پیامم ده
در گفتـــه امانم ده

این شعر نه اخطار است
آگاهی و هشدار است
زنگیست ز ناقوس طبیعت
پیکیست ز آزادی به ذلت
این شعر پیام است وخبرنیست
اندیشهٔ جان است و زبان نیست
آری اگر از غربت خودپند بگیریم
از ثانیه ها حکمت و اندرز بگیریم
باشد که دگربار ازاین دام رهاشیم
ازبند شَه و شیخ و شَررهاهمه واشیم
ازترس بلا خیزد و از یأس تباهی
در ظلمت شب نیست بجز رنگ سیاهی
این نکته نتیجه است، به خاطربسپارید
بر نکبت ریشوی وطن، دل مسپارید

سپتامبر ۱۹۹۴

پیام آور

من از ایران آمدم
از نسل شیران آمدم
من ز البرز و دماوند بزرگ
از تبار رستم و ذال آمدم
آمدم تا از برای زندگی
چاره ای از بهر فردا آمدم
آمدم از قله های افتخار
بر زمین مادر، ز خورشید آمدم
از نژادی دور از نسل بشر
از نژاد هور و مزدا آمدم
آمدم از سوی خورشید بزرگ
آمدم چون ساز و سوزان آمدم
کوله بارم پُر ز اخبار و پیام
گفته ها از بهر انسان آمدم
گفته ها کوتاه و فهمش مثل آب
قاصدم، پیک از اهورا آمدم
کار من آغاز شد از این زمان
من برای فتح ایران آمدم
من برای صلح و آزادی و عشق
از برای دفن دجال آمدم

کار من آغاز از ایران و شیخ
من برای نسل انسان آمدم

هر قدم در این جهت از مال و جان
کاروانی را بهمره، قصد پاداش آمدم

هر که آمد، بر خلاف عشق رفت
من برای جنگ، با قانون شکنها آمدم

اصل این قانون، اصل زندگیست
من بهمراه قوانین مساوات آمدم

کاسهٔ صبر زمین لبریز شد
من یه پیغامم، که از او آمدم

او ندایش را به من ابلاغ کرد
از زبان مادری، از دشت ایران آمدم

او دلش غمگین و روحش خسته است
بهریک آرامشی، جاوید و برپا آمدم

مادر از انسان شکایت می کند
من یه سرباز، ازعدالتخانهٔ جان آمدم

حال می گویم که ایمان آورید
بر همان جسمی، که از آن آمدم

او زمین است، مادری از کهکشان
من در او بودم، و از او آمدم

من همـــان زرتشت پیرم، ای بشر
بار دیگر چون جوانی، از اهــورا آمدم

۱۹۹۴/۱۰/۱۰

خورشید

پدر جانم فروزانم
تو ای خورشید سوزانم
نگاهی کن جوابی ده
که من مستانه خوشحالم
برایت نامه ای دارم
من از سوی زمین آیم
من انسانم از ایرانم
من از ایران و تورانم
مرا مادر فرستاده
حضورت گفته ای دارم
مرا مأمور این امر مهم کرده
چه از دیدار تو مسرور ودل شادم
اجازت می دهی سرور
که سر از نامه بگشایم؟
که این پیغام کتبی را
برایت با زبان خوانم
اطاعت مـــی کنم اختر
هـــم اکنون باز می خوانم

درود بی کرانم بر پدر باد
زمینم ، طفل سرگردان و سیارم
پدر جانم فروزانم
تو ای خورشید سوزانم
تو می دانی و می بینی
که من سر سبز و آبادم
من از آتش برون گشتم
و اکنون خاک عُریانم
نمی دانی چه مشکل بود
که من از چشمت افتادم
از آن روز بد تلخ جدایی
تا کنون، دلتنگ و گریانم
بروئید از تنم جاندار گوناگون
و اینک زخمی و بیمار انسانم
زمانی نسلشان میمون و عنتر بود
درآن دوران منم آسوده جان بودم
شرایط مغزشان راجا بجا کرد
و ازآن روزمن بیخواب و بیتابم
پدر جانم فروزانم
تو ای خورشید سوزانم
جـــوابی ده دوایی کن
که مـــن رنجور و بیمارم

۱۹۹۴/۱۰/۱۲

گُل

و نسرین زاده شد از مادرش با چهره‌ای شاد
و حـــک شـــد یاد او در گلشن یاد
خوشـی بخشـید ایـل و خانـدانـش را
معــطر کـرد بــا بوی خوشش اطرافیانش را
از آن دم مــاه مهتابــش درخــشان شد
زمین خندان و خــورشیدش فــروزان شد
و در آخر گل نسرین نصیب مردِ مردان شد
منور کـــرد قلبش را و همسازی بر آدم شد
مبارک باشـــد ایـــن روز خجسته
کـــه شـادی در وجـودش ریشـه بسته
هـــزاران ســال عمـرت باد شـادان
بـــه همـراه عـزیـزانت و یـــاران

اگوست ۱۹۹۳

بدرود

ای هموطنان با همه بدرود
با یار و رفیق و همنشینان بدرو
تلخ است جدائی ز شما لیک
راهی بجز این نیست، کنون با همه بدرو
باشد که دگر بار همه گرد هم آئیم
تا فرصت دیدار مجدد، همه بدرو
پیغام من از بارگه عشق چنین است
صد بار به عشاق درود و همه بدرو
بودیم صبائی بکنار همه یاران
گُل نقش رُخ خندهٔ یاران همه بدرو
ای هموطنان عمر به پوچی مگذارید
در فکر وطن، دست بدست، با همه بدرو
ما روی زمینیم به هر جا که دل آنجاست
دل را بسپردیم به یاران و به ایران همه بدرو

۱۸-۷-۹۴